# Creating Forms in SAP® ERP HCM

# SAP® Essentials

## Expert SAP knowledge for your day-to-day work

Whether you wish to expand your SAP knowledge, deepen it, or master a use case, SAP Essentials provide you with targeted expert knowledge that helps support you in your day-to-day work. To the point, detailed, and ready to use.

SAP PRESS is a joint initiative of SAP and Galileo Press. The know-how offered by SAP specialists combined with the expertise of the Galileo Press publishing house offers the reader expert books in the field. SAP PRESS features first-hand information and expert advice, and provides useful skills for professional decision-making.

SAP PRESS offers a variety of books on technical and business related topics for the SAP user. For further information, please visit our website: *www.sap-press.com.*

Brian Schaer
Time Management with SAP ERP HCM
2008, 579 pp.
978-1-59229-229-5

Jürgen Hauser
SAP Interactive Forms by Adobe
2009, 624 pp.
978-1-59229-254-7

Jeremy Masters and Christos Kotsakis
Implementing Employee and Manager Self-Services
In SAP ERP HCM
2008, 431 pp.
978-1-59229-188-5

Martin Esch, Anja Junold
Authorizations in SAP ERP HCM
2008, 336 pp.
978-1-59229-165-6

Stefan Kauf, Viktoria Papadopoulou

# Creating Forms in SAP® ERP HCM

Galileo Press

Bonn • Boston

**ISBN 978-1-59229-282-0**

© 2009 by Galileo Press Inc., Boston (MA)
1st Edition 2009

1st German edition published 2009 by Galileo Press, Bonn, Germany

Galileo Press is named after the Italian physicist, mathematician and philosopher Galileo Galilei (1564–1642). He is known as one of the founders of modern science and an advocate of our contemporary, heliocentric worldview. His words *Eppur si muove* (And yet it moves) have become legendary. The Galileo Press logo depicts Jupiter orbited by the four Galilean moons, which were discovered by Galileo in 1610.

**Editor**  Frank Paschen
**English Edition Editor**  Jenifer Niles
**Translation**  Lemoine International, Inc., Salt Lake City, UT
**Copyeditor**  Julie McNamee
**Cover Design**  Jill Winitzer
**Photo Credit**  Masterfile/Damir Frkovic
**Layout Design**  Vera Brauner
**Production Editor**  Kelly O'Callaghan
**Typesetting**  Publishers' Design and Production Services, Inc.
**Printed and bound in** Canada

# Contents

## 7 Integration with the Payroll and Time Management Components of SAP ERP HCM ... 183



## 8 Authorizations (Authorization Objects) ... 191



## 9 Outlook for SAP Interactive Forms by Adobe ... 195



## Appendices ... 201

Contents

# 1    Introduction

A form is the hallmark of every enterprise and should be accurate, clear, and have an attractive design. This applies to all areas of business, including HR. In this book, we will focus on two typical HR forms: the payslip and the time statement.

In the SAP world, different options for designing a form have developed over the years, so customers who have been using SAP software will recognize the primary tools used for form creation and output, including *SAPscript*, *Smart Forms* (in HR, also called *HR Forms*), and *SAP Interactive Forms by Adobe*. However, because SAPscript is used primarily in SAP components outside of HR, in this book, we'll focus on form design with Smart Forms and SAP Interactive Forms.



SAP Interactive Forms became available with SAP ERP Human Capital Management (SAP ERP HCM) 6.0 and SAP NetWeaver 7.0 (see Figure 1.1) and will be continuously extended in future. The integration of the Adobe technology provides you with extensive new options — particularly the more comprehensive and more convenient WYSIWYG (*What You See Is What You Get*) design functions directly in the SAP NetWeaver system as well as the direct printout of PDF forms.

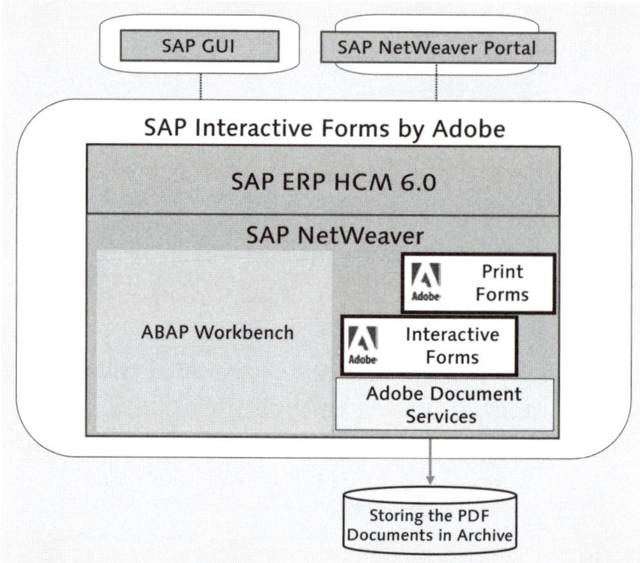



**Figure 1.1**  Integration of the Adobe Technology with SAP NetWeaver

Although the previous technologies for creating print forms continue to be supported within the framework of the release strategy, the future is geared toward SAP Interactive Forms. More functional and basic developments will be made based on the newly integrated Adobe technology today and in the future, but all existing forms will be gradually changed over to Adobe technology and delivered as such. The integration of SAP Interactive Forms with the standard functions of SAP ERP HCM means that these new technological components are integrated with *all* areas, so the forms based on Adobe components can be called directly from Customizing into the SAP ERP HCM system. The created forms are then provided by the system in an integrated manner within the framework of the application, for instance, for the call and creation of the payslip.

For the foreseeable future, you will be able to choose whether you want to design and create the form using Smart Forms or SAP Interactive Forms. So, this book focuses on the function and application of these two tools for designing and creating print forms. Notes for the selection of the technology are provided for cases in which forms are delivered both for Smart Forms and for SAP Interactive Forms.

Within SAP ERP Human Capital Management, the HR Forms Workplace provides the framework to create flexible evaluations of HR master data, time data, and payroll results in an attractive design using these two technologies. The HR Forms Workplace enables you to consistently and conveniently select, design, and print data from different sources. Unfortunately, applying the design and adjusting the forms to the enterprise requirements isn't always that easy, so throughout the book we will give you detailed, practical guidelines for creating forms using the HR Forms Workplace.

## 1.1 Target Audience of this Book

This book is written for:

▶ Consultants and developers who want to (or have to) deal with this subject

▶ Key users who create reports or forms and deploy the HR Forms Workplace tools for this purpose

The book will help you classify and apply the form design with Smart Forms and SAP Interactive Forms. Knowledge of ABAP and ABAP Workbench, Smart Forms, and Adobe LiveCycle Designer will be helpful.

## 1.2 Structure of this Book

The HR Forms Workplace is the interface to design and create forms in SAP ERP HCM, so in **Chapter 2**, Functions of the HR Forms Workplace, we will first explain the data retrieval for the form before discussing the functions and how to use the individual components, such as MetaNet, MetaFields, and so on. **Chapter 3**, Designing the Form Layout with the Form Builder, outlines how you can create and change forms using Smart Forms and SAP Interactive Forms. **Chapter 4**, Payslip — Creation and Customizing, guides you through all of the form setting steps, including customizing the selection screen and other processing steps. **Chapter 5**, Time Statement — Creation and Customizing, assumes that you understand the information in the previous chapters and focuses on the specifics in time management. **Chapter 6**, Enhancements with BAdIs, describes how you can use BAdIs (Business Add-Ins) to format business addresses or activate forms automatically after a transport. **Chapter 7**, Integration with the Payroll and Time Management Components of SAP ERP HCM, outlines how the payslip and time statement are integrated with the SAP ERP HCM components of Payroll and Time Management and how you can control the call via features. **Chapter 8**, Authorizations (Authorization Objects), considers the subject of authorizations, which is particularly important in HR. And, finally, **Chapter 9**, Outlook, answers the following questions: What are the future prospects in the area of form design? What happens to SAP Interactive Forms by Adobe? How can you use the same technical basic principles in other processes of HR? The many **appendices** summarize the most important SAP Notes, BAdIs, and other useful information.

We hope that you'll enjoy reading this book, and we wish you a lot of success in form design!

**Stefan Kauf** and **Viktoria Papadopoulou**

# 2     Functions of the HR Forms Workplace

The *HR Forms Workplace* (also referred to as *Forms Workplace*) enables you to design forms in SAP ERP Human Capital Management. It carries out the tasks of the data collection and retrieval processes for the form and also implements the graphical design using integrated but still independent tools, such as the Form Builder for Smart Forms and the Form Builder for SAP Interactive Forms. The Forms Workplace is used for form creation with the aim of evaluating data from the personnel administration, payroll, and time management areas.

Data retrieval is implemented using the HR *Metadata Workplace* (also referred to as *Metadata Workplace*). It describes, maintains, and retrieves the required data in fields, structures, and tables, that is, in the so-called *MetaNet*. All required objects are defined in the Metadata Workplace and are then available in the MetaNet. The MetaNet delivered in the SAP standard retrieves the data necessary for the payslip and time statement and can be enhanced with customer-specific structures and data. This is required, for example, if you want to output data from customer-specific infotypes or tables in a form. Section 2.1.2, Customizing and Enhancing the MetaNet, describes this procedure in detail.

Figure 2.1 shows how you can create forms with the Forms Workplace. In the left side of the figure, you see the *MetaNet* and the resulting data retrieval, and on the right side, you see the form-specific *InfoNet*. The InfoNet is used to design the layout of the form and consists of the structures defined via the MetaNet. The definition of the data and the description of the data collection (in this example, the payroll data) take place in the Metadata Workplace. The MetaNet, which is like a data catalog, provides the information that a form requires. The InfoNet is the form-specific data selection, which provides the form with data that has been optically formatted using a graphical tool. You can follow the arrows in Figure 2.1 to track the form design process.

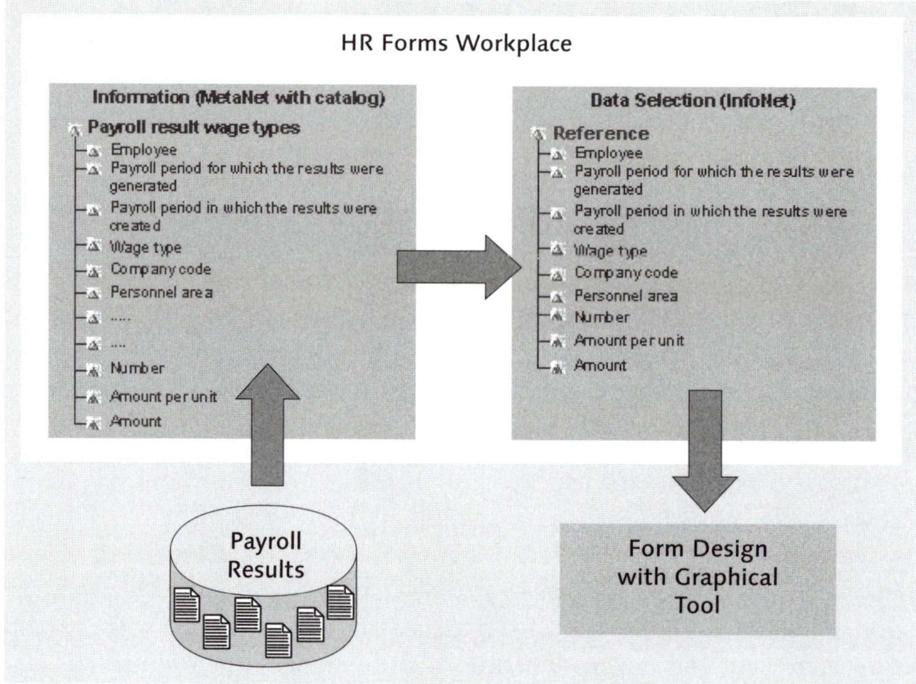


**Figure 2.1** Process-Oriented View of the HR Forms Workplace

You can also call the Forms Workplace directly via Transaction HRFORMS. In the SAP Customizing Implementation Guide (IMG), you can call the Forms Workplace via the following path: Payroll • Payroll International (or the respective country) • Forms Using HR Forms Workplace • Edit HR Forms Using Forms Workplace. Unfortunately, there is no path in the SAP Easy Access menu.

## 2.1 The SAP Standard MetaNet

The SAP standard MetaNet (SAP_DEFAULT), which already contains a comprehensive description of the data, is available in the Metadata Workplace. If required, SAP enhances it with support packages or objects for an upgrade, such as new fields from relevant infotypes. You can also add further required data to the MetaNet itself. You can integrate all data that you want to output in your form and that is contained in SAP ERP. The integration includes the definition of the individual objects and the read information. So let's look at how you can populate the objects with data.

The SAP standard MetaNet contains all data that is relevant for the payslip and time statement as well as a selection of critical master data, which means you can also use the MetaNet to create other evaluations and forms, for example, for a master data sheet. This is considerably easier if the data that is supposed to be evaluated is contained in the SAP standard MetaNet, and you can directly start selecting the data for your form.

During the form creation, you assign the MetaNet you created to the form in the Forms Workplace. You can only use the data that is available in the MetaNet as the output in the form. To position the data in the form, you must perform an additional step (besides customizing the MetaNet), which is defining the InfoNet.

You can call the Metadata Workplace via Transaction HRFORMS_METADATA. If you're already in the Forms Workplace, you can also navigate to the tool via the UTILITIES • HR METADATA WORKPLACE menu path (see Figure 2.2). But you can't call it directly from the IMG or the SAP Easy Access menu.

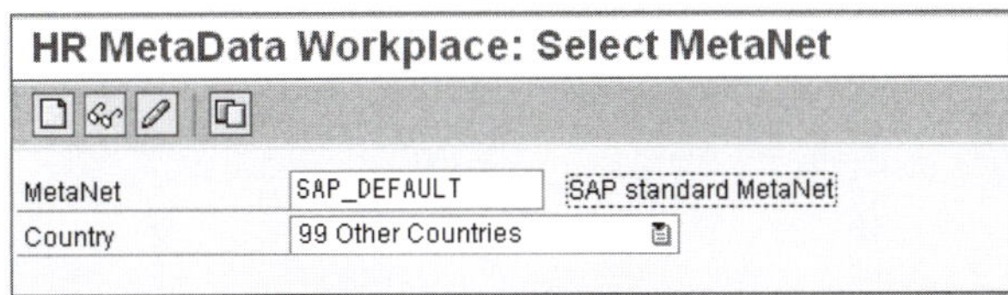

**Figure 2.2**  Initial Screen of the Metadata Workplace

Before creating your own MetaNet, look at the international SAP standard Meta-Net, SAP_DEFAULT (country grouping 99 OTHER COUNTRIES). Look at the existing objects of the MetaNet: The names of the objects indicate which data they contain. For example, the CUMULATED_PAY MetaStar displays the cumulated payroll results, and the TIM_ZES MetaStar displays the time balances for each day. For example, the object names of the MetaNet and the infotype and table structures sometimes match. Familiarize yourself with the tool and the individual objects of the MetaNet. The better you know the tool, the more easily you can enhance and maintain the standard MetaNet — or simply check it. For example, if you need to know whether it contains required data and how the data is defined, you open the required MetaNet using the DISPLAY button, the METANET •DISPLAY menu path, or the F7 key (see Figure 2.2).

The country dependency of the MetaNet enables you to define similarities for all countries but also provides the option to specify country-specific properties that are supposed to be available for particular countries only. Objects that can be created for a specific country in the MetaNet can also only be used in a form with the same country grouping, if required. The forms that have been created using the Forms Workplace are also country-dependent.

Objects with Country Grouping 99 can be used in any MetaNet. To maintain customer-specific objects, the country grouping of the object must correspond to the country grouping of the MetaNet. For example, an object with Country Grouping 99 can only be maintained in a MetaNet with the same country grouping but can be used in forms with a different country grouping. And objects with a particular country grouping can only be maintained and used in a MetaNet and form with the same country grouping.

> **Note**
>
> Don't change the SAP standard MetaNet, SAP_DEFAULT because you can use it as a template for your own MetaNet. Only if you use the international MetaNet — more specifically, the SAP standard MetaNet, SAP_DEFAULT, for Country Grouping 99 — as a template for your own MetaNet do MetaNets also exist for all other countries automatically. Because of this, you have MetaNets for every country. If required, you can then customize them based on the corresponding country.

### 2.1.1 MetaNet Objects

The objects of the MetaNet form the basis for the structures and data that are available in your form. This section deals with the relationships between the individual objects and their tasks in the MetaNet.

> **Note**
>
> Don't change standard objects because they may be overwritten when you import HR Support Packages or upgrades. Use the respective object as a template, and then customize it, or create your own objects.

You can find the following objects in the MetaNet:

- ▶ MetaFields
- ▶ MetaFigures
- ▶ MetaDimensions
- ▶ MetaStars

*MetaFields* describe MetaDimensions and are processed during the creation of a MetaDimension. They either map the keys or attributes of MetaDimensions.

MetaFigures are key figures that are used in MetaStars (see Figure 2.3). For example, if the key figure is an amount, the unit is also a part of the MetaFigure. Because MetaFigures depend on countries, they can only be assigned to the corresponding MetaStars. If you want to use MetaFigures across several countries, create it with Country Grouping 99.

*MetaDimensions* consist of *MetaFields* that map either a part of the key or an attribute of the MetaDimension and provide a comprehensive description of the MetaDimension. MetaDimensions can be used in multiple MetaStars. You must select the key of a MetaDimension in such a way that the attributes of the MetaDimension can be uniquely identified, similar to the key of a table in the ABAP Dictionary.

Like MetaFigures, MetaDimensions are country-dependent, too. If you want to use MetaDimensions across several countries, create a MetaDimension with Country Grouping 99. This ensures that you can assign the MetaDimension to a MetaStar, independent of the country grouping.

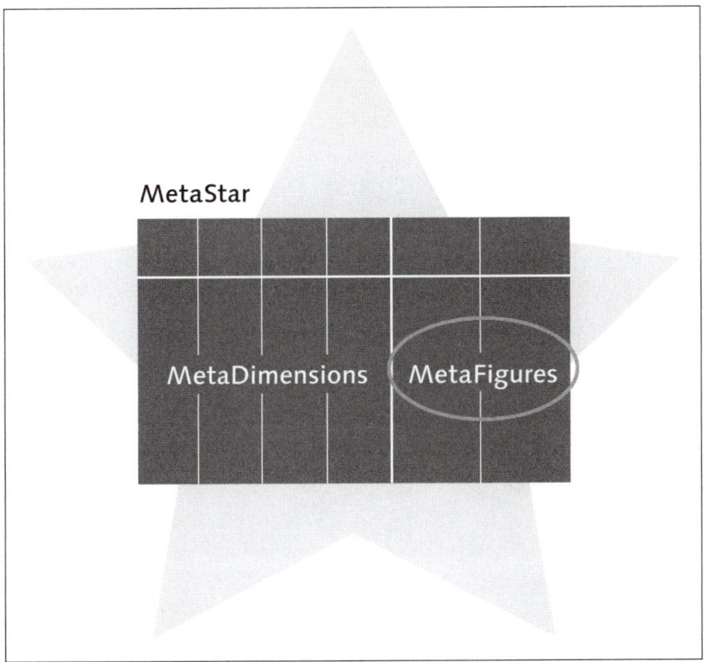


**Figure 2.3**  MetaFigures Within a MetaDimension

*MetaStars* consist of *MetaDimensions* and *MetaFigures*, which allows for a meaningful grouping of information (see Figure 2.4). This includes information on infotypes, such as organizational data or address data of an employee from one of the payroll tables, such as Table RT (Result Table), or from one of the time evaluation tables, such as Table ZES (Daily Time Balances). MetaFigures aren't absolutely necessary here. If it contains both MetaDimensions and MetaFigures, you can populate a MetaFigure and the corresponding unit via the MetaStar table or via a read function. You can also combine the two procedures. Later in the book in Chapter 5, Section 5.2.5, Converting Industrial Times to Standard Hours and Minutes, there is an example where a MetaFigure is populated via the MetaStar table, and a second MetaFigure via the read function.

> **Tip**
>
> If you work with an international MetaNet, create the MetaStars that are supposed to contain cross-country data using Country Grouping 99. They are then automatically provided for all other country groupings.

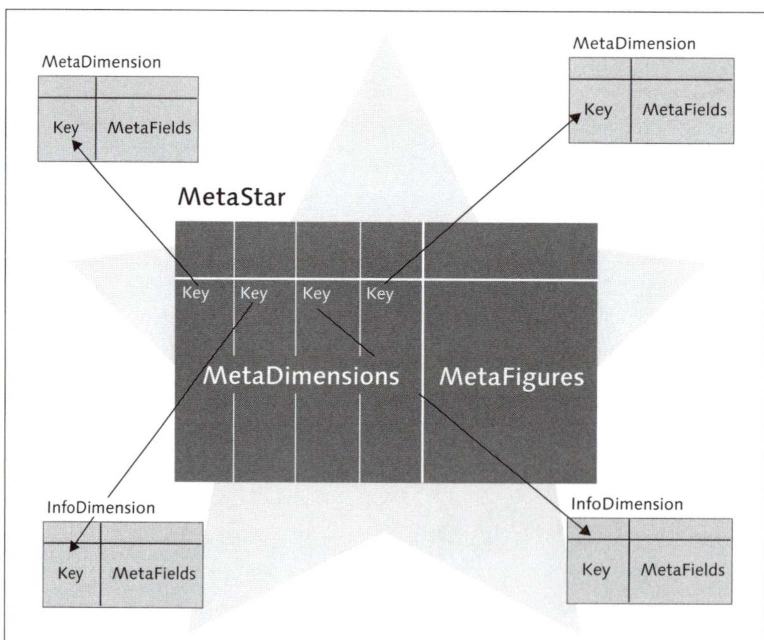


**Figure 2.4** Illustration of a MetaStar and Its Objects

The listed and described objects are assigned to your form as the MetaNet. Within a form, this is called an *InfoNet*. The same applies to all objects of the InfoNet: Within the system and language usage, *Meta* is replaced by *Info*. You can restrict the MetaStars and their MetaDimensions for your form in your InfoNet. For your form, only the data that you actually require is relevant. Section 2.2.3, Defining and Selecting Form-Specific Data, describes the exact procedure in detail.

> **Note**
>
> The *MetaNet* contains general data and the description of its origin. The *InfoNet* contains form-specific formatted data as InfoStars.

### 2.1.2  Customizing and Enhancing the MetaNet

To call the Metadata Workplace, you use Transaction HRFORMS_METADATE (refer back to Figure 2.2). You then select the SAP_DEFAULT MetaNet and OTHER COUNTRIES or Country Grouping 99. If you want to create the MetaNet for a specific country only, and this isn't supposed to be changed in the future, you can also select a particular country grouping and generate the MetaNet for only one country. Select the COPY function, or press Ctrl + F5, and then enter the name for your MetaNet (see Figure 2.5).

> **Note**
>
> The naming convention for customer-specific MetaNets only allows for the letter Z in the first place. You can use digits after the first place and underscores after the third place.

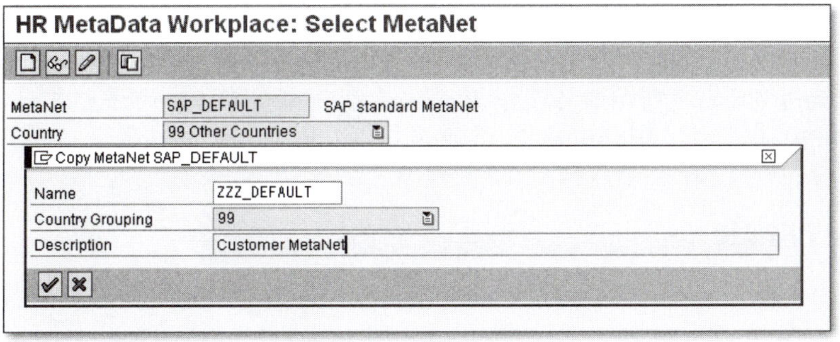

**HR MetaData Workplace: Select MetaNet**

| | |
|---|---|
| MetaNet | SAP_DEFAULT    SAP standard MetaNet |
| Country | 99 Other Countries |

Copy MetaNet SAP_DEFAULT

| | |
|---|---|
| Name | ZZZ_DEFAULT |
| Country Grouping | 99 |
| Description | Customer MetaNet |

**Figure 2.5**  Copying the SAP Standard MetaNet

Next, you assign the MetaNet to a customer-specific package, and save it locally or in a Workbench transport request to ensure the automatic integration with the transport system. All objects of the MetaNet are Workbench objects and consequently don't have to be imported into all used clients as is the case for customizing objects. If you've saved an object locally, you can retroactively assign a package, which is supposed to be transported to a target system, to the object. To do this, you need to modify the object catalog entry, which is described later on in this chapter. After saving the MetaNet, you navigate to the maintenance interface of the Metadata Workplace (see Figure 2.6).

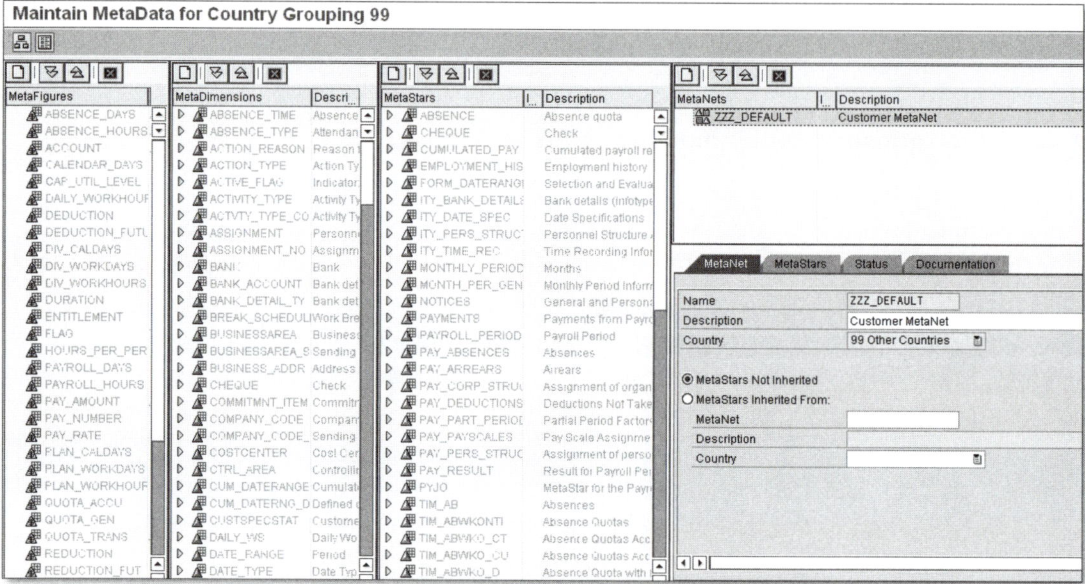

**Figure 2.6**  Maintenance Interface of the Metadata Workplace

MetaFigures, MetaDimensions, MetaStars, and the MetaNet itself are mapped in four selection trees (from left to right). This is also the logical order for the creation of new objects. Each window contains the following four buttons (see Figure 2.7):

▶  ☐  — Create a new object

▶  ▽  — Expand tree

▶  △  — Collapse tree

▶  ☒  — Hide tree

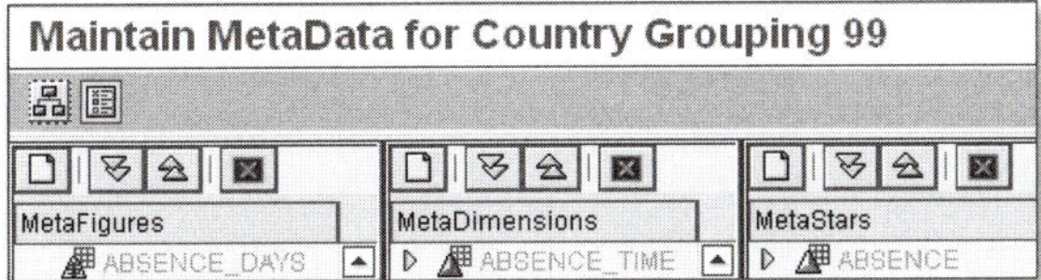

**Figure 2.7**  Buttons in the Metadata Workplace

You can also use the SHOW TREES button ⊞ or press F5 to display all hidden selection trees, and use the LEGEND button ▦ next to it or press F6 to display the legend.

The right mouse button provides the following functions:

▶ Copy the object

▶ Check the object

▶ Display and change the object catalog entry of the object

The EDIT menu item provides numerous functions, such as CREATE OBJECT, EXPAND NODE, COLLAPSE NODE, EXPAND TREE, COLLAPSE TREE, HIDE TREE, or SHOW TREES, which you can use to edit your MetaNet (see Figure 2.8).

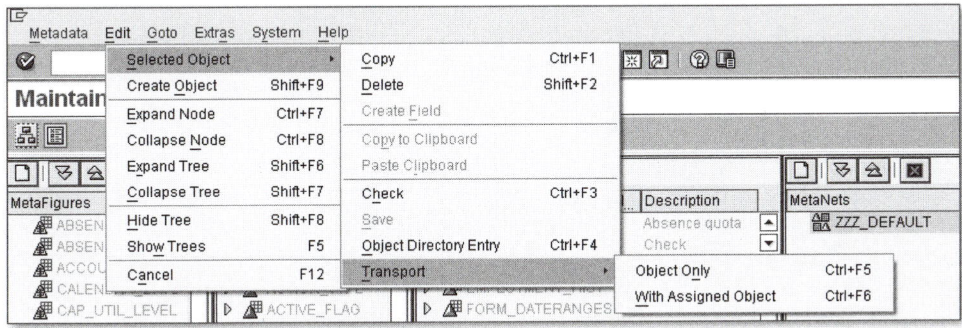

**Figure 2.8**  Functions for Editing the MetaNet

The tabs in the lower-right part of the screen enable you to maintain the attributes of an object (see Figure 2.6 or Figure 2.9). Depending on which object you double-click, the system displays different tabs with the corresponding input and maintenance options.

Before you start checking and editing the objects of the MetaNet, you should decide whether your MetaNet is supposed to inherit the MetaStars of another MetaNet or whether it's supposed to be independent. *Inheritance* has the advantage that changes to the SAP_DEFAULT standard MetaNet are automatically transferred to your MetaNet.

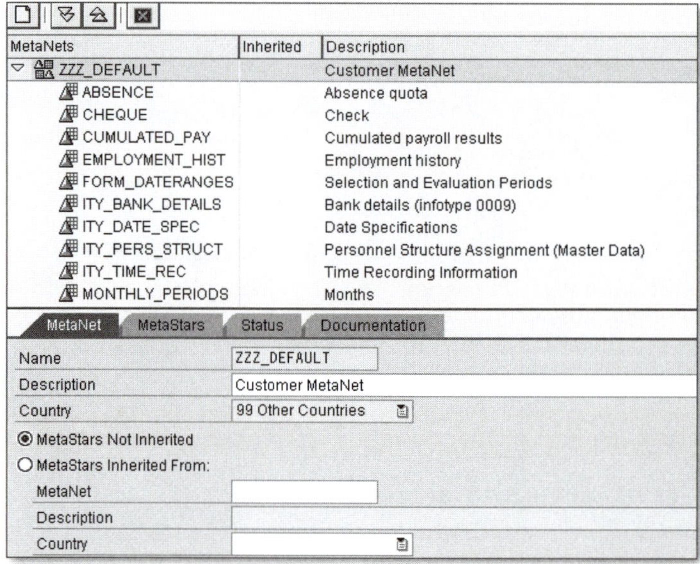

**Figure 2.9** Tabs of the MetaNet

To set up inheritance, select the MetaStars Inherited From option, enter "SAP_DEFAULT" (the standard MetaNet) into the MetaNet field, and enter "99 Other Countries" in the Country field (see Figure 2.10). Inherited MetaStars will have a ⬔ icon in the Inherited column (see Figure 2.10).

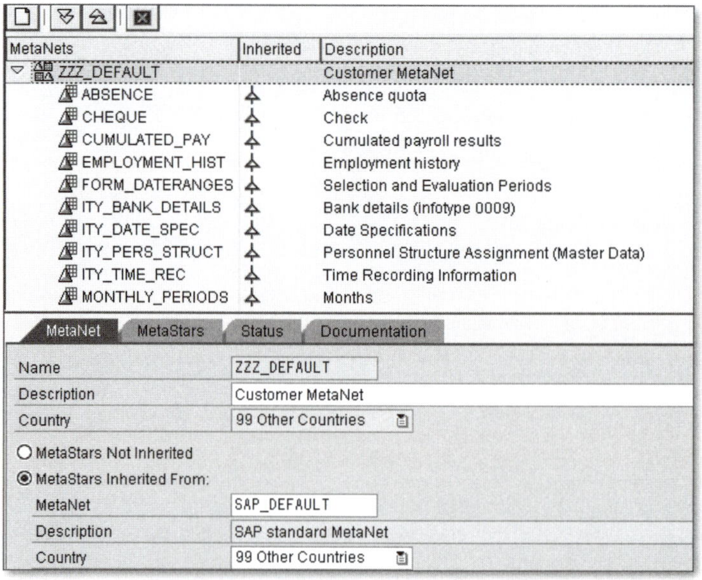

**Figure 2.10** Maintaining the MetaNet Tab — Inheritance of MetaStars

You can maintain objects that you create in a MetaNet for a specific country grouping within any MetaNet with the same country grouping. Objects of the MetaNet aren't dependent on the MetaNet but on the country grouping. For example, if you create a MetaDimension and a MetaStar with Country Grouping 99 and then call these objects in a MetaNet with Country Grouping 01, you can use these objects, but you can't change them. Objects that you can't change because they have been created in a different country grouping are called inherited objects, as illustrated in Figure 2.11.

| | | |
|---|---|---|
| ▷ ZTAB_T536A | Addresses | |
| ▽ ZTAB_T549Q | Payroll Periods | |
| ▷ FORPERIOD | For-Period | |
| ▷ ZZT549Q | Payroll Periods | |
| ▽ ZTIM_BEZUG | BEZUG | |
| ▷ ASSIGNMENT | Personnel Assignment Number | |
| ▷ ZTIM_BEZUG | Recalculation data | |

**Figure 2.11**  Inherited MetaNet Objects

Use a copy of the standard MetaNet or the standard MetaNet itself, if all data are provided, and no additional data are needed. If you *do* need additional data, you can create your own MetaStars, MetaDimensions, and MetaFigures. If you want to extend an existing and inherited object, copy it and customize it accordingly. However, before we explain how to create MetaStars, the following section describes the objects that make up a MetaStar. You can extend your MetaStar by newly created MetaFigures and MetaDimensions at any time.

> **Tip**
>
> Ask yourself the following questions before creating a MetaStar:
>
> ▶ Which data do I want to retrieve?
>
> ▶ What is the structure of my MetaStar supposed to look like?
>
> ▶ Can I use already-existing MetaDimensions?
>
> ▶ Do I need my own MetaDimensions?
>
> ▶ Which key fields and attributes is my MetaDimension supposed to contain?
>
> ▶ In which database tables and in which form are the data stored, and what is the best way to select the data?
>
> ▶ Do I need additional MetaFigures?
>
> You shouldn't begin creating your own objects until you've answered these questions and checked the existing objects of the MetaNet. This also enables you to get to know the MetaNet and its objects.

You can't delete a created MetaNet via the menu of the Metadata Workplace. Instead, you must right-click on the MetaNet, and then select DELETE (see Figure 2.12).

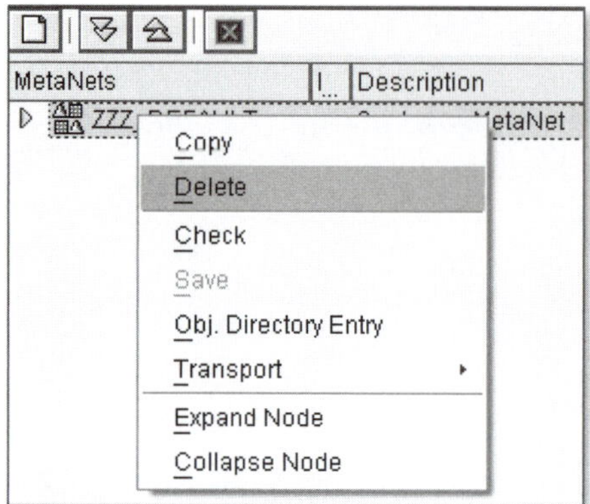

**Figure 2.12** Deleting the MetaNet

The following sections discuss the individual objects of the MetaNet in more detail. They describe how you can create new objects, how you can maintain properties, and which properties you can maintain, as well as the aspects you should consider. The properties of objects are described in tabs, which are explained for each object separately. The names for the tabs are identical for all objects, but they contain different input fields that describe the objects.

### Creating a MetaFigure

The standard MetaNet provides numerous MetaFigures. If you still need your own MetaFigure, follow the steps explained next.

Select the CREATE ▢ function in the MetaFigures menu selection tree. The system now prompts you to specify the NAME and DESCRIPTION of your new MetaFigure (see Figure 2.13). The naming convention corresponds to the naming convention for the MetaNet; that is, the name may only begin with a Z, and underscores can be used after the third place only. The country grouping is transferred automatically and corresponds to the country grouping of the MetaNet. The country grouping can be used in the corresponding MetaNets as long as you have multiple MetaNets with the same grouping, or the MetaFigure is created with Country Grouping 99. A MetaFigure with Grouping 99 exists in all MetaNets. These naming conventions are valid for all objects of the MetaNet.

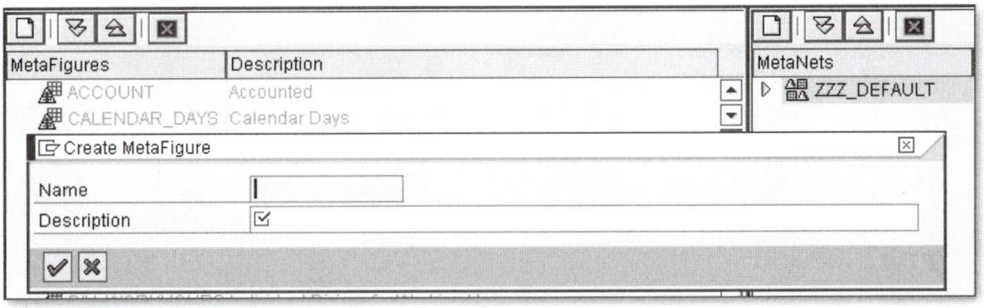

**Figure 2.13**  Creating a MetaFigure

Enter the type of the MetaFigure into the FIELD TYPE field of the METAFIGURE tab (see Figure 2.14). Press  F4  for help with this field.

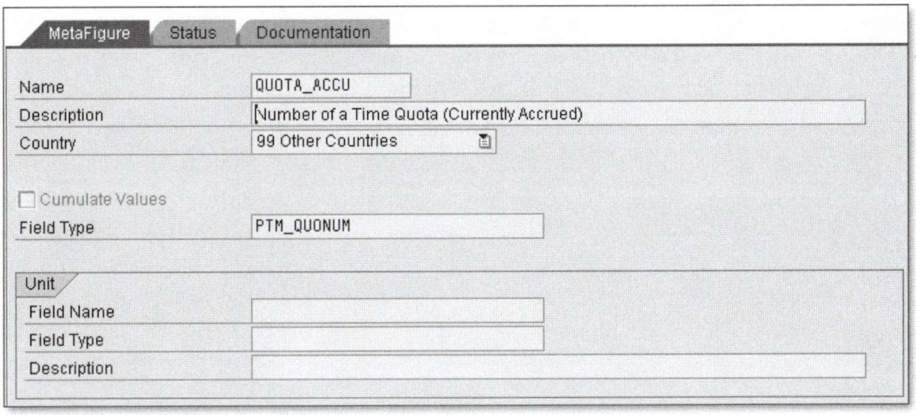

**Figure 2.14**  MetaFigure Tab

You only maintain the UNIT area if the MetaFigure is a key figure with a unit, such as the PAY_AMOUNT MetaFigure. Here, you expect a reference of the amount to a currency (see Figure 2.15). If you later assign a MetaFigure to a MetaStar whose line structure contains a field that could provide the unit for the MetaFigure, you don't have to maintain the unit in the MetaFigure. You can directly assign the field for the unit in the MetaStar.

Select the CUMULATE VALUES field if the system isn't supposed to manage the field in the MetaStar structure as a key field. This means that lines with identical values are cumulated in the key fields. For example, the PAY_DEDUCTIONS MetaStar contains all deductions that haven't been implemented yet. With the contained PAY_AMOUNT MetaFigure, the respective table lines are cumulated as already described.

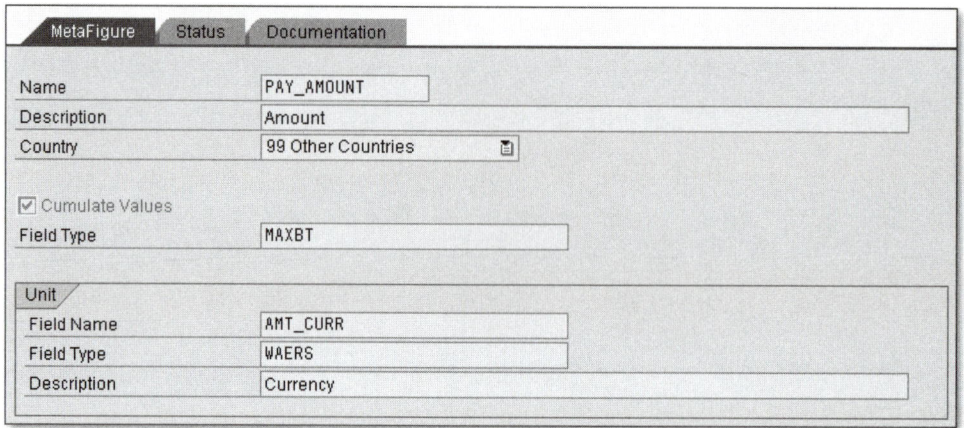

**Figure 2.15** MetaFigure with Unit

The STATUS tab contains technical information, such as the MetaFigure NAME and DESCRIPTION, STATUS, PACKAGE to which the MetaFigure is assigned, PERSON RESPONSIBLE, ORIGINAL SYSTEM, and ORIGINAL LANGUAGE (see Figure 2.16).

**Figure 2.16** Status Tab

In the last tab, DOCUMENTATION, you create the documentation of the MetaFigure. The documentation is automatically stored in the documentation maintenance (Transaction PDSY) (see Figure 2.17). The DOCUMENTATION tab is provided for all objects. You can use it to enter information on the data origin and usage, for example, to facilitate future maintenance and for the use of new users or consultants. The documentation is really helpful when you have to deal with a form and its components again after a longer period of time.

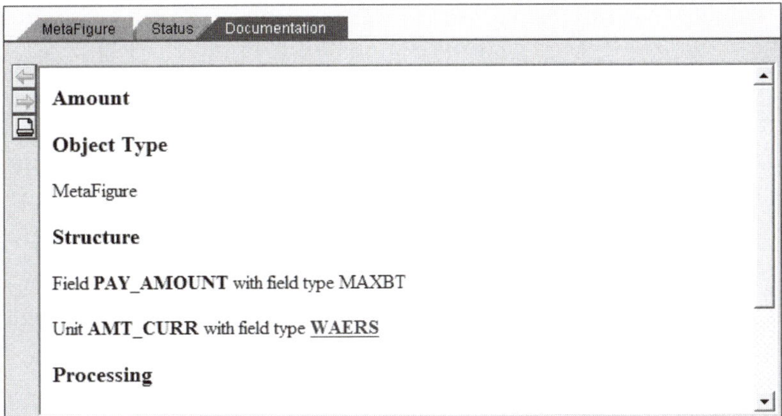

**Figure 2.17**  Documentation Tab

The descriptions of the STATUS tab and the DOCUMENTATION tab aren't repeated here for MetaDimensions and MetaStars because their structure and content are identical. As already mentioned, you should maintain the DOCUMENTATION tab for each object by writing one or two sentences that describe the object, its properties, and its usage.

### Creating a MetaDimension

As for MetaFigures, you should check whether there is already a MetaDimension that meets your requirements before creating your own MetaDimension or copying and customizing an existing MetaDimension. If you want to create a MetaDimension, use the same steps described for MetaFigures (see Figure 2.18). If you want to copy a MetaDimension, select the MetaDimension, right-click, and choose COPY. Alternatively, you can navigate to the function via the menu. In this case, you must also select the MetaDimension and then EDIT • SELECTED • COPY OBJECT. The system then prompts you to enter the name for your MetaDimension and a description. In this context, consider the naming convention for objects of the MetaNet, which was described in Section 2.1.2, Customizing and Enhancing the MetaNet.

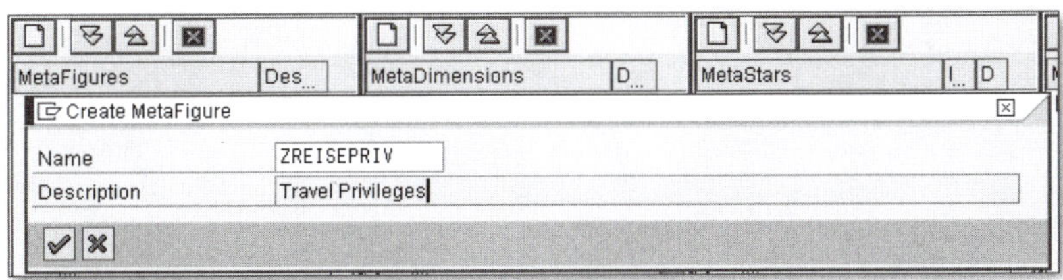

**Figure 2.18**  Creating a MetaDimension

After you've created a MetaDimension, you need to maintain the key fields and attributes of this dimension. As already explained in Section 2.1.1, MetaNet Objects, the content of a MetaDimension (as a data record) is uniquely described by the key fields. The attributes of a MetaDimension can be identified by means of the key fields. However, before defining a field as the key field or as an attribute, you must create it (see Figure 2.19). For this purpose, select the MetaDimension. You can create a field via the menu function to which you can navigate via the EDIT • SELECTED • CREATE FIELD path or by right-clicking.

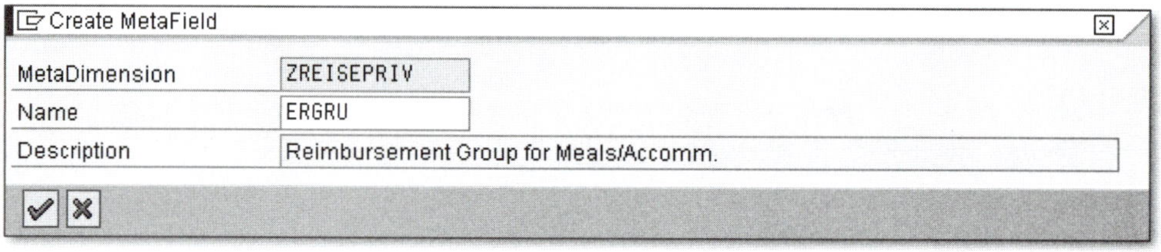

**Figure 2.19** Creating a MetaField

After you've created all of the fields, select the METAFIELDS tab of the MetaDimension. Now the system displays all existing MetaFields (see Figure 2.20). Enter the appropriate data item from the ABAP Dictionary into the FIELD TYPE column. If required, use the input help to select the appropriate type. Now you must define whether it's a *key field* or an *attribute*. Select the corresponding field of the KEY column. A field that is defined as a key contains the icon in the KEY column. An attribute has the icon. If a data item has domain fixed values, you can use them to populate an attribute. Enter the "VAL_TEXT" value into the FIELD TYPE field of the attribute, and enter the MetaField whose domain fixed values the attribute is supposed to contain into the FIXED VALUE OF field.

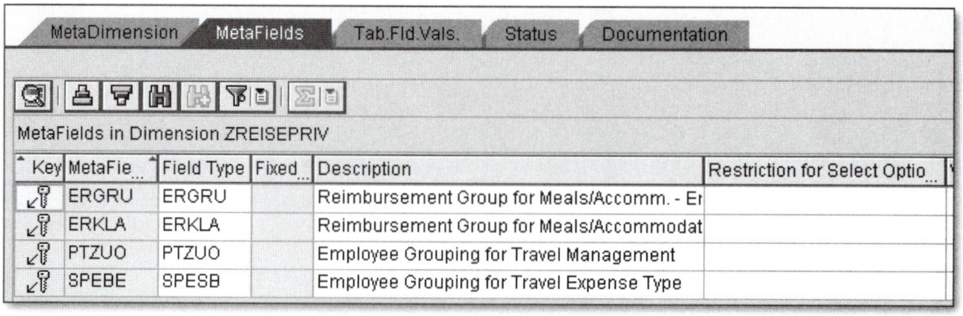

**Figure 2.20** Maintaining the MetaFields Tab

In the additional two columns, you can implement the restrictions regarding the selection conditions for the individual MetaFields. Entries in the RESTRICTION FOR SELECT OPTIONS column enable you to define whether you want to allow for multiple selections, single selections, or no selections at all. In the VALIDITY OF THE SELECT OPTIONS column (not displayed in the figure), you specify whether the previously defined restriction is globally or locally valid. These definitions become effective when you maintain the InfoNet and InfoStars for your forms. For example, if the selection is globally valid, the selection that you implement in the Info-Star for the InfoDimension is also automatically adapted for all InfoStars in which this InfoDimension is used. If the selection is locally valid, you can maintain the selection in different ways for all InfoStars that use the InfoDimension.

In the EMPLOYEE MetaDimension, a global restriction is valid for the selection conditions of some MetaFields, for example, ADRS1_NAME_FMT. As a result, only one selection can be maintained (see Figure 2.21) if you use this MetaDimension in your InfoNet and implement a selection for the InfoDimension, as in the case mentioned.

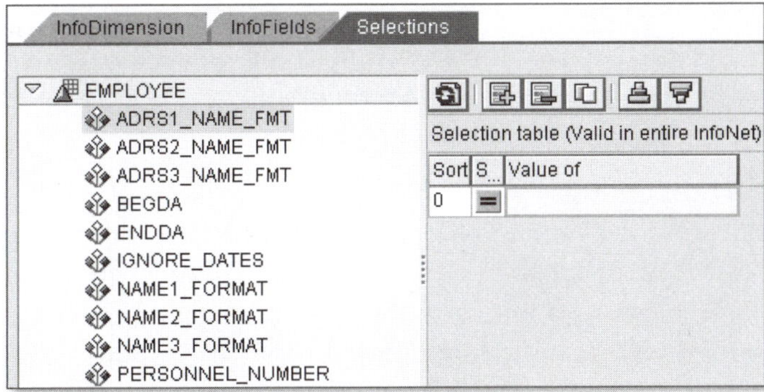


**Figure 2.21** Restricted Selection for the InfoDimension

At this point, you should only consider whether and how you want to allow fields to be selected. The actual selection is then made in the InfoNet of the form. The effect of the selected flag is only obvious here. However, changes can also be made at a later stage. Section 2.2.3, Defining and Selecting Form-Specific Data, describes how you insert a selection in the InfoNet.

After creating the MetaFields of the MetaDimension, you need to think about how the attributes of the MetaDimension will be populated. The key fields are populated when the MetaStar to which these fields are assigned is processed. The values that are contained in the key fields are then used to read the attributes. The METADIMENSION tab provides the following alternatives (see Figure 2.22):

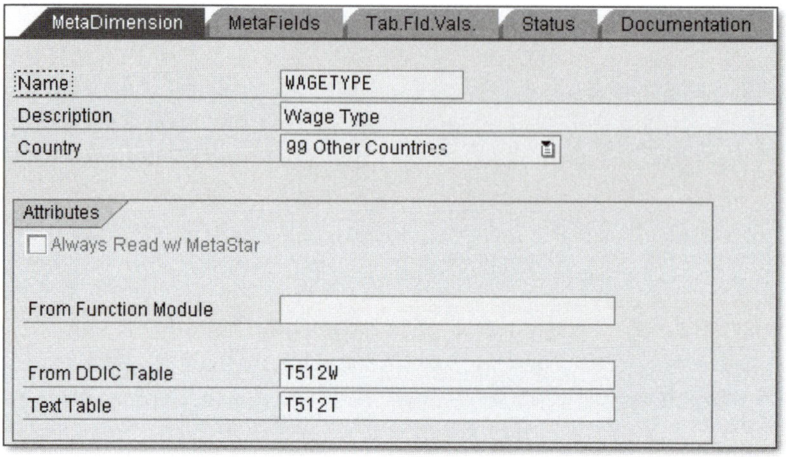

**Figure 2.22** MetaDimension Tab

▸ ALWAYS READ W/ METASTAR
This option populates the attributes of the MetaDimension when the system reads the MetaStar. In this case, you define a function module as the read function in the METADIMENSIONS tab of the MetaStar.

▸ FROM FUNCTION MODULE
The key values are transferred to a function module that populates the attribute fields. If you enter a new function module into the FUNCTION MODULE field, the system displays the CREATE READ FUNCTION button ▢ after you press the Enter key. If you create the function module here, the system automatically defines the interface of the function module.

▸ FROM DDIC TABLE
If a database table or a view exists in the Data Dictionary whose entries can be read via the key fields of the MetaDimension, use them to populate the attribute fields. For example, the WAGETYPE: MetaDimension attributes are populated via Table T512W and the corresponding TEXT TABLE T512T. If you use this alternative, you must now implement the assignment between the MetaFields and the table fields in the METAFIELDS tab. In this context, the key fields serve as the selection criteria for reading the table entry (see Figure 2.23).

MetaFields in Dimension WAGETYPE

| Key | Table Field | Operator for the Select. | MetaField | from text table | Field Type | Fixed value of | Description |
|---|---|---|---|---|---|---|---|
| 🔑 | MOLGA | = | COUNTRY | ☐ | MOLGA | | Country Grouping |
| 🔑 | LGART | = | WAGETYPE | ☐ | LGART | | Wage Type |
| 🔳 | LGTXT | | LONGTEXT | ☑ | LGTXT | | Long Text |
| 🔳 | KZTXT | | SHORTTEXT | ☑ | KZTXT | | Short Text |

**Figure 2.23**  Selection for Populating the Attributes of a MetaDimension via a DDIC Table

You can enter additional key fields for reading the database table in the TABLE FIELD VALUES tab. This is possible if the key fields contain constant values that are identical for all dimension values that need to be determined. For example, the EVALCLASS02 MetaDimension attribute is populated from Database Table T52D4 and Text Table T52DB. The evaluation class is an additional key field of these tables that contains the constant value "02" (see Figures 2.24 to 2.26) to read the characteristics of this evaluation class.

| Name | EVALCLASS02 |
|---|---|
| Description | Wage Type Grouping in Evaluation Class 02 |
| Country | 99 Other Countries |

**Attributes**

☐ Always Read w/ MetaStar

| From Function Module | |
|---|---|
| From DDIC Table | T52D4 |
| Text Table | T52DB |

**Figure 2.24**  MetaDimension for Evaluation Class 02

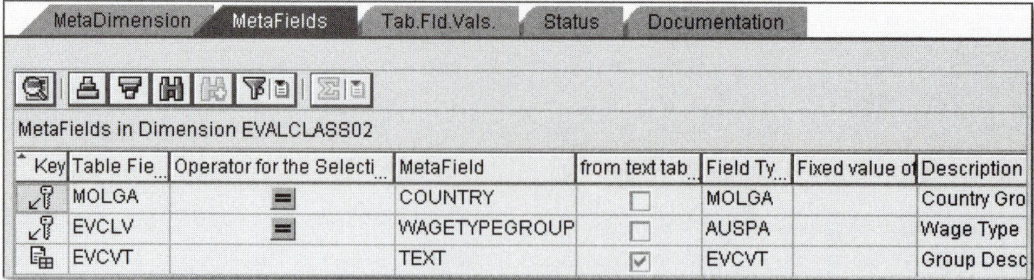

**Figure 2.25**  Assignment of the Table Fields to the MetaFields

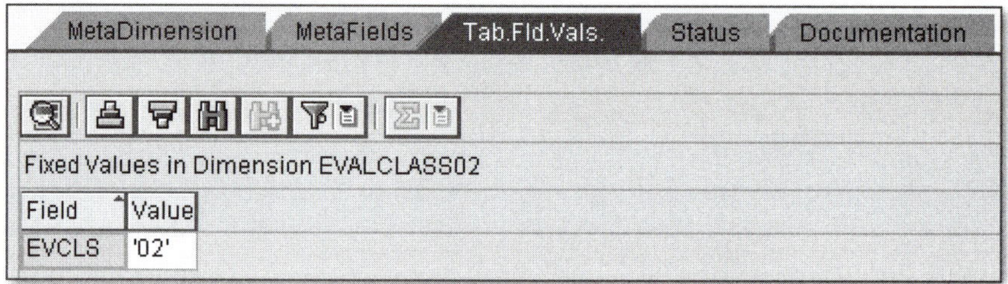

**Figure 2.26**  Additional Constant for Populating the Attributes

The two additional tabs, STATUS and DOCUMENTATION, are identical to the tabs for the MetaFigures with the same name and aren't discussed here again.

You assign your own or already-existing MetaDimensions to your MetaStars via drag and drop. The following section describes how you create MetaStars.

### Creating a MetaStar

Section 2.1.1, MetaNet Objects, already defined the objects of the MetaNet. This section describes how you can create your own MetaStar in the Metadata Workplace and which attributes and properties you need to maintain.

> **Tip**
>
> Don't change provided MetaStars; instead, use them as templates, and then customize your MetaStars accordingly.

To create MetaStars, click the CREATE button ☐ in the MetaStars selection tree. The system now prompts you to specify the NAME and DESCRIPTION of your MetaStar (see Figure 2.27).

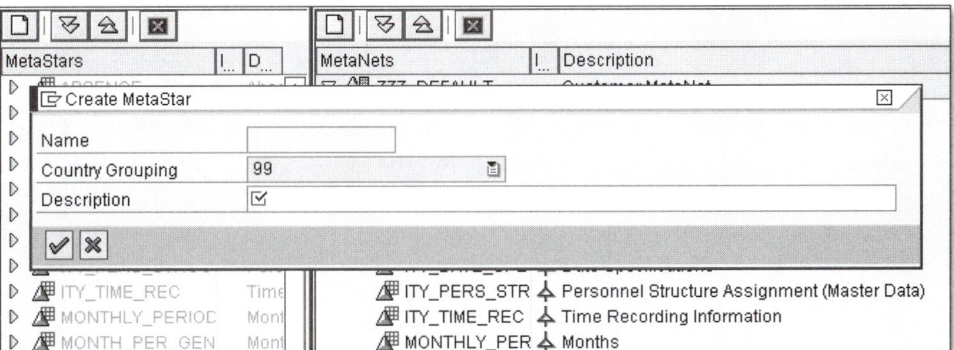

**Figure 2.27**  Creating a MetaStar

You maintain the attributes and properties of a MetaStar in the MetaStar, MetaDimensions, MetaFields, MetaFigures, Status, and Documentation tabs (see Figure 2.28).

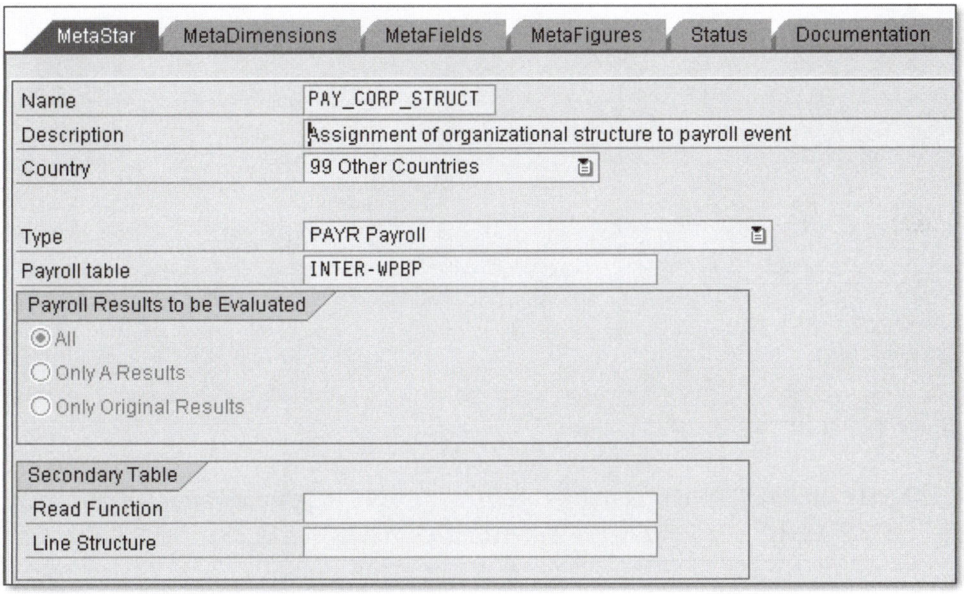

**Figure 2.28**  Attributes and Properties of a MetaStar

The Name, Description, and Country are automatically transferred to the MetaStar tab when the MetaStar is created and can't be maintained. To continue with the definition of your MetaStar, you must select a Type, which defines the type of data that will be read and when. This is the first information you must specify in the attributes of the MetaStar when creating a MetaStar. The system won't display the type-dependent attributes for maintenance until you enter the TYPE. Note that you can't modify the type at a later stage or by creating a new MetaStar. If you use a MetaStar as a template, the system automatically copies the type of the MetaStar. The following types are available:

▶ **Master data**

Use the "Master data" type if you want to integrate data from infotypes (see Figure 2.29). In the print program, the structures of the MetaStar are populated at the time of `GET PERSON`. The methods of the `CL_HRPAY99_IR_4_PNPCEREPORTING` class assume the process of reading the data.

Enter the infotype whose data you want to read. In the SECONDARY TABLE area, you can specify a READ FUNCTION and LINE STRUCTURE that is called and populated after the data on the respective infotype has been retrieved.

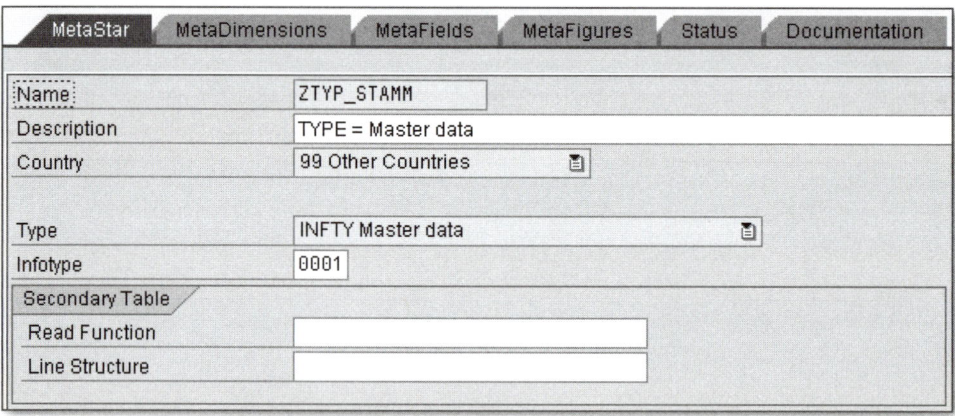

**Figure 2.29** MetaStar Tab for the "Master Data" Type

The ITY_PERS_STRUCT (contains INFOTYPE "0001" [Organizational Assignment]) and ITY_DATE_SPEC (contains data from INFOTYPE "0041" [Date Specifications]) MetaStars are examples of this type. Because you can save up to 12 date specifications in a line of INFOTYPE 0041, the read function populates a secondary table with single records for each date specification.

▶ **Payroll**

Assign the "Payroll" type to MetaStars that you want to populate with data from payroll results (see Figure 2.30). You can select the table whose data your

MetaStar is supposed to contain via the input help of the PAYROLL TABLE field. However, if you want to populate a secondary table with another line structure, you can do this via the READ FUNCTION field. You can only select one alternative because the entries exclude each other.

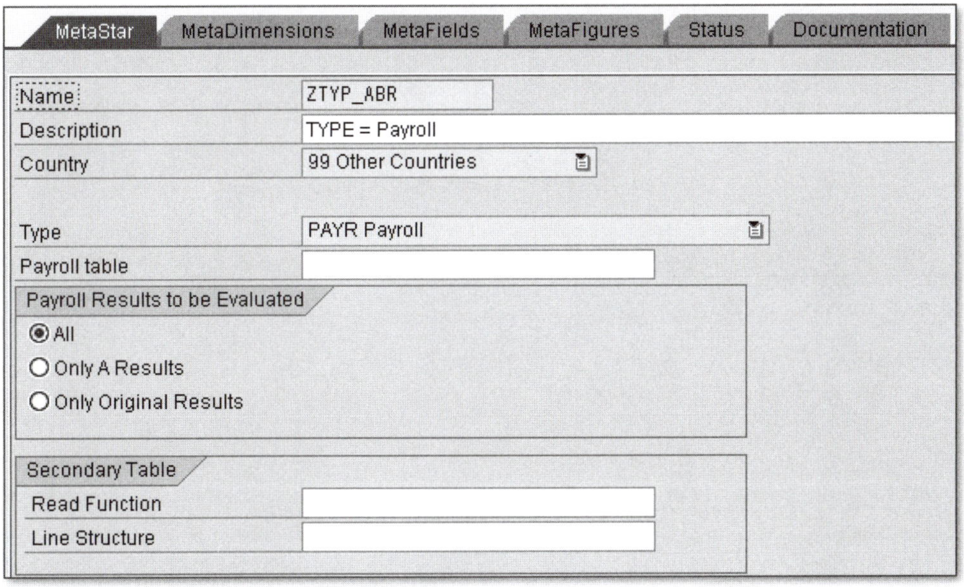

MetaStar    MetaDimensions    MetaFields    MetaFigures    Status    Documentation

Name    ZTYP_ABR
Description    TYPE = Payroll
Country    99 Other Countries
Type    PAYR Payroll
Payroll table
Payroll Results to be Evaluated
All
Only A Results
Only Original Results
Secondary Table
Read Function
Line Structure

**Figure 2.30**  MetaStar Tab for the "Payroll" Type

Both cases are mapped in the PAYMENTS and PAY_RESULT MetaStars. In the PAYROLL RESULTS TO BE EVALUATED area, you can limit the selected payroll results through the status indicator. If payroll results with the A (current result) or P (previous result) status indicator are selected, retroactive accounting differences occur, which aren't always useful in MetaStars. If you set the ALL flag, the system evaluates all payroll results; that is, for retroactive accounting the values in the summarizable fields are deducted from the current values, which lead to retroactive accounting differences.

For example, the PAY_RESULT MetaStar contains the results for the selected payroll dates. You can use the ONLY A RESULTS flag to evaluate results with the A status indicator without calculating retroactive accounting differences. This is the case for the CUMULATED_PAY MetaStar, which contains the cumulated payroll results that don't require calculating the retroactive accounting differences.

If you only want to evaluate original results, set the ONLY ORIGINAL RESULTS flag. For original results, the system evaluates only the results for which the in-period corresponds to the for-period. For example, the PAYMENTS MetaStar contains the payments that aren't changed in retroactive accounting so that retroactive accounting results don't have to be considered.

▶ **Time Evaluation Data**
Use the "Time Evaluation Data" type if you want to integrate data from the time evaluation (see Figure 2.31). In the print program, the structures of the MetaStar are populated at the time of GET PERSON. All tables of the time evaluation are available that are read via the HR_FORMS_TIM_GET_B2_RESULTS function module.

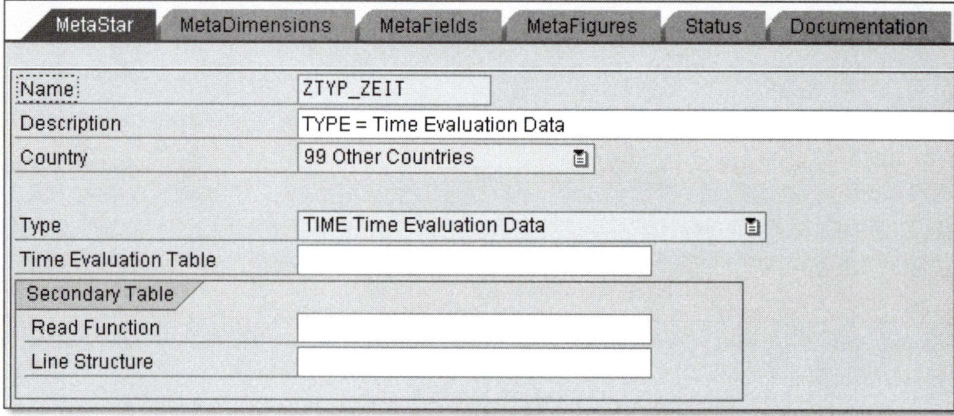


**Figure 2.31** MetaStar Tab for the "Time Evaluation Data" Type

Just as you can for the "Payroll" type, you can specify a read function (instead of a table from the time evaluation tables) that populates the line structure of a secondary table. If you populate both areas, the secondary table is ignored. Existing MetaStars for the time statement have the TIM_ prefix.

▶ **Special Type A (Dependent on Pers. No.)**
Data that depends on a person is indicated by the "Special Type A" type and is read at the time of GET PERSON in the print program (see Figure 2.32).

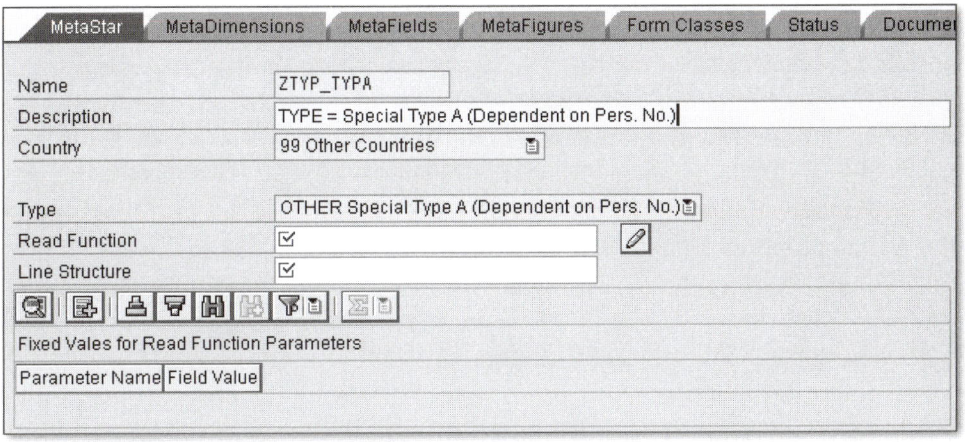

**Figure 2.32** MetaStar Tab for the "Special Type A" Type

You enter a Read Function and the Line Structure that is to be populated. In addition, you can specify Fixed Values that the system considers when it calls the read routine. The reading of the absence quota is performed based on this type and populates the ABSENCE MetaStar.

▶ **Special Type U (Independent of Pers. No.)**
"Special Type U" is similar to "Special Type A." However, the data for this type is read at the time of START-OF-SELECTION because the data is person-independent. Here, you also specify a Read Function, a Line Structure, and optionally Fixed Values For Read Function Parameters (see Figure 2.33).

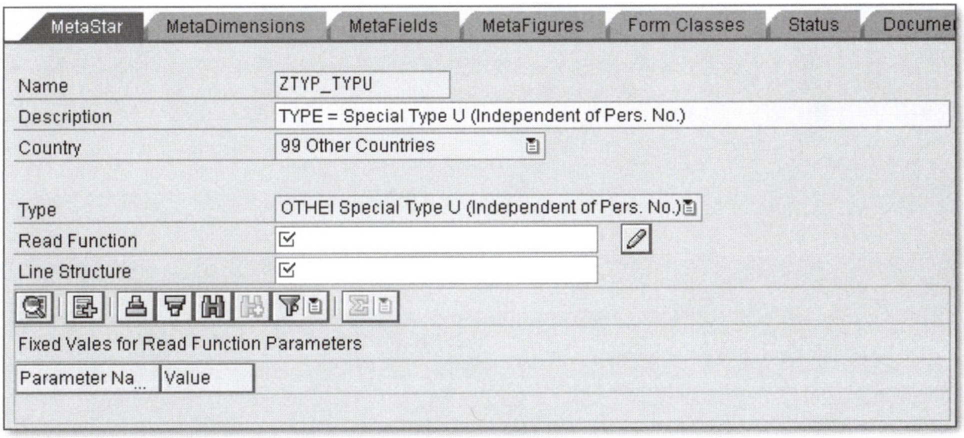

**Figure 2.33** MetaStar Tab for the "Special Type U" Type

For example, the MONTHLY_PERIODS MetaStar contains the periods for the selected period parameter in the selection period. The period parameter is transferred to the read function by specifying a fixed value.

If you want to create a read function, enter a function module into the corresponding field in the METASTAR tab. Compared to the creation of the function module via the Function Builder (Transaction SE37), the advantage of this procedure is that the system proposes the interface parameters. If required, you can then customize the function modules that you created with this procedure. In our example, after you've pressed the Enter key, the system displays the message that the specified function module does not exist (see Figure 2.34).

**Figure 2.34** Message If the Function Module Does Not Exist

Next to the READ FUNCTION field, the system now displays the button for creating the function module (see Figure 2.35). After you've clicked this button, the system asks you to assign the module to a function group. If you haven't created a function group yet, you can do this via Transaction SE37 (Function Builder). You can also call the Function Builder using the SAP Easy Access menu: TOOLS • ABAP WORKBENCH • DEVELOPMENT • FUNCTION BUILDER. You can then create a function group via the GOTO • FUNCTION GROUP MANAGEMENT • CREATE GROUP path.

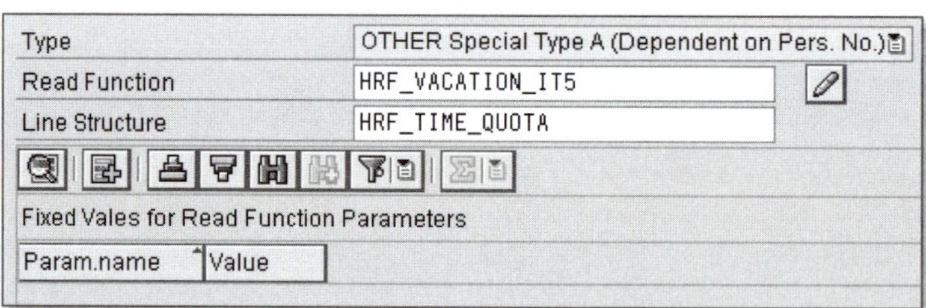


**Figure 2.35** Button for Creating the Function Module

> **Tip**
>
> You can create your own function group for your MetaNet so that you keep an overview of which function modules are used in the MetaNet.

After creating a MetaStar and editing the METASTAR tab, check which MetaDimensions you must assign to the MetaStar. If a MetaStar is employee-dependent, you should assign the two MetaDimensions, ASSIGNMENT and EMPLOYEE, for example. Both MetaDimensions contain information on the employee.

## Assigning MetaStars to a MetaDimension

This section provides details on MetaDimensions by first describing how to assign a MetaStar and how the MetaStar influences the METADIMENSIONS tab, which lists the MetaDimensions assigned to the MetaStar. Here you can define whether the key fields of a MetaDimension are populated by a read function or the line structure of the MetaStar. If you want to populate the key fields of the MetaDimension with a read function, that is, a function module, you should create the module as described previously for the MetaStar. You can't change the read functions of a provided MetaStar. You can view the function module by clicking on the glasses icon (see Figure 2.36).

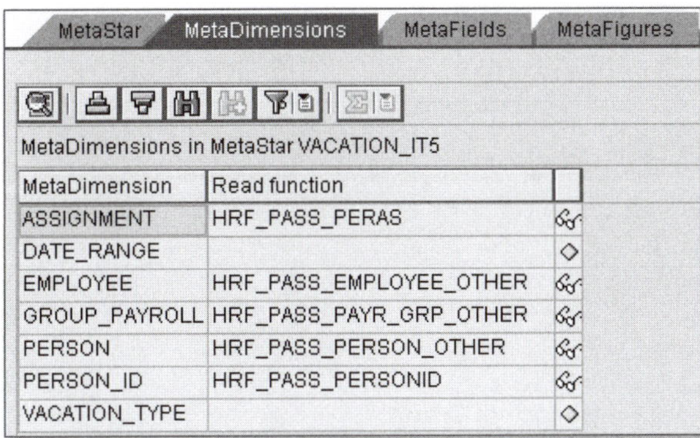

**Figure 2.36**  Provided MetaDimensions

If you copy a MetaStar, it already contains the read functions that the original object includes. If you create a new MetaStar and assign MetaDimensions to it, the READ FUNCTION field is always empty (see Figure 2.37).

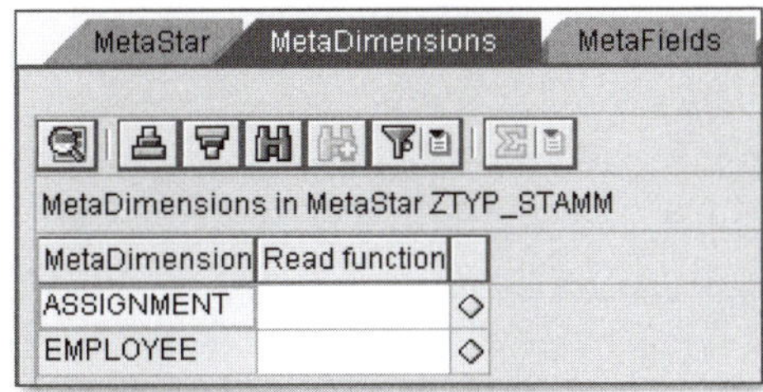

**Figure 2.37**  Own MetaStar

If you don't specify a specific read function for a provided MetaDimension (this option is available), find the corresponding function module from another MetaStar, and enter this one.

The entries that you make in the METADIMENSIONS tab affect the METAFIELDS tab (see Figure 2.38). MetaDimensions that have a read function are ignored here.

| MetaStar | MetaDimensions | MetaFields | MetaFigures | Status | Documentation |

MetaFields Filled by MetaStar PAY_ABSENCES

| MetaDimension | Read function | MetaField | Table | Table Field |
| --- | --- | --- | --- | --- |
| ABSENCE_TIME | ☐ | BEGIN_DATE | INTER-AB | BEGDA |
| ABSENCE_TIME | ☐ | BEGIN_TIME | INTER-AB | BEGUZ |
| ABSENCE_TIME | ☐ | END_DATE | INTER-AB | ENDDA |
| ABSENCE_TIME | ☐ | END_TIME | INTER-AB | ENDUZ |
| ABSENCE_TYPE | ☐ | ABSENCE_TYPE | INTER-AB | AWART |
| ABSENCE_TYPE | ☐ | BEGDA | INTER-WPBP | BEGDA |
| ABSENCE_TYPE | ☐ | ENDDA | INTER-WPBP | ENDDA |
| ABSENCE_TYPE | ☐ | PERS_AREA | INTER-WPBP | WERKS |
| ABSENCE_TYPE | ☐ | PERS_SUBAREA | INTER-WPBP | BTRTL |
| ASSIGNMENT | ☑ | PERAS | | |
| EMPLOYEE | ☑ | ADRS1_NAME_FMT | | |
| EMPLOYEE | ☑ | ADRS2_NAME_FMT | | |
| EMPLOYEE | ☑ | ADRS3_NAME_FMT | | |

**Figure 2.38** MetaFields Tab

You maintain the MetaFields directly in the MetaDimension, as we discussed earlier. If no read function is specified for populating the MetaFields, you must populate the fields via the MetaStar and its line structure. The METADIMENSION, READ FUNCTION, and METAFIELD columns are just display columns. In the TABLE and TABLE FIELD columns, you assign the tables and fields that are available for the MetaStar to the fields of the corresponding MetaDimension. If only one table or line structure is available, the TABLE column is omitted. The PAY_ABSENCES and ITY_DATE_SPEC MetaStars are examples of these two cases.

Whether only one table or multiple tables are provided depends on the MetaStar type. For the PAYROLL and TIME EVALUATION DATA MetaStar types, the TABLE column is available. Here, you can assign all available table fields to the fields of the MetaDimensions that are assigned to the MetaStar. For the mentioned MetaStar types, you can select the tables of the corresponding cluster.

The MetaFigures tab (see Figure 2.39) lists the MetaFigures that are assigned to the MetaStar. These are populated from the tables of the MetaStars. You can also specify a read function here. Consequently, the MetaFigures aren't immediately populated. Instead, they are populated after the MetaStar table has been populated. For each line of this table, the system calls the read function to populate the MetaFigures. The columns in this tab also depend on the MetaStar type. For the Payroll type, for example, you can use the Payroll Currency If Unit Is Empty column to define how the system is supposed to proceed if no currency is transferred for fields that contain an amount (see Figure 2.39).

| MetaStar | MetaDimensions | MetaFields | MetaFigures | Status | Documentation |

MetaFigures in MetaStar ZPAY_RESULT

| MetaFigure | Read function | | Table Field | Table Field for Unit | Payroll Currency if Unit is Empty |
| --- | --- | --- | --- | --- | --- |
| PAY_AMOUNT | | ◇ | BETRG | AMT_CURR | ☐ |
| PAY_NUMBER | | ◇ | ANZHL | ZEINH | ◉ |
| PAY_RATE | | ◇ | BETPE | RTE_CURR | ☐ |

**Figure 2.39**  MetaFigures Tab

The Special Type A and Special Type U MetaStar types have an additional tab, Form Classes (see Figure 2.40). By specifying a form class, you can exclude the MetaStar if the form belongs to this class. Both MetaStar types can generally be used in any form class and, if required, may not be provided in one or more form classes in the tab. However, this only makes sense if the developer of a form that is categorized via the form class isn't supposed to be provided with certain MetaStars, or if you want to minimize the number of MetaStars for a form due to the form class.

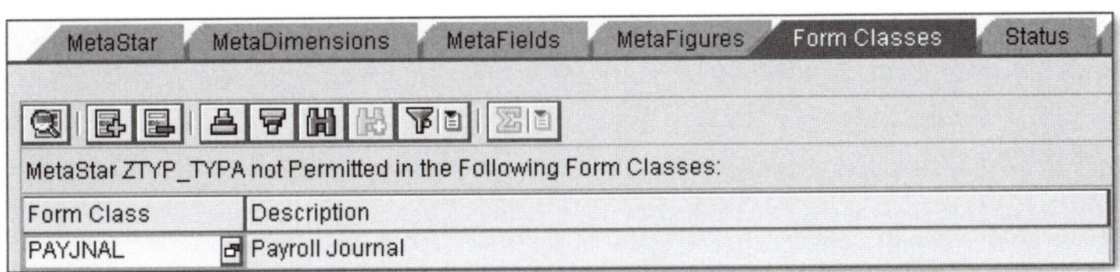

| MetaStar | MetaDimensions | MetaFields | MetaFigures | Form Classes | Status |

MetaStar ZTYP_TYPA not Permitted in the Following Form Classes:

| Form Class | Description |
| --- | --- |
| PAYJNAL | Payroll Journal |

**Figure 2.40**  Form Classes Tab

The system automatically hides the other MetaStar types if a form class in which the type isn't allowed is assigned to the form. For example, MetaStars of the Time Evaluation type aren't displayed in the payslip that is assigned to the PAYSLIP form class because of the properties of the form classes, which you can view via the Forms Workplace menu. For this purpose, call the UTILITIES • FORM CLASSES • DISPLAY menu item.

## 2.2  Creating a Form

Forms you create with the Forms Workplace are based on the data that has been selected from the assigned MetaNet. When the form is generated, the system automatically creates the application program and the data definitions that are defined in the InfoNet. The selection screen and its fields depend on the report category and form class of the form. Note that you can't extend the selection screen by customer-specific parameters or selection options. If you want to output the form as a Smart Form or SAP Interactive Form, you can also replace the data collection using a customer-specific program rather than the Forms Workplace. The limitation of the person selection due to additional parameters can be managed by including a report that assumes this task. Then you call your actual form within the program and transfer the previously selected personnel numbers to it.

In the following sections we describe the structure of the Forms Workplace, and how to create and maintain forms and their properties and attributes. Because Chapters 4 and 5 discuss the creation of payslips and time statements in detail, a specific form is used that you create by following the steps described here. The Forms Workplace is particularly used to create payslips and time statements because templates are available for both forms. These templates can then be copied. The same applies to the objects that are contained in the SAP standard MetaNet, SAP_DEFAULT. However, the following sections only describe a procedure that is independent of this procedure because it can be used for all forms that you create with the Forms Workplace.

### 2.2.1  Getting Started with the HR Forms Workplace

To get started, call the Forms Workplace by using Transaction HRFORMS (see Figure 2.41). The initial screen displays an overview list of all existing forms. For the payslip and time statement, templates are available for your use.

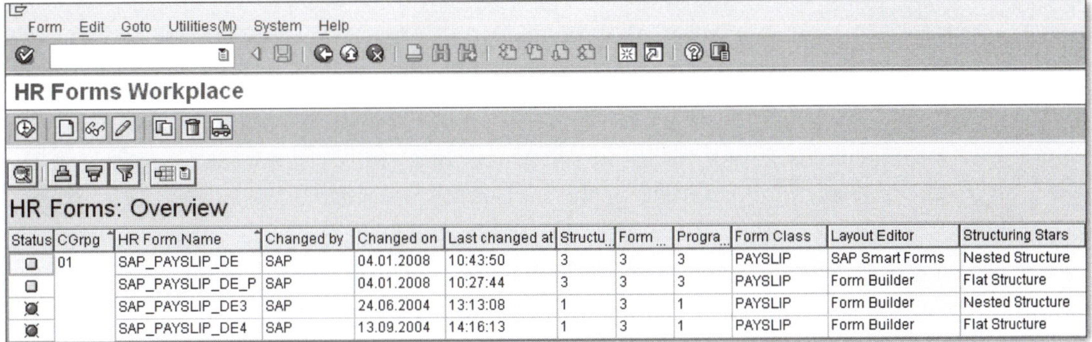

**Figure 2.41** Initial Screen of the HR Forms Workplace

The columns in the overview list are described here:

- **Status Of The Form**
  The green traffic light indicates the form is active; the red traffic light indicates the form is inactive.

- **CGRPG (Country Grouping)**
  The country grouping supports country-dependent and country-independent forms. For the payslip, this affects the data that is accessed. When you call the payroll for a specific country, the system only provides the forms for selection that correspond either to the country grouping or to the international version (99). This doesn't apply to the time statement because it's only available in the international version (like the cluster, which is country-independent).

- **HR Form Name**
  You select the name of the form when creating the form. Consider the naming convention, and select a meaningful name that indicates the form type.

- **Changed By**
  The system displays the SAP user name of the last person who changed the form.

- **Changed On and Last Changed At**
  These two columns list the date and time of the last change of the form. If the up-to-dateness of a form template isn't indicated by the name, always select the template with the most recent date.

- **Structure Status, Form Definition Status, Program Status**
  The status of one of these components of a form provides information on its status. The possible statuses correspond to the values "1" for inactive, "2" for in process, and "3" for active.

▶ **Form Class**
The following form classes are available: OTHER FORMS, PAYROLL JOURNAL, PAYROLL ACCOUNT, PAYSLIP, and TIME STATEMENT. When the form is created, the form class defines which MetaNet and report categories are proposed. The additional fields in the selection screen of the print program also depend on the form class. You can then display or hide the permitted fields. The data that you can access in the form is also affected by the form class. For example, you can't access data from the time evaluation in a form that contains the PAYSLIP form class.

▶ **Layout Editor**
For the graphical design, you can choose between the Form Builder for Smart Forms or for SAP Interactive Forms. After you've selected a variant and created your form, you can't change this any longer.

▶ **Structuring Stars**
You can choose either a nested or a flat structure. In a *nested structure* of the InfoStar tables, they only contain the key fields of the assigned InfoDimensions and the InfoFigures. You must retrieve the attribute fields directly from the InfoDimension. As a result, you must collect the data from several tables using loop statements. If you use *flat structures*, the InfoStar tables also contain the attribute fields of the InfoDimensions. Consequently, you can avoid additional loop statements. If possible, you should use flat structures for the InfoStars because this makes creating forms much easier.

After ensuring that the data required for your form is available in the standard MetaNet or your own MetaNet, you can continue creating your form. If you notice that you need additional data, you can always extend the MetaNet retroactively. You can even assign a new MetaNet if it contains all of the data that you already use in your form-specific MetaNet, that is, the InfoNet.

If a form template that you can use exists, you can copy it to create your own form. Otherwise, you can create a new form.

To copy a template and create a form, follow these steps:

1. Select the form that you want to copy, and select the COPY button 🗗.

2. Specify the required form name and the country grouping. The system automatically copies all other attributes. The same function is provided via the FORM • COPY menu path.

To create a new form, follow these steps:

1. Select the CREATE button ☐.
2. Specify the form name, the country grouping, and the form class. In this case, you can use the same function via the FORM • CREATE menu path.

### 2.2.2 Defining Form Attributes

Now that you've created your form, you need to maintain further attributes and activate the form parts (see Figure 2.42). To get started, enter the DESCRIPTION, and then select the METANET, the LAYOUT EDITOR, and the STAR STRUCTURING for your form as illustrated in Figure 2.42. Section 2.2.1, Getting Started with the HR Forms Workplace, includes the description of the inputs and objects mentioned here. If you've created your own MetaNet, which you also want to use for your form, specify this MetaNet in the METANET field. Otherwise, use the SAP standard MetaNet, SAP_DEFAULT.

| HR Form | InfoStars | Documentation | Select. Screen | Cumulation WTs |
|---|---|---|---|---|

| | |
|---|---|
| HR Form Name | ZZZ_FORMULAR |
| Description | Template |
| Form Class | NONE Other Forms |
| MetaNet | SAP_DEFAULT SAP standard MetaNet |
| Layout Editor | X Form Builder |
| Star Structuring | X Flat Structure |

**Status**

| | | | |
|---|---|---|---|
| Status | ☒ Inactive | | |
| Created by | MAES | on 08.01.2009 | at 13:23:53 |
| Changed by | | on | at 00:00:00 |

**Form Parts**

| | |
|---|---|
| ABAP Dictionary Structure | ☒ Inactive |
| SAP Smart Form Name | ☒ Inactive |
| Print Program | ☒ Inactive |

**Figure 2.42** Form Attributes in the HR Form Tab

The INFOSTARS tab provides an overview of the InfoStars that are already available in your InfoNet. If your form isn't based on a template in which the InfoNet is already defined, it's empty at first. You can also define a description for your form in the DOCUMENTATION tab. This description can be called in the initial screen of the Forms Workplace via the GOTO • DOCUMENTATION menu path.

The SELECT. SCREEN tab provides numerous optional parameters. You can display or hide these options and predefine values for them (see Figure 2.43). They mainly refer to the payslip, so Section 4.2.1 describes them in detail in Chapter 4. The SELECT. SCREEN tab enables you to enter the REPORT CATEGORY for the selection screen of the print program, which generally controls the limitation of the data to be selected and the data retrieval.

| HR Form | InfoStars | Documentation | Select. Screen | Cumulation WTs |

Report category     `HRF_ONOC`    HRFORMS: Other Forms - No Off-cycle

Optional fields in the selection screen

| Show | Selection Field | Set Default ... | Default Value |
| --- | --- | --- | --- |
| ☐ | Include retroactive accounting: no, yes, also retr accg runs | ☐ | |
| ☐ | Consider and Display Archived Payroll Results | ☐ | |
| ☐ | Currency conversion | ☐ | |
| ☐ | Only Read Infotype Records in the Time Interval | ☐ | |
| ☐ | In-view payroll periods | ☐ | |
| ☐ | Alternative Currency | ☐ | |
| ☐ | Number of Employees per Form (0= All) | ☐ | |
| ☐ | Simulate multiple payroll | ☐ | |

**Figure 2.43** Select. Screen Tab

In the CUMULATION WTS (Wage Types) tab, you define the PART APPLICATION in which you maintained the Customizing for the cumulation wage types (see Figure 2.44). The "CEDT" part application includes the cumulation wage types that SAP predefined for the sample form of the payslip. You usually use cumulation wage types for the payslip or a form in which you want to output the payroll results. Section 4.2.3, Defining and Outputting Cumulation Wage Types, describes the steps that are necessary for the Customizing.

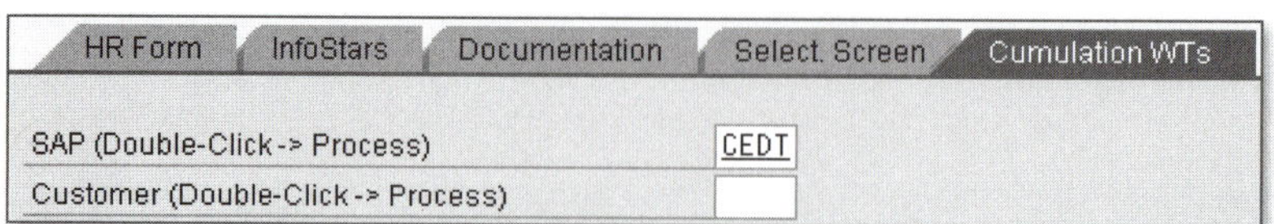

| HR Form | InfoStars | Documentation | Select. Screen | Cumulation WTs |

| SAP (Double-Click -> Process) | `CEDT` |
| Customer (Double-Click -> Process) | |

**Figure 2.44** Cumulation Wage Types Tab

### 2.2.3    Defining and Selecting Form-Specific Data

Before you can activate your form, you need at least one InfoStar in your InfoNet. The MetaNet that is assigned via the attributes and the MetaStars that are defined in the MetaNet are available for structuring your InfoNet. The MetaNet is in the left selection tree, and the InfoNet is in the right. You can move MetaStar, MetaDimensions, and MetaFigures to your InfoNet via drag and drop (see Figure 2.45).

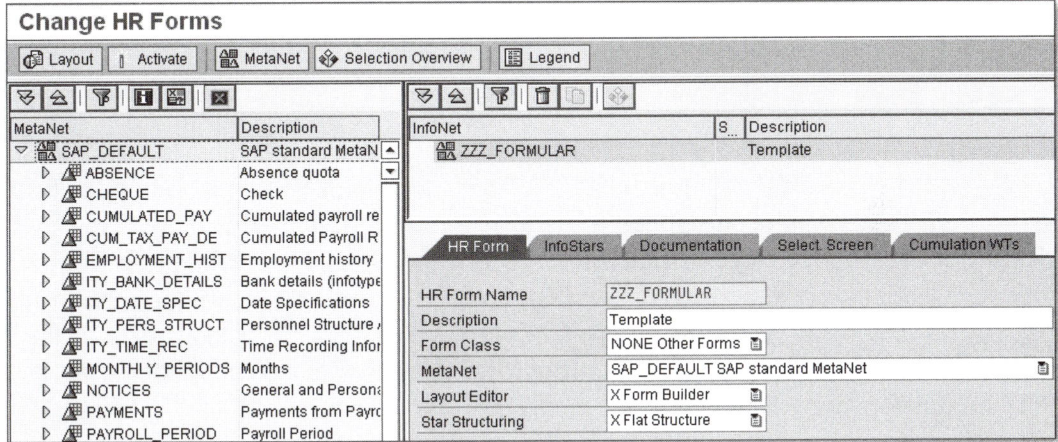

**Figure 2.45**    Structuring the InfoNet

First, select and move the MetaStar to your InfoNet. Select the InfoStar to adapt the name of the InfoStar in the INFOSTARS tab, if required. This is particularly useful if you create multiple InfoStars that are based on the same MetaStar. Apart from that, no InfoStars with identical names can exist in an InfoNet. If you don't change the name of the InfoStar and you repeat the procedure, the name of the new InfoStar is extended by a numerical value that is incremented to ensure unique naming.

Next, move the required MetaDimensions and MetaFigures to the InfoStar (see Figure 2.46). The basis of your InfoStar is the MetaStar that you inserted in the InfoNet via drag and drop. This means that you can only use MetaDimensions and MetaFigures that the MetaStar contains.

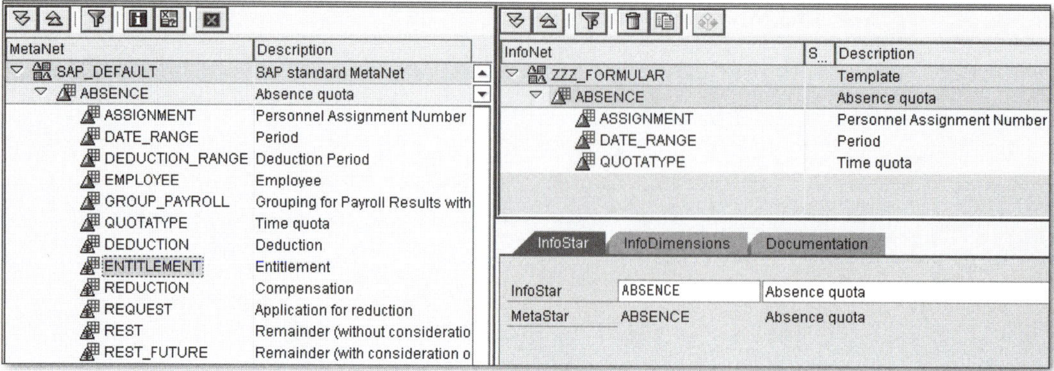

**Figure 2.46**  Creating an InfoStar in the InfoNet

When you create an InfoStar, you can limit the data that are retrieved in the Info-Star. (This only applies to the InfoFields of the InfoDimensions.) This means that you can implement a selection for one or more InfoFields to specifically limit the data. If you copy an existing standard form, selections are already available at the InfoStar or InfoField level, which you can display with the SELECTION OVERVIEW button. This button enables you to view the InfoFields and InfoStars that are affected by a selection (see Figure 2.47).

If you want to return to the initial screen, click on the METANET button, which enables you to display and hide the MetaNet so that you can control your InfoNet only or your InfoNet *and* MetaNet.

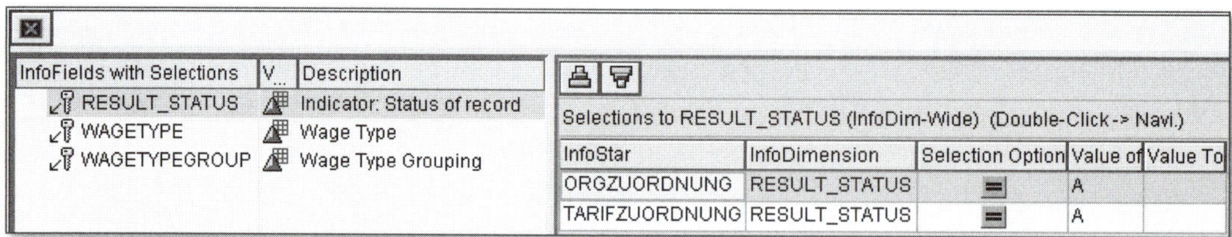

**Figure 2.47**  Selection Overview

If you want to set selections yourself, select the InfoDimension of an InfoStar whose InfoFields you want to consider for a selection. After selecting the InfoDi-mension, click on the INSERT SELECTION button ⊞. The system adds a new tab to the attributes of the InfoStar. The tab provides a list of the InfoFields for which you can implement a selection. Select an InfoField, and add a selection using the INSERT LINE button ⊞ (see Figure 2.48). The additional buttons enable you to delete or copy lines, sort them in descending or ascending order, and update them. You can add an explicit sorting for the lines of the InfoStar with the InfoField and the select values via the SORT column. Here, you can enter only numerical values between 0 and 99. The system sorts the line by the sorting criterion and then transfers them to the layout. However, you can retroactively sort the lines in the Form Builder.

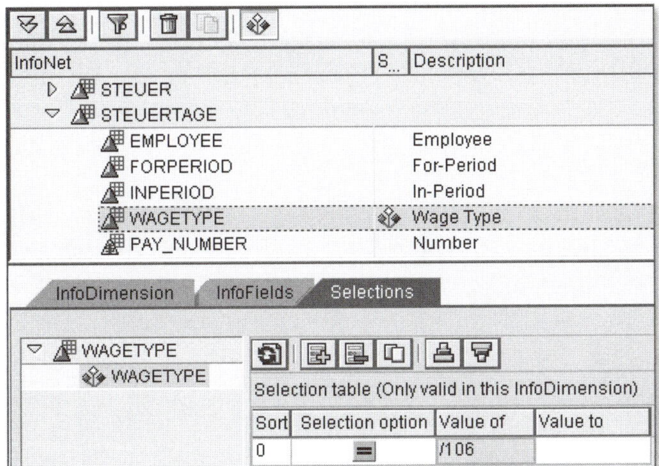

**Figure 2.48**  Selection at the InfoField Level of an InfoStar

After setting up your InfoNet, you call the form definition to activate it. As soon as you've clicked the LAYOUT button, the system calls the Form Builder for Smart Forms or for SAP Interactive Forms. Activate the form definition via the ▯ button.

After you select the Form Builder for the design of the layout, you must modify the predefined layout type before you can activate the form definition. You can find the LAYOUT TYPE entry in the PROPERTIES tab. Click on the BACK button ▣ to return to the Forms Workplace. Now, activate the print program of the form by clicking on the ACTIVATE button. In the attributes of the form, you can view the status of the form parts. All three parts should be in an active status, as illustrated in Figure 2.49.

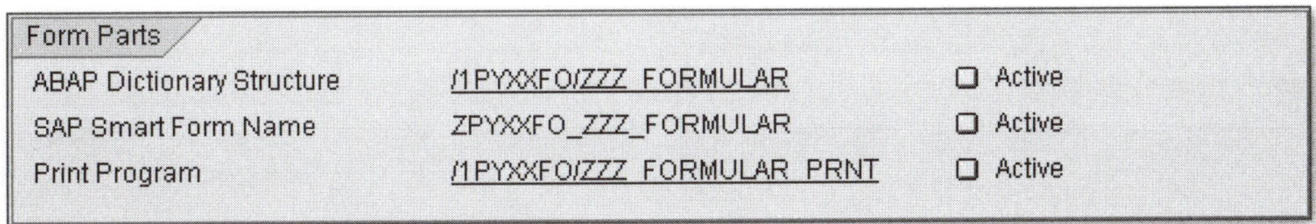

**Figure 2.49**  Status of the Form Parts

### 2.2.4 Form Printing from the Forms Workplace

When you're in the development stage of a form, the Forms Workplace provides two functions so that you can easily and quickly test the form:

▶ Calling the print program

▶ Calling the print program in the test mode

You can only call the print program if the ABAP DICTIONARY STRUCTURE, the FORM DEFINITION, and the PRINT PROGRAM are active. Follow these steps to access these functions:

1. Call your form via the overview of the Forms Workplace.

2. Select the form that you want to print, click on the EXECUTE THE PRINT PROGRAM button ⊕, or press F8, as illustrated in Figure 2.50. Alternatively, you can also select the FORM • PRINT PROGRAM menu path.

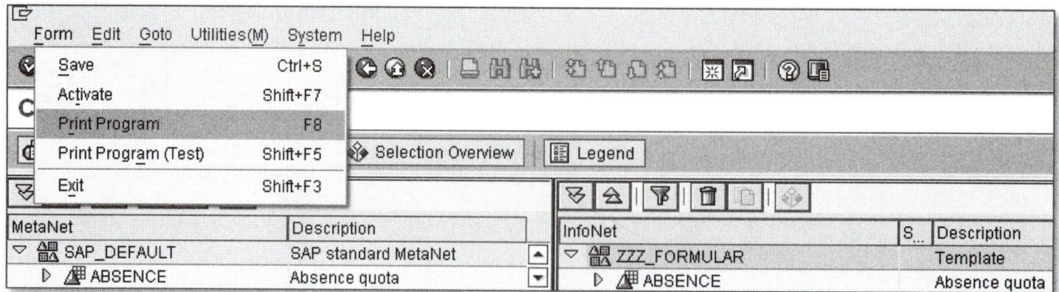

Figure 2.50 Calling the Print Program in the Forms Workplace

3. If you're in the Forms Workplace, select the described menu path or press the F8 key (see Figure 2.51).

Figure 2.51 Menu Path — Calling the Print Program

Another option is to call the print program in test mode. If you want to check which data your InfoNet contains in live mode, start the print program in test mode so that the system populates the structures and tables but doesn't generate a form.

The left area of Figure 2.52 shows the InfoStar structure of the form. If you want to view the selected data, select one of the objects. For our example, we chose the ABW_ABSENCE InfoStar. The right screen area displays the content of the selected objects.

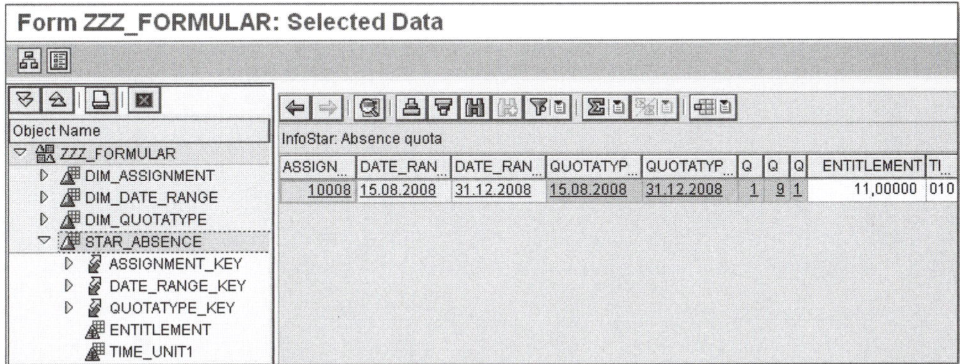

**Figure 2.52**  Calling the Print Program in Test Mode

Chapter 7, Integration with the Payroll and Time Management Components of SAP ERP HCM, outlines more call options in the print program, particularly within the SAP ERP HCM components, Payroll and Time Management, as well as in the SAP Easy Access menu.

## 2.3    Conclusion

This chapter introduced the Forms and Metadata Workplace as well as the available functions so that you can now use both tools to design forms. We listed the objects of the MetaNet and described how you can use or copy the SAP_DEFAULT standard MetaNet. And we showed you how to create your own MetaFigures, MetaDimensions, and MetaStars, as well as how to maintain their properties and attributes. Consequently, you should be able to analyze the standard MetaNet for existing objects to determine whether you need your own objects or you can use the provided objects.

In addition to the objects of the MetaNet, we used a sample form to introduce the functions of the Forms Workplace and explain the properties and attributes of the form that you need to maintain. So you now know how to create a form or copy an existing template to create your own form.

A critical aspect of generating a form is the design of its layout. In the next chapter, we will introduce you to the two tools, the Form Builder for Smart Forms and the Form Builder for SAP Interactive Forms, which you can use to position data provided via your previously defined InfoNet in your form. You will also learn that in addition to positioning data, elements such as templates, tables, lines, or texts highlighted by font formatting are used to design the layout.

# 3 Designing the Form Layout with the Form Builder

Two tools are available to help you define the logical structure and the graphical design of a form: the Form Builder for Smart Forms and the Form Builder for SAP Interactive Forms. Both tools are integrated with the Forms Workplace and are linked to the respective form via the attributes of the form (see Figure 3.1).

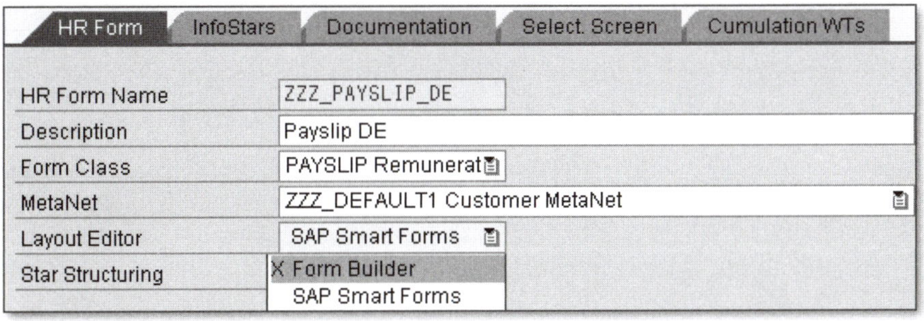

**Figure 3.1** Layout Editor

> **Note**
>
> Using the Form Builder for SAP Interactive Forms requires, at least, that *Adobe LiveCycle Designer* is installed locally. Section 3.2.2, Prerequisites for Using SAP Interactive Forms, describes the other technical prerequisites.

There are templates for both output formats of the payslip; however, the structure of the layout is similar. Currently, there is only one template for Smart Forms for time statements; for the payroll journal, there is also only one template for selected country groupings for both layout editors.

> **Note**
>
> The payroll journal is a form that contains selected payroll results for a group of employees for a selected period.

In the following sections we will discuss the Form Builder for Smart Forms and then the Form Builder for SAP Interactive Forms.

> **Tip**
>
> The SAP documentation on Transaction SMARTFORMS provides more information on a migration of the forms from Smart Forms to SAP Interactive Forms.

## 3.1    Using the Form Builder for Smart Forms

This section first provides a brief overview of the Form Builder for Smart Forms. Then, you'll learn about the selected functions that are often used in real-life scenarios to help you create your form layout, including how to create font formats with the Style Builder, define text modules, integrate graphics, and output bar codes. Finally, you'll see how to activate and deactivate areas in the layout.

> **Tip**
>
> If you need more detailed information, read *SAP Smart Forms*, which is also published by SAP PRESS (see Appendix H, Additional Information).

First, you need to know where the Form Builder for Smart Forms is defined in your SAP system: In the Forms Workplace, click on the LAYOUT button to navigate to the layout maintenance. You can find the tool in the SAP Easy Access menu via the following path: TOOLS • FORM PRINTING. Here, you can determine the name of the form using the F4 help and directly edit the layout of the form. Alternatively, you can also directly call the Form Builder for Smart Forms via Transaction SMARTFORMS.

### 3.1.1    A Brief Overview

This description of the Form Builder for Smart Forms focuses on the most important functions that help you manage most of the real-world application cases.

The initial screen of the Form Builder for Smart Forms (Form Builder for short) is divided into three areas (see Figure 3.2):

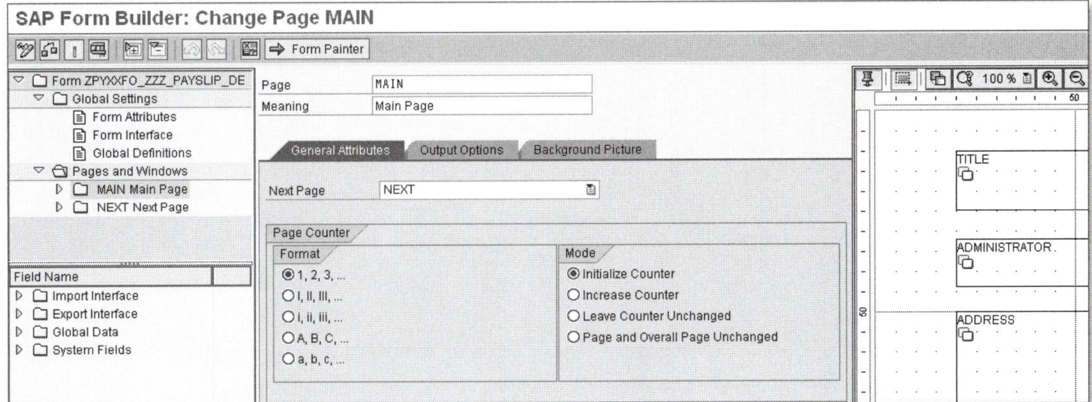

**Figure 3.2**  Initial Screen of the SAP Form Builder for Smart Forms

▶ The left area lists the elements (see Table 3.1 later in this chapter) of your form mapped in a tree structure as well as the global settings that consist of the form attributes that are to be maintained: FORM INTERFACE and the GLOBAL DEFINITIONS.

▶ The right area contains the tabs in which you can maintain the attributes of the elements. You select the elements from the tree structure by double-clicking on them. The number and type of tabs depends on the element selected.

▶ In addition, you can display and hide the *Form Painter* using the FORM PAINTER button; the Form Painter maps the positions of the windows on a form page. Except for windows, background picture, and graphics, no additional elements, such as tables or texts, are visible.

Within a window, that is, a kind of output area, you output your data in a particular position in the form. The FIELD LIST contains the available data as fields, structures, and tables. You use the FIELD LIST ON/OFF button to retrieve the data.

The FORM ATTRIBUTES enable you to define settings regarding the read out loud function and further details that refer to output options, such as used style and page format (see Figure 3.3).

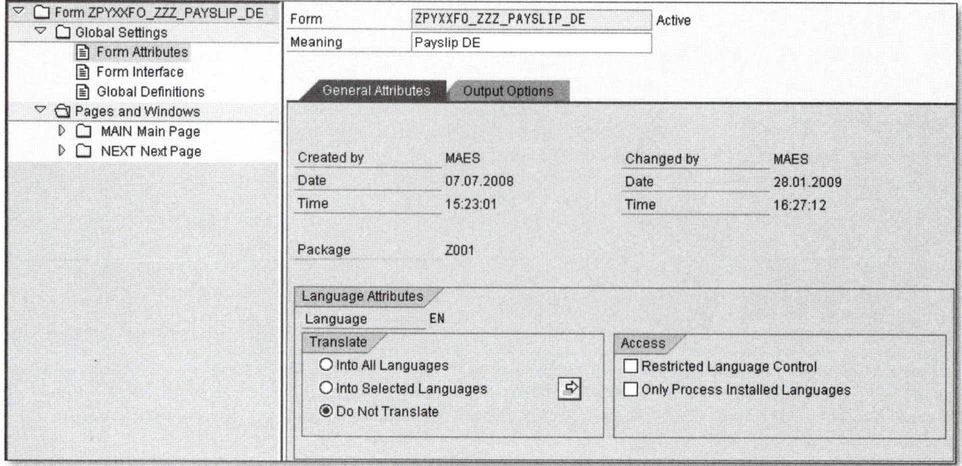

**Figure 3.3** Form Attributes in the Form Builder

The FORM INTERFACE provides you with the data of the InfoNet, which you set up previously (see Figure 3.4). The HRDATA parameter contains the structure that is generated from the InfoNet. This structure contains all of the InfoStars and InfoDimensions.

| Parameter Name | Type Assignment | Associated Type |
|---|---|---|
| ARCHIVE_INDEX | TYPE | TOA_DARA |
| ARCHIVE_INDEX_TAB | TYPE | TSFDARA |
| ARCHIVE_PARAMETERS | TYPE | ARC_PARAMS |
| CONTROL_PARAMETERS | TYPE | SSFCTRLOP |
| MAIL_APPL_OBJ | TYPE | SWOTOBJID |
| MAIL_RECIPIENT | TYPE | SWOTOBJID |
| MAIL_SENDER | TYPE | SWOTOBJID |
| OUTPUT_OPTIONS | TYPE | SSFCOMPOP |
| USER_SETTINGS | TYPE | TDBOOL |
| HRDATA | TYPE | /1PYXXFO/ZZZ_PAYSLIP_DE |
| LAST | TYPE | XFELD |

**Figure 3.4** Form Interface in the Form Builder

The GLOBAL DEFINITIONS area contains the constants, workspaces for tables, structures, and variables that you need during the form creation; for example, to read the data of an InfoStar in a loop, you need to use a work area (see Figure 3.5).

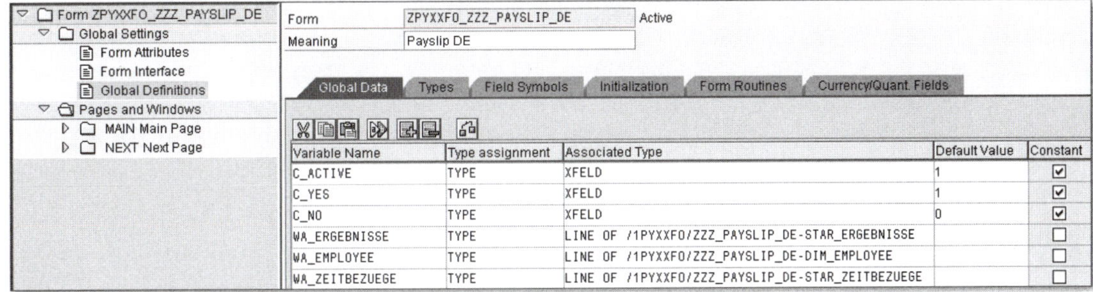

**Figure 3.5**  Global Data in the Form Builder

Table 3.1 describes the icons of the elements that you can use in a form. Because the elements are arranged in a tree structure, they are also called *nodes*. Consequently, the term *node type* is often used instead of element type.

| Icon | Node Type | Short Description |
|---|---|---|
|  | Page of a form | A form consists of one or more *pages*. You define the following features via the attributes of a page:<br><br>Next page of a page<br><br>Page counter<br><br>Output format of the page<br><br>Output of a background picture. |
|  | Main window (max. 1) | As a maximum, only one *main window* may exist in a form. The main window adapts to the data volume (continuous text) that is supposed to be output in the next page dynamically using a page break. The width of the window must remain the same, but the height of the window may vary. |
|  | Secondary window | In a *secondary window*, data has a fixed position. Continuous texts that don't fit into the output area of the window are truncated. |
|  | Copies window/final window | You use *copies windows* if you want to define an output area as a copy. The final window is skipped during processing and not processed until all elements of the tree structure have been processed. This makes sense if you want to output a total amount on the first page, and the total amount hasn't been determined at this stage. |

**Table 3.1**  Node Types in the Form Builder

| Icon | Node Type | Short Description |
|---|---|---|
| | Text | All *texts* are output via the text node — this also applies to texts that you output within templates, loops, and tables. The following *text types* are discussed in Section 3.1.3, Defining Text Modules:<br><br>Text element<br><br>Text module<br><br>Include text<br><br>Dynamic text. |
| | Graphic | *Graphics*, for example, logos, that you've imported to the SAP system using Transaction SE78 can be integrated via this node type (see Section 3.1.4, Integrating Graphics). You can create background pictures via the attributes of a page. |
| | Address | *Addresses* that you've created within the Central Address Management (CAM) can be integrated with a form using this node type. They are identified by a number and formatted according to the postal rules of the sender country. |
| | Template | A *template* is a static table with a strictly defined layout. Its rows and fields are strictly defined, too. If content doesn't fit into a field, it isn't output. |
| | Table | For a *table*, you define the format of its rows and fields. Tables are dynamic, so they adapt to the content. A table may contain a header and a footer area. The number of rows depends on the content of the table that is supposed to be output via a table node. Because a table may span several pages, you should use it within the main window. |
| | Table entry | *Table entries* are output within templates or tables. |
| | Table cell | *Table cells* are a part of table entries. |

**Table 3.1** Node Types in the Form Builder (Cont.)

| Icon | Node Type | Short Description |
| --- | --- | --- |
| | Command | You can use *command nodes* to change page breaks, paragraph numbering, and print control. You can only use commands for page breaks within the main window. |
| | Loop | You use *loops* if you want to output or process table content. The content in a workspace can be output as a plain text or via a template. Besides templates, you can navigate to a table also within a template, for example, to use a value from the loop as a key for reading entries in a table. |
| | Alternative | *Alternatives* enable you to use different procedures, depending on the condition. Below alternatives, the system automatically creates the TRUE and FALSE nodes, which map the result of the condition. Below these nodes, in turn, you then create further nodes, which are processed based on the result of the condition. |
| | Folder | *Folders* provide more clarity and can be used to protect objects against page breaks. This is useful for related table rows, for example. |
| | Program line | You can enter any ABAP code, for example, for calculations, complex checks, or retroactive data retrievals in a *program line*. It's also possible to call a function module or routine that you created in the FORM ROUTINES of the global definitions. You transfer variables, structures, and tables that you created in the global definitions to the program node via the import and export parameters. |

**Table 3.1**  Node Types in the Form Builder (Cont.)

### 3.1.2  Creating Font Formats Using the Style Builder

The style of a form defines which paragraph and character formats you can implement in output texts. You create styles using the Style Builder (see Figure 3.6). Basically, the style of a form is the group of the available font formats.

You can access the Style Builder for style maintenance in the SAP Easy Access menu via the TOOLS • FORM PRINTING path or via Transaction SMARTSTYLES or SMARTFORMS.

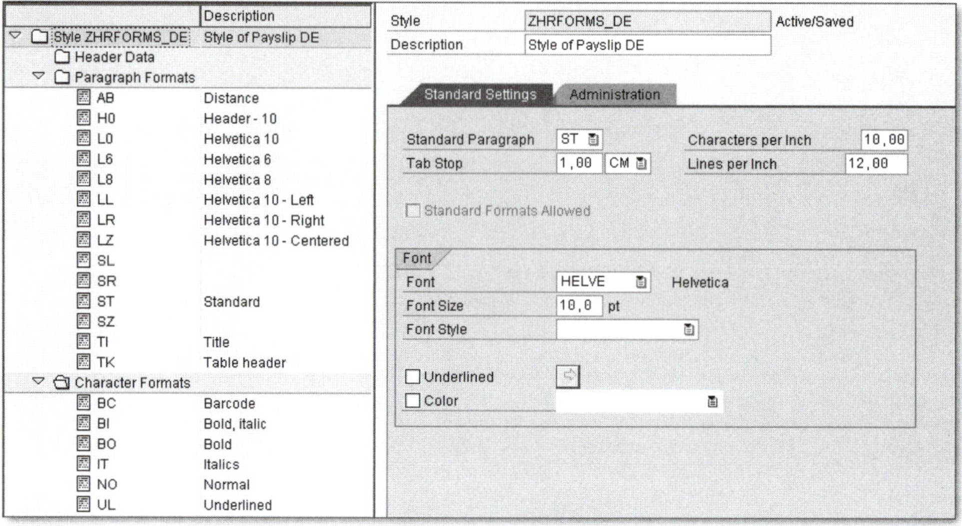

**Figure 3.6**  User Interface of the Style Builder for Style Maintenance

In the form attributes of the form, you maintain the style to be used in the Output Options tab (see Figure 3.7). For our example, this is the ZHRFORMS_DE style, which is a copy of the standard style HRFORMS_DE.

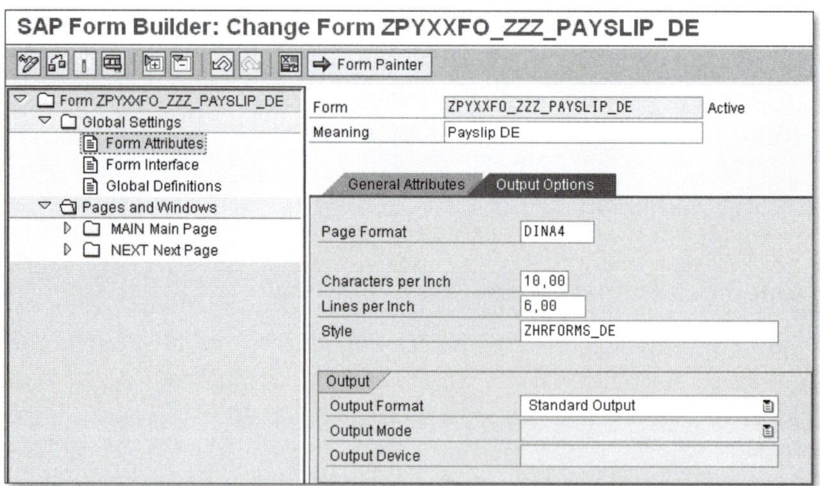

**Figure 3.7**  Maintaining the Style of the Form in the Output Options Tab

If you copy a form, the system also copies the style. If you want to add font formats, you should first copy the style and then add your own font formats. You should only delete font formats if you're sure that you will no longer need or use them. Otherwise, the system displays warnings that prompt you to adapt all text elements in which a nonexisting font format is used.

To copy a style and then add your own font format, follow these steps:

1. Call one of the transactions mentioned (SMARTSTYLES, SMARTFORMS) to copy the HRFORMS_DE standard style, which is also copied when a form template is copied, to your customer name space, for example, ZSTIL_FORMULAR (see Figure 3.8).

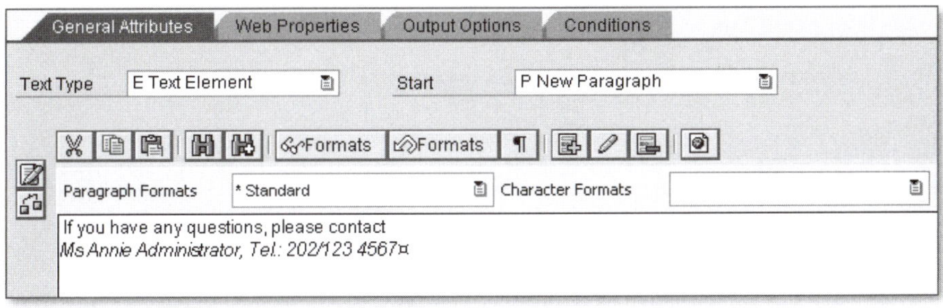

**Figure 3.8**  Copying the Standard Style with the Style Builder

2. Enter the name of the HRFORMS_DE standard style into the Style field, and click on the Copy button. You can now use the Create button to generate a new style.

3. Assign the paragraph and character formats to the text elements of a form within the editor using the PARAGRAPH FORMATS and CHARACTER FORMATS fields (see Figure 3.9).

4. You assign paragraph formats to entire text paragraphs, and character formats to individual words within a paragraph. If you want to delete the assignments of a character format, you can use the FORMATS button.

**Figure 3.9**  Selecting Paragraph and Character Format in the PC Editor

### 3.1.3    Defining Text Modules

To position texts in your form, you have four options:

▶ Text elements

▶ Text modules

▶ Dynamic text

▶ Include text

Depending on the text type you've selected, the layout of the GENERAL ATTRIBUTES tab of the text node changes (see Figure 3.10). If the DYNAMIC FIELD VALUE button ▶ is displayed next to the input field, you can enter a variable field instead of a fixed value. The field is populated at runtime and determines the values of the fields. You can define variable fields in the form interface or in the global definitions.

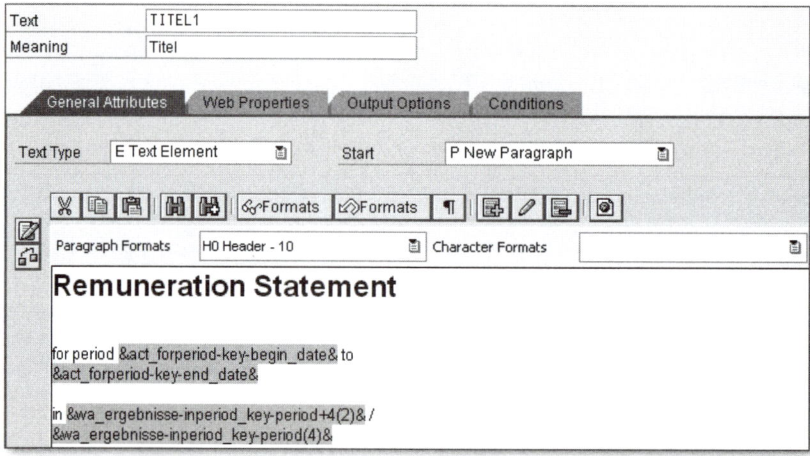


**Figure 3.10**    Plain Text Element

In the following sections we will detail the individual text types, that is, the text element, the text module, the dynamic text, and finally the include text.

**Text Type "Text Element"**

You create plain text elements, as illustrated in Figure 3.10, with the "text" node type. In the editor area, you enter the text that is supposed to be output. You can integrate all other text types with your form in the same way; only the text type changes.

### Text Type "Text Module"

You create text modules in the initial screen of the Form Builder (see Figure 3.11). This allows you to easily use texts in multiple forms.

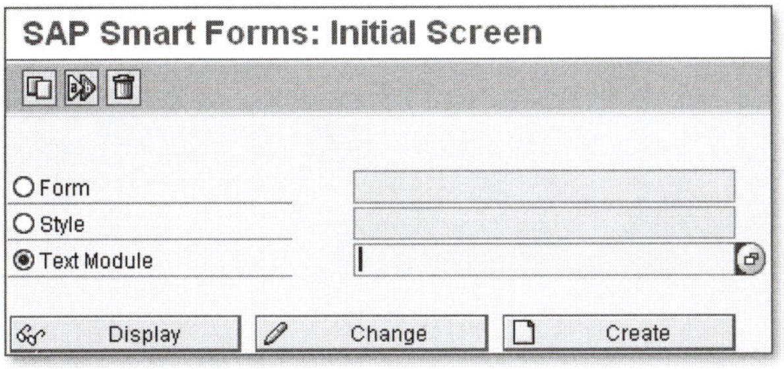

**Figure 3.11** Creating Text Modules

Select the respective text type to integrate a text module. Then, enter the name of the existing text module, and specify a language in which you want to integrate the text module, if necessary (see Figure 3.12). You can also define the language dynamically, for example, using the CONTROL_PARAMETERS interface parameter and the LANGUAGE field (see Figure 3.13). This parameter is populated when the program that calls the form and transfers the data to the form is started.

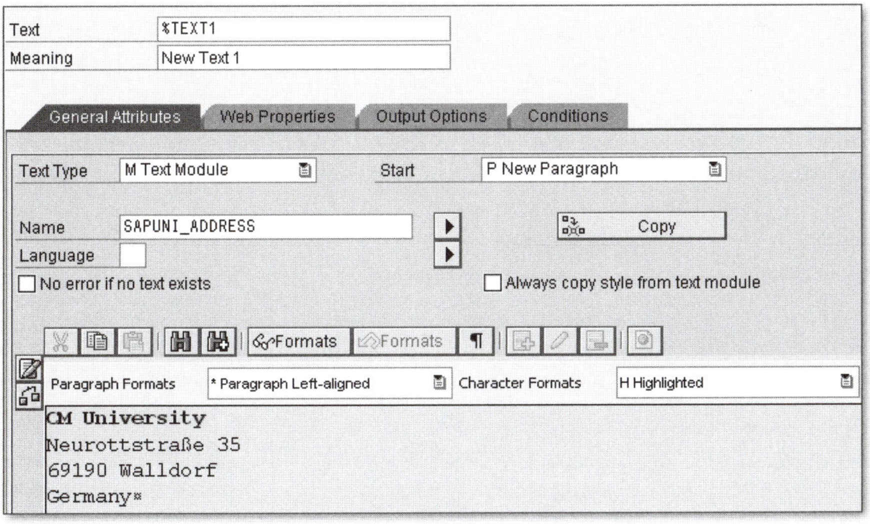

**Figure 3.12** Integrating a Text Module with a Form

To avoid the output of errors if no text module exists, select the No Error If No Text Exists option (see Figure 3.13).

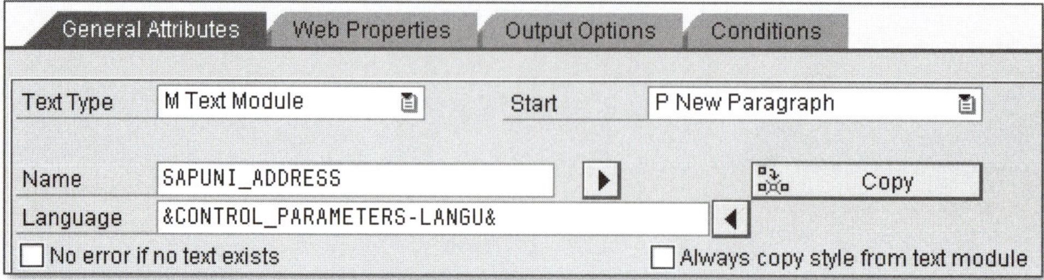

**Figure 3.13** Setting the Language Dynamically

> **Note**
>
> Text modules are client-independent and connected to the transport system. Text modules are preferred because Include Texts are client-dependent and must be transported manually. If you want to use already-existing Include Texts, always choose text modules.

### Text Type "Dynamic Text"

Dynamic texts correspond to the TSFTEXT table type and consist of plain text lines of the TLINE type. The TLINE type contains a format column and a text line. For example, if a table of this format is included in your program, and you want to transfer the table to your Smart Form, create a table of the TSFTEXT type in the form interface. Then, insert the table name (here, TEXT_TAB) in the Field Name field of the text node (see Figure 3.14).

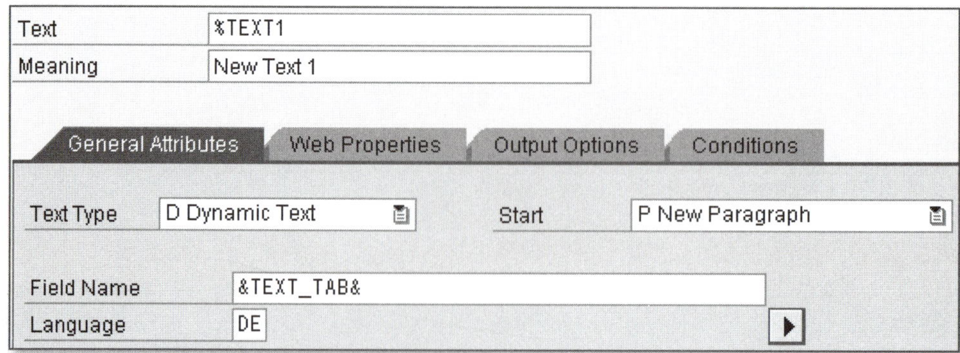

**Figure 3.14** Integrating Dynamic Text with a Form

Information in tables of this format might be provided by function modules that you use in your program for the collection of data. This means you can output a table and its text lines via a text node of the DYNAMIC TEXT type in a form without changing the table content provided.

**Text Type "Include Text"**

You create Include Texts (also called *SAPscript standard texts*) via Transaction SO10 (see Figure 3.15). You can also access this application in the SAP Easy Access menu by selecting the TOOLS • FORM PRINTING • SAPSCRIPT path.

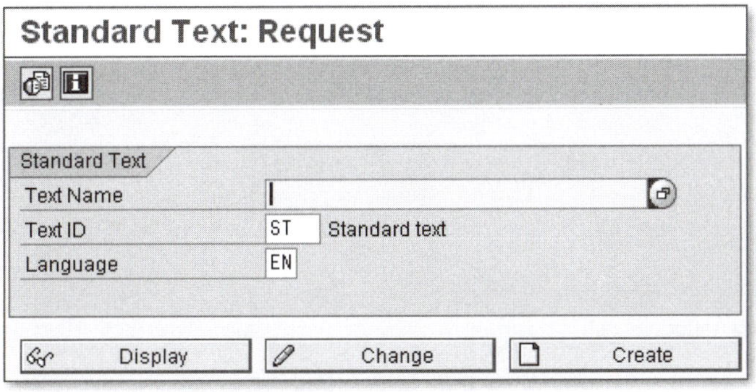

**Figure 3.15**  Creating Include Texts

You create a text node, and then select the Include Text type in the TYPE field to integrate the already-created Include Text (see Figure 3.16).

Just as you can for text modules, you can determine the fixed values for the text key dynamically for include texts by determining the fields using variable fields.

> **Note**
>
> Because Include Texts are client-dependent, you can also copy them to another client using Transaction QCYT (QM Standard Texts [General]). Include Texts aren't connected to the transport system and must be included in a transport request using the RSTX-TRAN report.
>
> Because of this, you shouldn't use Include Texts if you can use Text Modules instead.

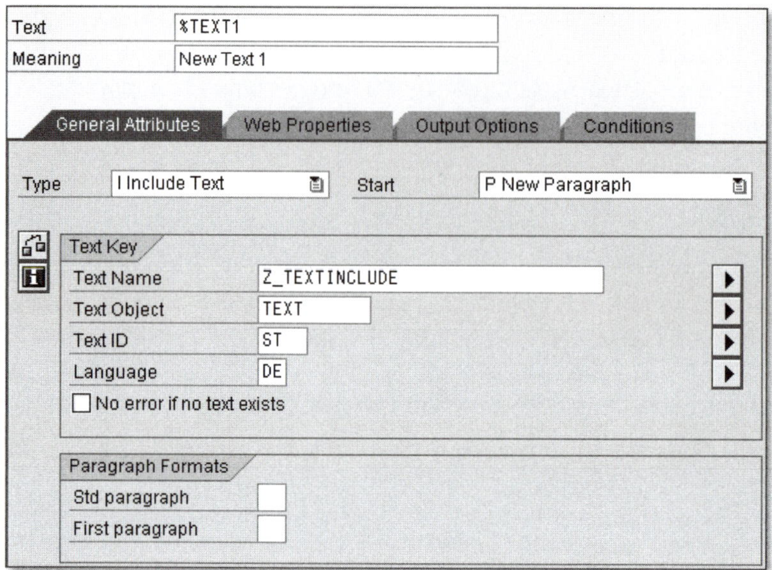

**Figure 3.16**  Integrating Include Text with a Form

### 3.1.4  Integrating Graphics

You can integrate graphics, such as company logos, with your Smart Form using the graphic node (see Figure 3.17). You can also use a graphic as a background picture on a form page. In this case, integrate the graphic as a background picture of a page via the BACKGROUND PICTURE tab (see Figure 3.18).

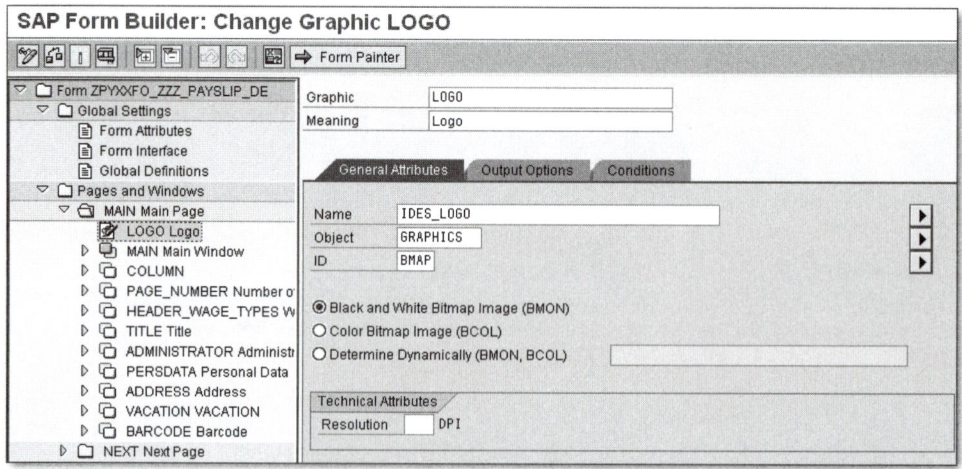

**Figure 3.17**  Integrating a Graphic with a Form

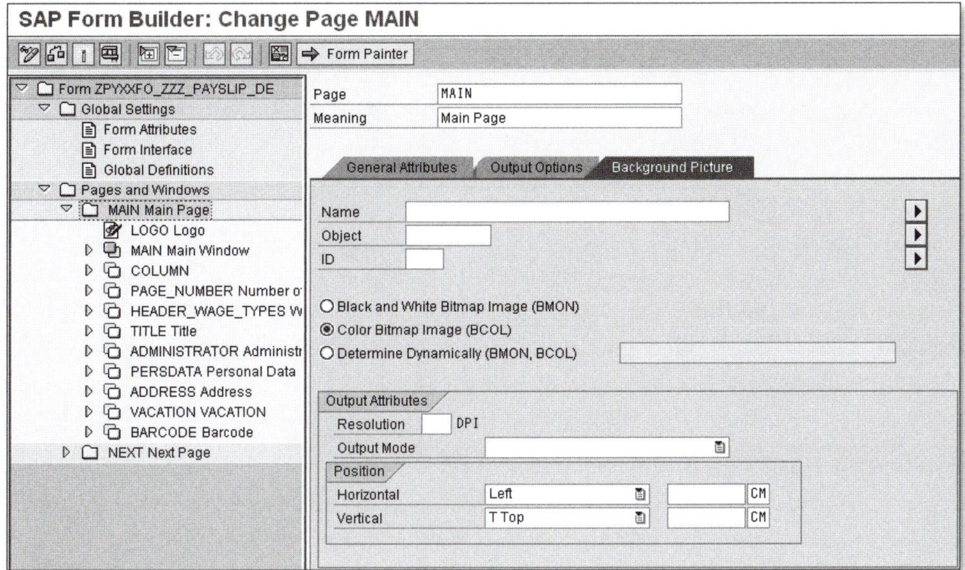

**Figure 3.18**  Using a Graphic as a Background Picture in a Form

To integrate graphics or use them as background pictures, you must first import the graphic to your SAP system (in both cases). For this purpose, use Transaction SE78 (Administration of Form Graphics). To call the application, select the SAP MENU • TOOLS • FORM PRINTOUT • ADMINISTRATION path in the SAP Easy Access menu (see Figure 3.19).

**Figure 3.19**  Administration of Form Graphics

The next step is to select the IMPORT button and then the TRANSPORT button after saving the graphic to store and provide your graphic in the required systems on the document server (or *Business Document Server, BDS*).

At the time this book went to press, support was provided for all graphics that were imported as TIFF or BMP files. Any other graphic formats should be converted into the supported formats.

### 3.1.5 Outputting Bar Codes

To output a bar code in your form, you first need to create it or use an existing bar code. Then, you must define a character format, which uses this bar code, within the scope of your specified form style (see Section 3.2.1, Creating Font Formats Using the Style Builder). You use this character format to convert a text into the previously defined bar code. A bar code enables the SAP system to generate a graphic, which can be immediately output in a form.

You create and maintain bar codes (see Figure 3.20) via the SAPscript font maintenance (Transaction SE73, menu path: SAP MENU • TOOLS • FORM PRINTOUT • ADMINISTRATION).

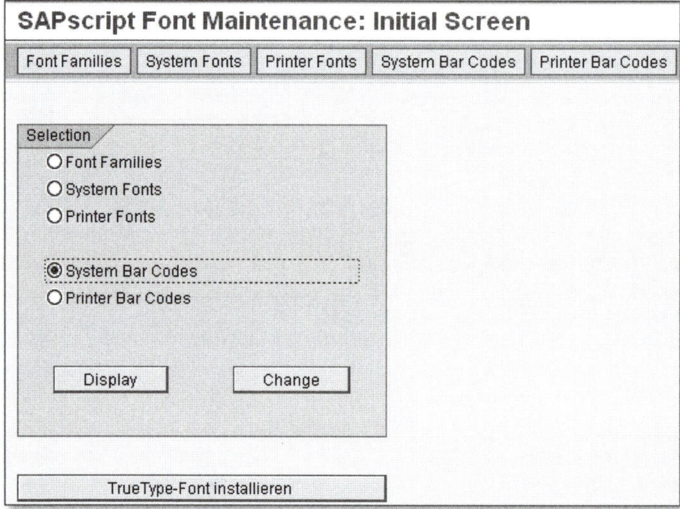


**Figure 3.20**　Initial Screen of the SAPscript Font Maintenance

Check whether you can use one of the existing bar codes. For this purpose, call the SYSTEM BAR CODES option in the CHANGE mode to create your own bar code, if required. The system displays a list of the existing bar codes and their properties (see Figure 3.21).

You can create your own bar code from the user interface for the system bar code maintenance by clicking on the CREATE button. If the system asks you which bar code technology you want to use, select the *new technology* (also referred to as *new bar code printing*). This technology enables the SAP system to convert the bar codes into printable graphics during the form processing instead of generating them in the printer, as before. The benefit of this is that no additional hardware is required that generates the bar code in the printer.

**SAPscript Font Maintenance: Display System Bar Codes**

| Bar Code | Description | | Min. | Max. | Width | Unit | Height | Unit | BCode Type | Rotatn. |
|---|---|---|---|---|---|---|---|---|---|---|
| ARTNR | Artikelnummer | | 01 | 10 | 4,80 | CM | 1,20 | CM | | 000 |
| AUFNR | Auftragsnummer | | 01 | 08 | 4,80 | CM | 1,20 | CM | | 000 |
| BARCLVS | Test Barcode im LVS | | 01 | 20 | 5,00 | CM | 2,00 | CM | | 000 |
| BC_93 | Code 93 | | 01 | 40 | 7,00 | CM | 1,30 | CM | C93 | 000 |
| BC_C128B | Code 128 B, | n.txt,h=13mm | 01 | 40 | 9,00 | CM | 1,30 | CM | | 000 |
| BC_CD39 | Code 39 no chk, | n.txt,h=13mm | 01 | 40 | 5,00 | CM | 1,30 | CM | | 000 |
| BC_CD39C | Code 39 w.chk, | n.txt,h=13mm | 01 | 40 | 9,00 | CM | 1,30 | CM | | 000 |
| BC_EAN13 | EAN 13, | n.txt,h=13mm | 12 | 12 | 5,00 | CM | 1,30 | CM | | 000 |
| BC_EAN8 | EAN 8, | n.txt,h=13mm | 07 | 07 | 3,00 | CM | 1,30 | CM | | 000 |
| BC_EANH | EAN 128, | n.txt,h=13mm | 01 | 40 | 9,00 | CM | 1,30 | CM | | 000 |
| BC_ESC | ESC character (hex 1B) | | 01 | 01 | 0,00 | TW | 0,00 | TW | | 000 |
| BC_I25 | Int.2of5 no chk, | n.txt,h=13mm | 02 | 26 | 5,00 | CM | 1,30 | CM | | 000 |
| BC_I25C | Int.2of5 w.chk, | n.txt,h=13mm | 01 | 25 | 5,00 | CM | 1,30 | CM | | 000 |

**Figure 3.21**  List of the Existing Bar Codes

**Note**

This new technology can't be used for SAPscript forms. You can find more information on the new bar code technology in SAP Notes 430887 and 645158.

The following bar code symbologies, which define the technical character set of a bar code, are currently supported and available for selection:

- ▶ Code39 (alphanumeric code)
- ▶ Code128 (alphanumeric code)
- ▶ Interleaved 2of5 (numeric code)
- ▶ PDF417 (two-dimensional bar code)
- ▶ Code93 (alphanumeric code)

In addition to the bar code symbology, you also define the page orientation of the bar code. SAP Note 645158, which is updated in regular intervals, provides the input values for additional parameters that depend on the selected bar code symbology.

**Tip**

Appendix B lists numerous useful SAP Notes on the Forms Workplace.

To use the created bar code in your form, create a character format with the style that you assigned to the form (see Figure 3.22).

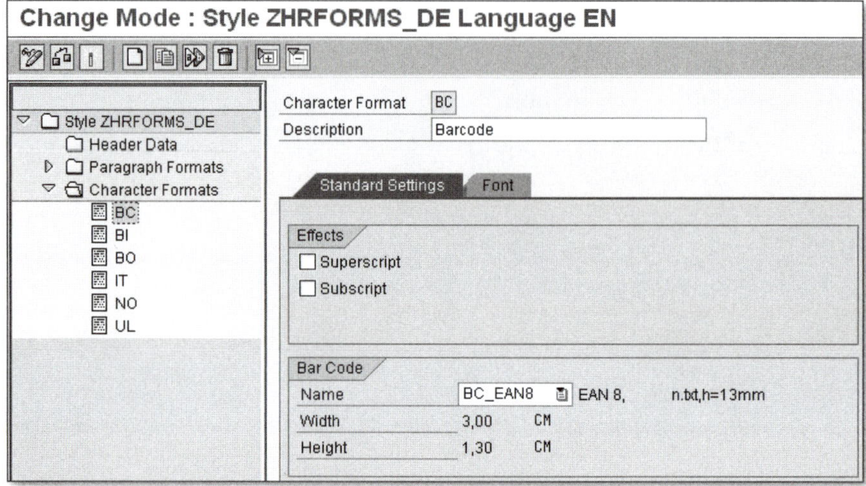

**Figure 3.22** Defining the Character Format of the Bar Code

Next, you define a variable in your form, and populate it with the character string that is supposed to be implemented in the bar code. The character string can be determined in a program node in the form. You then assign the corresponding character format to the variable (see Figure 3.23).

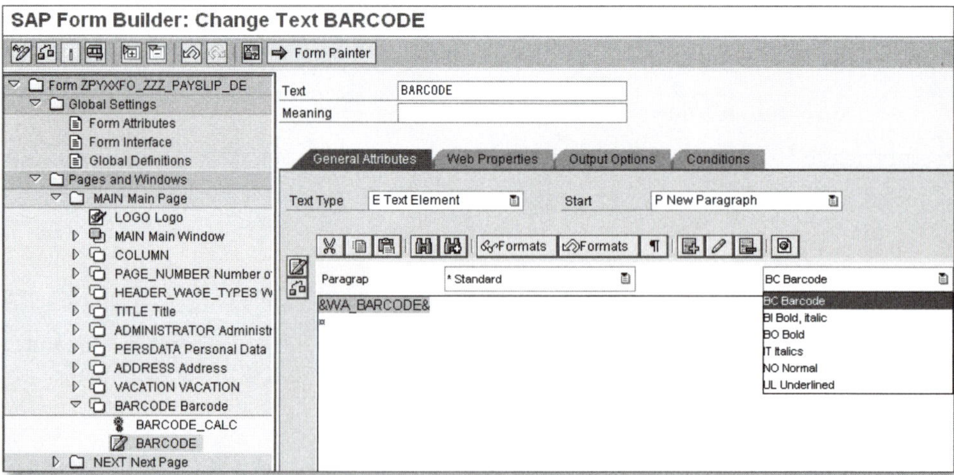

**Figure 3.23** Assigning the Character Format of the Bar Code in the Form

### 3.1.6 Activating and Deactivating Areas in the Layout

You'll probably have to change your layout from time to time. To easily integrate and test these changes, you can create constants in the global definitions of your form. You can then use these constants to activate and deactivate areas in the layout. Your form template may possibly already contain these constants. If not, you can create them as shown in Figure 3.24.

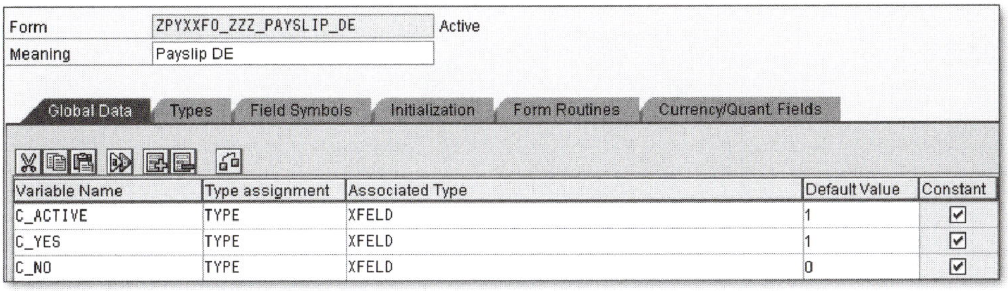

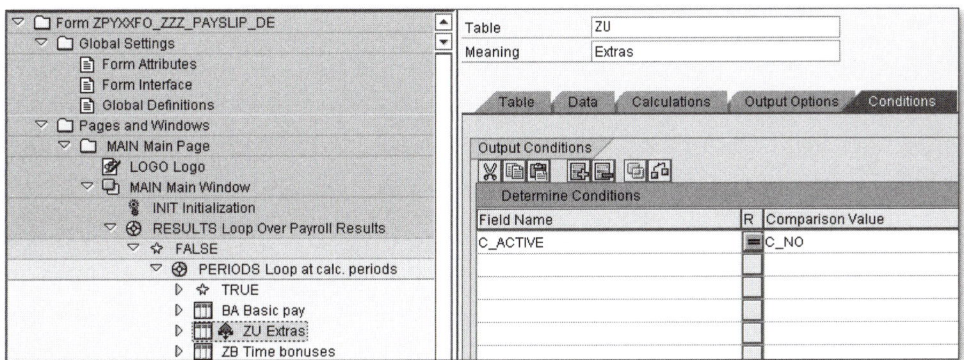

**Figure 3.24**  Creating Constants

For example, if you want to temporarily deactivate an area in the form of a folder, table, or plain text field, select the Conditions tab, and enter the constants so that the condition is met or not met (see Figure 3.25).

**Figure 3.25**  Deactivating a Table

If you create a new area and want to delete an old area for it, you can also use the constants to temporarily deactivate the old area. In this case, you can still reuse it, if required.

As you can see in Figure 3.26, the international SAP_TIM_99_0002 template has been provided for the time statement with the corresponding variables. Here, you see form ZZZ_TIM_01_0002, which is a copy of the SAP_TIM_99_0002 template. We will discuss this in more detail in Chapter 5, Time Statement — Creation and Customizing.

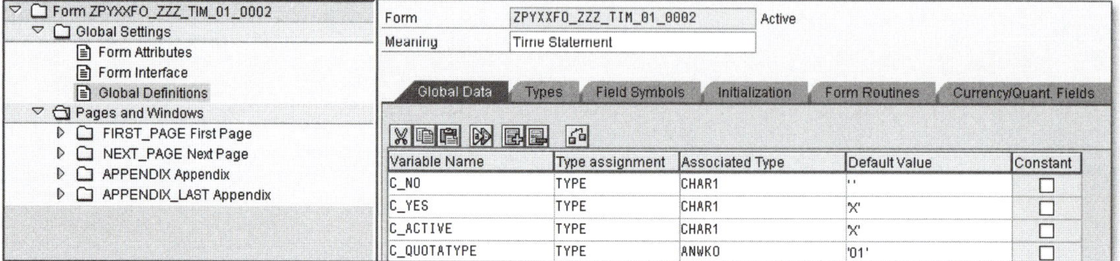

**Figure 3.26**  Global Definitions of the Time Statement

Now we will detail the use of the Form Builder for SAP Interactive Forms.

## 3.2    Using the Form Builder for SAP Interactive Forms

This section introduces the Form Builder for SAP Interactive Forms and describes how you can use this tool. In this context, the focus is on the differences in the Form Builder for Smart Forms.

### 3.2.1    A Brief Overview

In 2002, SAP and Adobe Systems entered a strategic partnership with the aim to integrate interactive forms as well as Adobe's print and design expertise with the SAP NetWeaver platform. In 2005, SAP finally brought SAP Interactive Forms by Adobe to market. Since then, numerous print forms have been converted, that is, changed from SAPscript or SAP Smart Forms to the PDF technology. With the release of enhancement package 4 for SAP ERP 6.0, SAP now provides more than 2,200 PDF-based print forms across all components.

> **Note**
>
> The same SAP NetWeaver components are used both for PDF-based print forms and for interactive PDF forms. Section 3.2.2, Prerequisites for Using SAP Interactive Forms, describes the technical prerequisites for using PDF-based forms.

When using Adobe technologies in the SAP system, the *data retrieval* and *layout* are strictly separated; that is, the data is retrieved from the SAP Dictionary through the interface, and the form is processed in Adobe LiveCycle Designer. This separation also requires a strict task separation and consequently allows for task sharing. This makes it easier to create forms and programs and implement necessary adaptations and changes in an easier and more cost-effective way.

When creating a form, it always needs to be assigned to a form interface. This means that there is always an interface for data retrieval. This data interface can be addressed using Transaction SFP in the SAP system or has a corresponding navigation in Customizing for the payslip or time statement. Figures 3.27 and 3.28 illustrate the process of calling the interface in Transaction SFP.

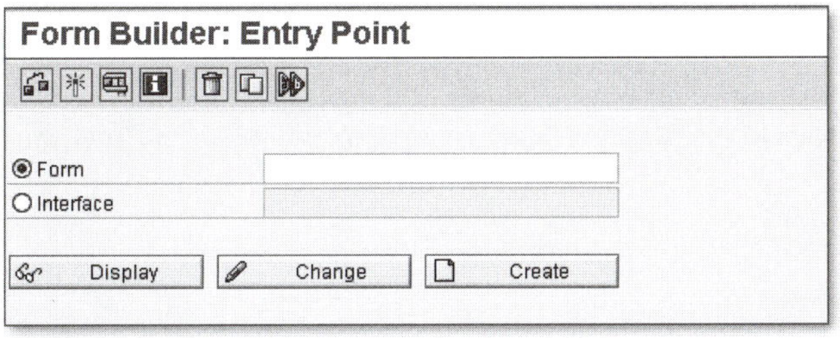

**Figure 3.27**  Interface and Form — Call

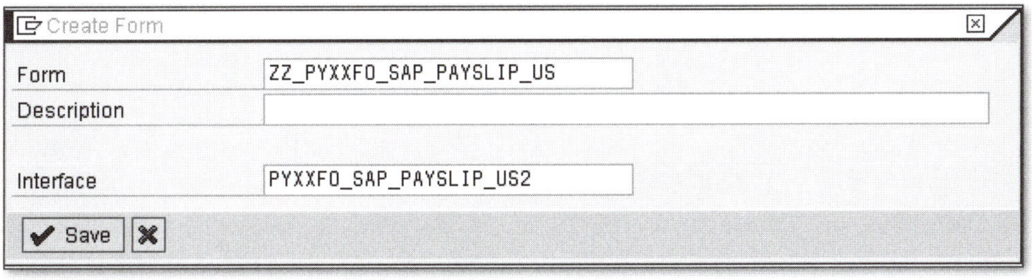

**Figure 3.28**  Interface and Form — Assignment

You could already generate a PDF document from an SAP print output (SP01), for example, using function modules or downstream tools or services, but the difference in the use of the Adobe technology is that both the data retrieval and the generation of the result document are implemented in the SAP system when SAP Interactive Forms are used. So, all modules of the software development are integrated with the known *Software Lifecycle Management* (Correction and Transport System) of SAP. This applies to ABAP Workbench (ABAP) and SAP NetWeaver Developer Studio (Java).

The same entry point through the interface for data retrieval is used both for Smart Forms and for SAP Interactive Forms. The two technology components only differ in Customizing and later processing, so you can call both technologies in SAP ERP HCM using Transaction HRFORMS. The following sections discuss this aspect in more detail.

### 3.2.2 Prerequisites for Using SAP Interactive Forms

To use the Adobe components in the SAP environment, you must meet some prerequisites:

- Adobe Document Services (ADS) must be installed in the SAP system.
- To use the payslip and time statement for HR, the corresponding enhancement packages must be implemented.
  - For the payslip, Release SAP ERP 6.0 and SAP Enterprise Extension HR (EA-HR 0002) are required.
  - The time statement isn't currently available for customers and will be delivered with EA-HR 0004.

To use the Adobe technology, the following components must be available (see Figure 3.29):

❶ **Form design**
Adobe LiveCycle Designer must be installed locally on the client and is automatically called by the SAP GUI when it's called from the SAP environment, for example, from Transaction HRFORMS or Transaction SFP. The necessary steps for the installation are described in SAP Notes 962762 and 1121176.

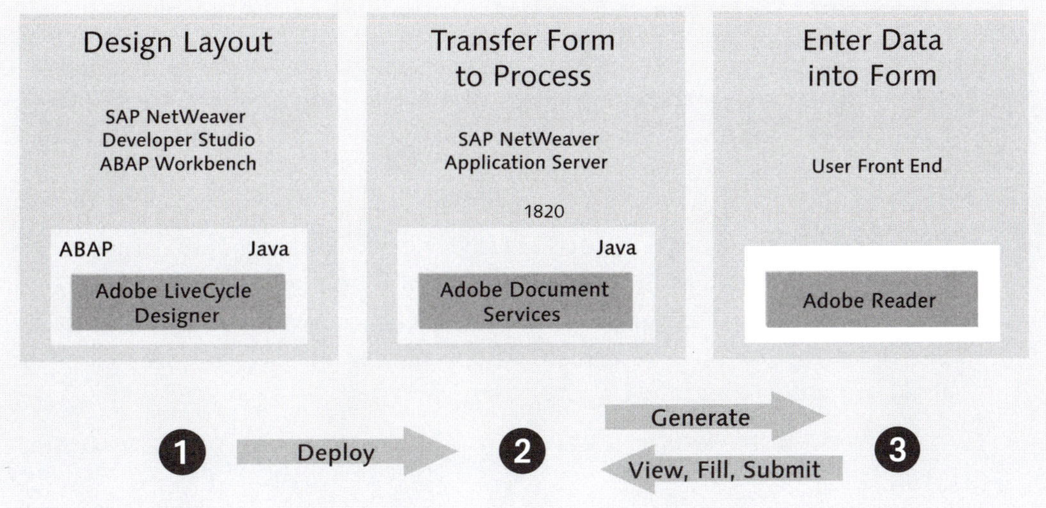


**Figure 3.29**  Workflow with SAP Interactive Forms

**❷ Form usage**

To convert the generated templates into PDF documents within the SAP environment, you need Adobe Document Services (ADS) installed as a component of the basis. The ADS installation must be implemented in a Java environment. The installation steps are described in the SDN under Adobe: SAP Interactive Forms By Adobe • Installation And Configuration • SAP Interactive Forms • Configuration Guide.

**❸ Form display**

At the minimum, Adobe Reader must be installed to display the created forms. The Adobe Reader software can be downloaded from the Adobe website (*www. adobe.com*) free of charge.

| Note |
| --- |
| You can check the installation of ADS anytime by calling the FP_PDF_TEST_00 report. The return message then displays the ADS version information. Use the FP_PDF_TEST_01 report to generate and display a form for testing purposes. |

### 3.2.3 Font Formats and Graphical Options of Adobe LiveCycle Designer

All SAP customers can download Adobe LiveCycle Designer from the SAP Service Marketplace. This tool is the new form development environment in the SAP system and is called from the respective Customizing. Chapter 4, Payslip — Creation and Customizing, and Chapter 5, Time Statement — Creation and Customizing, describe in detail how you can access Adobe LiveCycle Designer to design the payslip and time statement. In addition to the entry point via Customizing, you can also directly access it using Transaction HRFORMS in SAP ERP HCM or Transaction SFP in the application development. These entry points navigate you to the Form Builder and thus to Adobe LiveCycle Designer.

> **Note**
>
> The individual form functions depend on the respective SAP release and the corresponding Adobe LiveCycle Designer version. The descriptions and examples here are based on Adobe LiveCycle Designer Version 7.1.
>
> You can install Adobe LiveCycle Designer in the Windows C: directory under PROGRAMS • ADOBE • DESIGNER 7.1. For additional information on this installation, refer to SAP Note 962763. After the installation, the entire environment of Adobe LiveCycle Designer — integrated with the SAP system — is available.

You should call Adobe LiveCycle Designer from the SAP environment to use the data fields of the SAP Data Dictionary. They aren't available if you call Adobe LiveCycle Designer locally. Additionally, you must ensure that the installation of Adobe LiveCycle Designer isn't updated and, for example, replaced by another version when you process or create a form because such changes may lead to problems.

**Main Areas of Adobe LiveCycle Designer**

Adobe LiveCycle Designer consists of one workspace, which is divided into four main areas (see Figure 3.30):

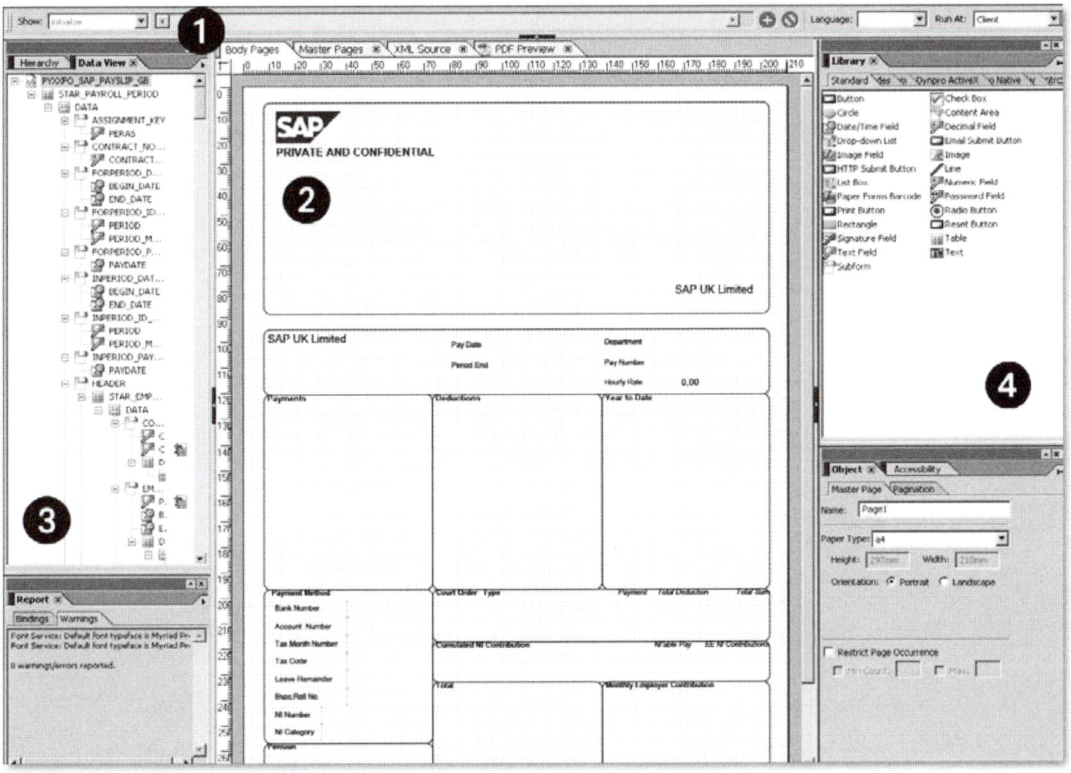

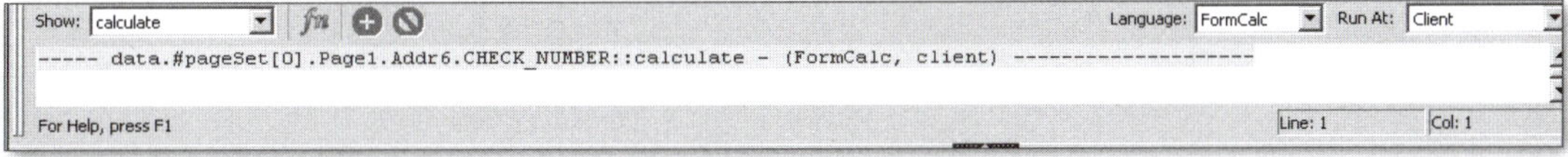

**Figure 3.30** The Four Main Areas of Adobe LiveCycle Designer

## ❶ Script Editor

The upper area contains the Script Editor, which you can activate or deactivate using the SCRIPT EDITOR palette or pressing the Ctrl + ⬆ + F5 key combination (see Figure 3.31). Here, for example, you can enter scripts in the two supported script languages, JavaScript and FormCalc, to create advanced form templates. This aspect is further discussed in the context of XML sources.

**Figure 3.31** Script Editor

**❷ Central area**

The structure of the area in the center is predefined. This area contains the BODY PAGES, MASTER PAGES, XML SOURCE, and PDF PREVIEW tabs. In "The Central Area of Adobe LiveCycle Designer" section later in this chapter you will find more information on this.

**❸ Left area**

You can customize the left area according to your individual requirements via the PALETTES menu item.

**❹ Right area**

In addition to the left area, you can also customize the right area according to your individual requirements via the PALETTES menu item.

Before detailing the central area, let's consider the right area and the left area, which provide the following functions:

▶ The PALETTES • WORKSPACE menu item enables you to display or hide the left and right workspace (palettes) and the upper workspace (palettes or Script Editor).

▶ You can also use PALETTES • WORKSPACE to display and access the individual functions, such as TOOLBARS, HIERARCHY, DATA VIEW, LIBRARY, LAYOUT, BORDER, OBJECT, and so on, in the right, left, and upper workspace.

▶ If you want to "clean up" the areas, you can select PALETTES • WORKSPACE • RESET PALETTE OPTIONS to reset all of your settings and restore the default state.

Figure 3.30 shows the individual palettes in detail. The TOOLBAR palette enables you to display or hide specific functions, such as grids or sizes. The STANDARD, FONT, PARAGRAPH, LAYOUT, and TABLE toolbars can be individually customized using the TOOLS • TOOLBARS menu path. The HIERARCHY palette maps the structure of the form and the nesting of the lines and blocks. The DATA VIEW palette displays the dictionary structures, that is, the fields with which the form is provided via the interface and context. You have the following options:

▶ **Positioning a field**
Double-clicking in the navigation directly takes you to the central area and the respective field in the form.

▶ **Additional information**
Right-clicking on the required field causes the system to display additional information, such as OPTIONS, SHOW DATA NAMES, and SHOW DATA DESCRIPTIONS.

▶ **Active integration of the Form Designer**
A red/green double arrow indicates an active integration of the Form Designer in the SAP development environment. This enables you to identify which fields have an active binding to SAP Dictionary fields (see Figure 3.32).

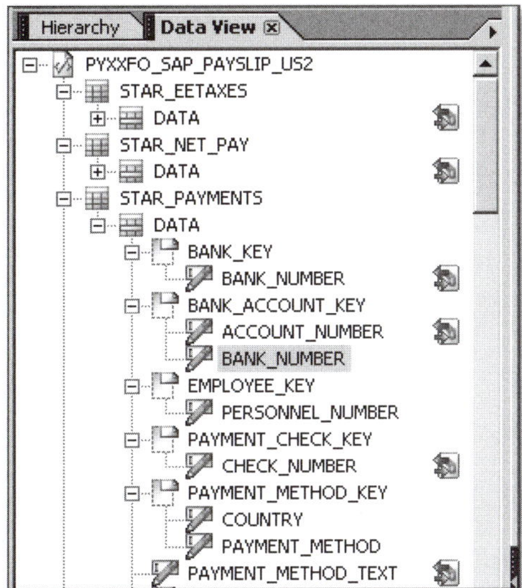

**Figure 3.32** Data View — Active Integration of the Form Designer

The LIBRARY palette (see Figure 3.33) contains all available objects; it also includes, for example, STANDARD libraries, which are provided within Adobe LiveCycle Designer, or various BARCODE libraries. The STANDARD library displays all available form field types:

▶ Static form fields, such as image, text, line, or rectangle

▶ Form fields in which data is input or output, such as text fields or check boxes

▶ Interactive form fields, such as buttons or drop-down lists

In the context of the integration of the Form Designer by Adobe, SAP has extended these libraries, for example, by *Web Dynpro ActiveX*, *Web Dynpro Native*, and *ISR Control*. (Internet Service Request is a library for interactive online forms in the HR environment.) You can also add your own libraries to these existing libraries. To do this, click on the arrow in the top-right corner as shown in Figure 3.33, and wait until another window opens in which you can create a new group. Then, you can use the options, for example, ADD GROUP, to add your own objects to the library.

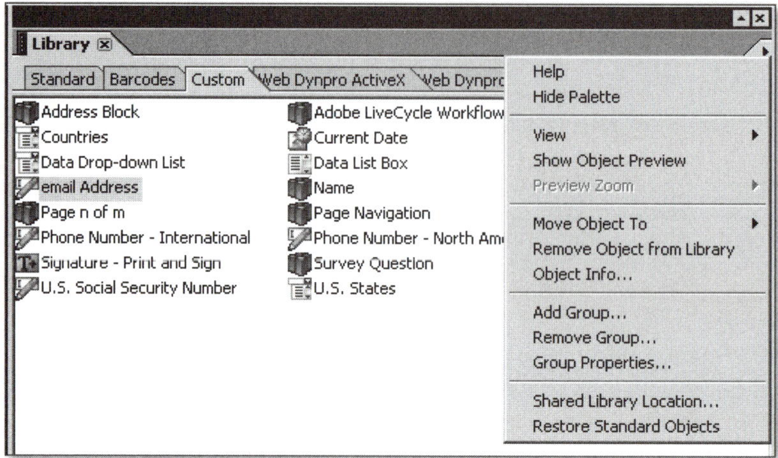

**Figure 3.33** Creating Your Own Library

> **Note**
>
> Always make sure that your libraries can be accessed appropriately by using a shared file server or a shared directory, for example.

The LAYOUT palette enables you to define the size and position of the objects. You can also specify whether the height and width of objects (e.g., fields) can be dynamically adapted to the field content (e.g., text). This is particularly interesting for interactive forms because the option to dynamically adapt the field size is used more often for interactive forms than for print forms.

In addition to defining the size of the objects, you can also define their position, such as top left or bottom right. Various rotations are also possible, and you can configure details for the borders or define the position and distance of the caption.

You have various options for designing the document border, which can be done via the BORDER PALETTE: You can configure the design of the border and corners (e.g., inverted rectangles, notched corners), the color, and the background fill according to your individual requirements. Figure 3.34 shows an overview of these options.

> **Tip**
>
> There are many design options for the color, border, and so on. If you need a detailed design image, you should implement additional design tests that enable you to test possible designs.

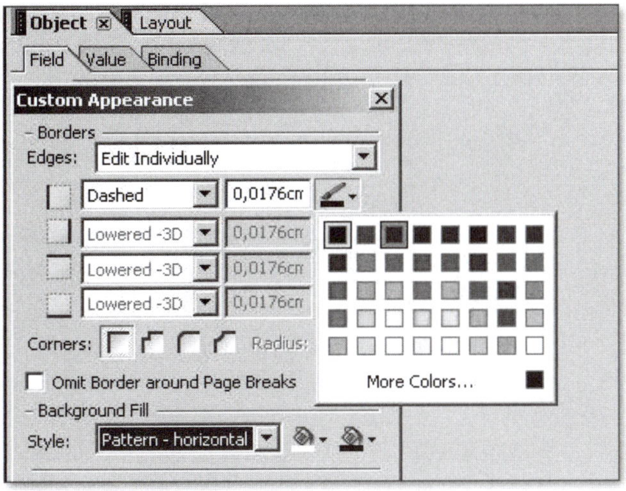

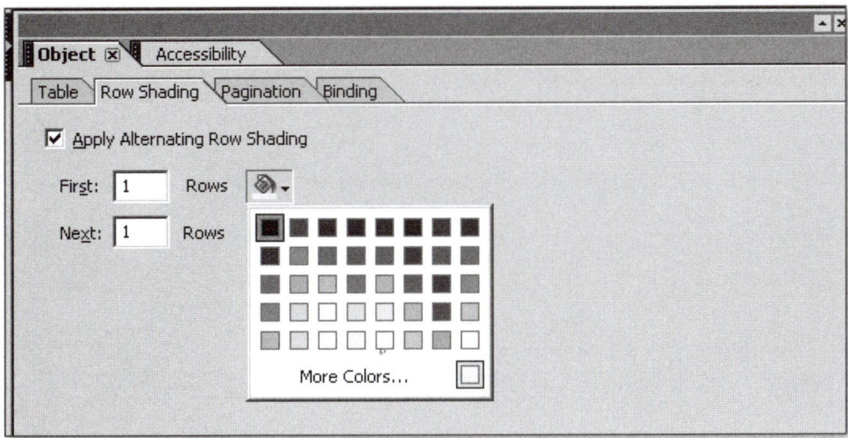

**Figure 3.34**  The Borders Palette

The OBJECT palette enables you to define fields. Fields from the SAP system, such as the personnel number, are already provided. Figure 3.35 shows the palette in Adobe LiveCycle Designer.

**Figure 3.35**  The Object Palette

The left area (DATA VIEW) displays the PERSONNEL NUMBER field as a technical definition from the SAP Data Dictionary (see Figure 3.36). The central area (MASTER PAGES or BODY PAGES) maps the PERSONNEL NUMBER field accordingly. In this example, the right area shows the object with the PERSONNEL NUMBER field as well as the definition. In the OBJECT window, the FIELD tab is active, and the appearance and type assignment are mapped. When navigating to the VALUE tab, the read only option is selected for this field because it has been provided from the SAP environment.

You also can change the *value of the field* by determining whether the user input is optional or mandatory and whether you want to define validation patterns. These decisions can be specified in the OBJECT palette.

In addition to these mainly optional functions, you can also define the corresponding *data binding* of the field to the fields in the SAP system (see Figure 3.36), which is much more important here. The workspace on the right contains the form field that is bound to the appropriate SAP Dictionary field through the assignment of the STANDARD BINDING field and the values provided in the dropdown list. The BINDING tab and the respective icon in the data view illustrate the connection to the HCM system.

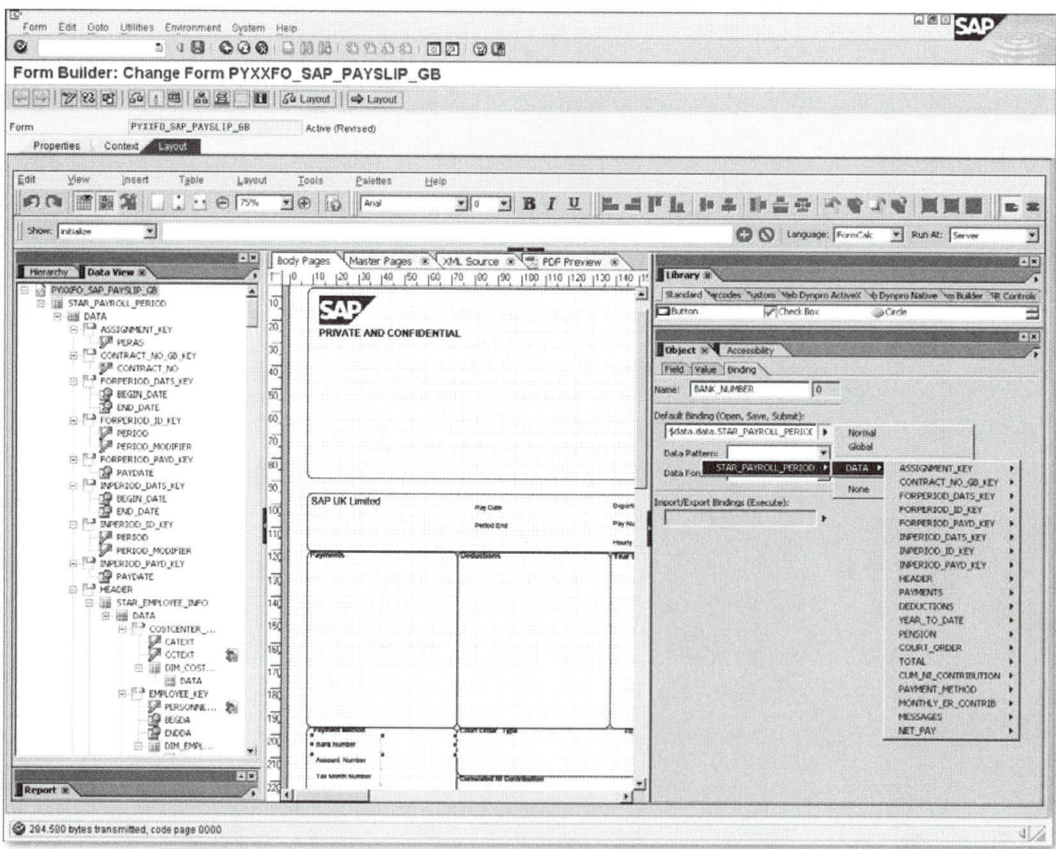

**Figure 3.36**  Data Binding

In Figure 3.37, you can also see the following critical options:

▶ **Accessibility**
Define information on fields.

▶ **Font**
Define formats for the font types, font styles, and sizes of individual fonts.

▶ **Paragraph**
Specify the respective paragraph formats, such as indentation, line spacing, and justification.

▶ **Drawing Aids**
Implement layout changes, loggings, and documentations by using Drawing Aids, Info, Report, and Procedure entries.

You can activate and deactivate these settings when you need to, and you can call some of these functions directly using key combinations. Figure 3.37 provides an overview of the functions for which this is possible as well as the corresponding shortcuts.

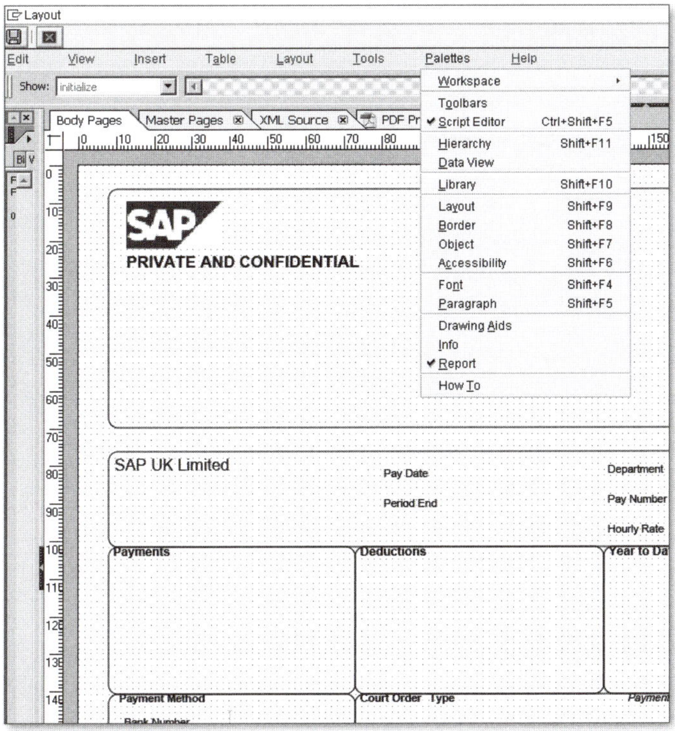

**Figure 3.37**  Palettes

In the following section we will briefly explain the central area of Adobe LiveCycle Designer. Chapter 4, Payslip — Creation and Customizing, and Chapter 5, Time Statement — Creation and Customizing, provide more information on structuring the payslip and time statement in the design environment of Adobe LiveCycle Designer.

### The Central Area of Adobe LiveCycle Designer

The central area or the layout area of Adobe LiveCycle Designer consists of the BODY PAGES, MASTER PAGES, XML SOURCE, and PDF PREVIEW tabs (see Figure 3.38).

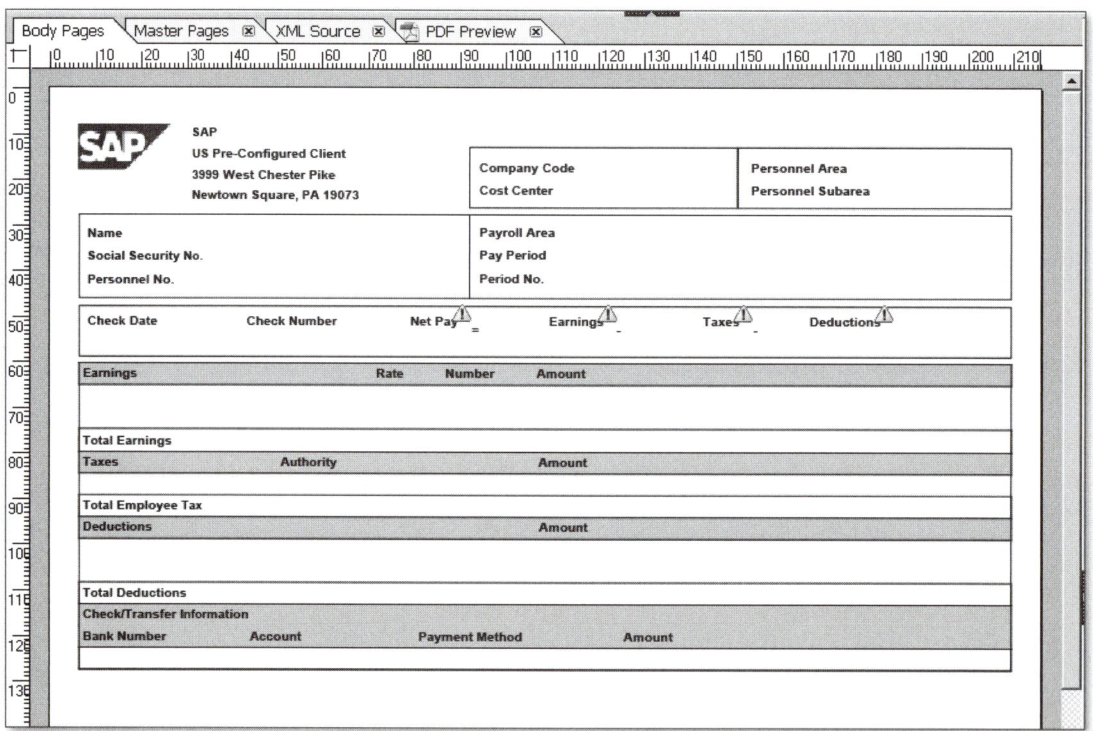

**Figure 3.38** Adobe LiveCycle Designer — Central Area

Each form contains at least one *master page,* which is stored automatically (see Figure 3.39). The content and modules of the master page are also mapped on each output page of the form. Each master page must include at least one content area that is used to output the company logo — in the simplest case — or specific header data on each page.

To create an annex that will be displayed at the end of the form, you define an additional master page. Common examples of these attached master pages are general terms and conditions or nondisclosure agreements.

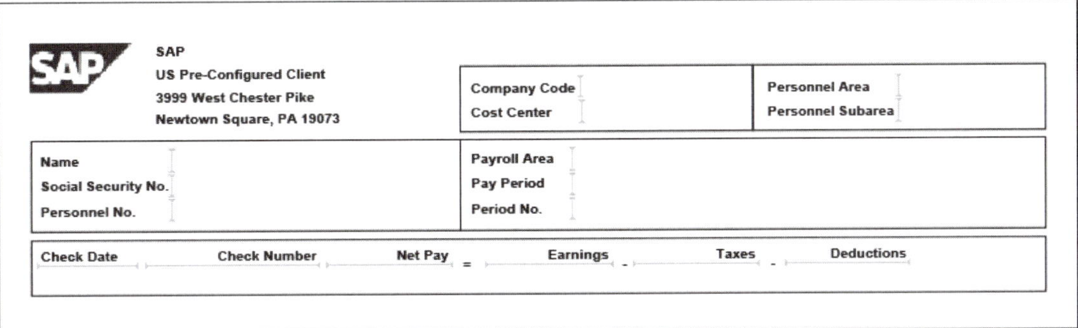


**Figure 3.39** Master Page

A *body page* is a subform that is stored at the highest level. A new body page can be inserted if a page break will be enforced. The *hierarchy* indicates when the respective body page is executed or how the individual body pages are arranged. You can control this via the settings of the object and in the PAGINATION tab. Figure 3.40 shows an example of this.

You can integrate dynamic content with the body pages, and for each body page, the system uses the content that has been defined for the corresponding page. Basically this means that a body page isn't only an empty shell or a container for dynamic content. The body pages are filled at runtime, that is, when the print program is executed. Even if only one body page is populated, the concrete print may span several pages because the scope of the dynamic content is that extensive, depending on the number of objects and their defined order.

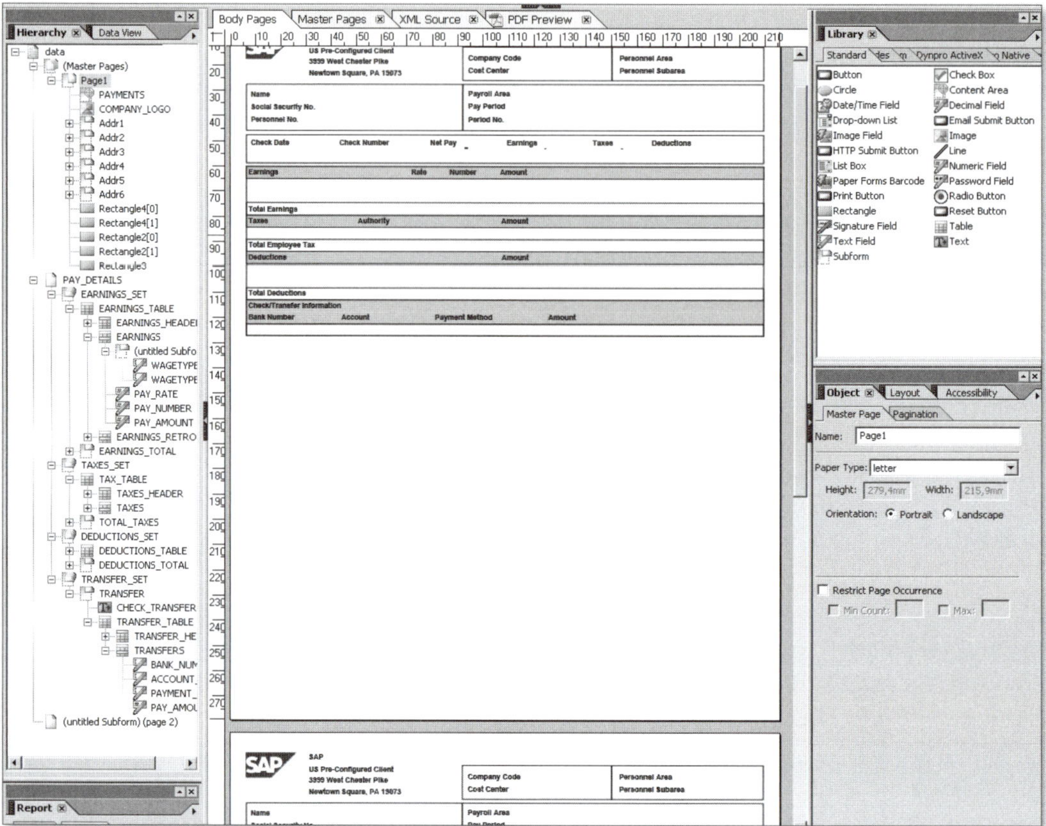

**Figure 3.40**  Controlling the Order with Body Pages

These elements, and many additional functions that can't be described here, enable you to structure and map forms according to your requirements (also refer to the SAP PRESS book *SAP Interactive Forms by Adobe*).

Let's now take a look at the *XML source*. Adobe LiveCycle Designer uses the XML format as an architecture (*Adobe XML Forms Architecture, XFA*); that is, it uses XML-based language elements as form templates or to design the respective form templates. XFA supports scripting in JavaScript and FormCalc as the scripting elements by Adobe (see Figure 3.41).

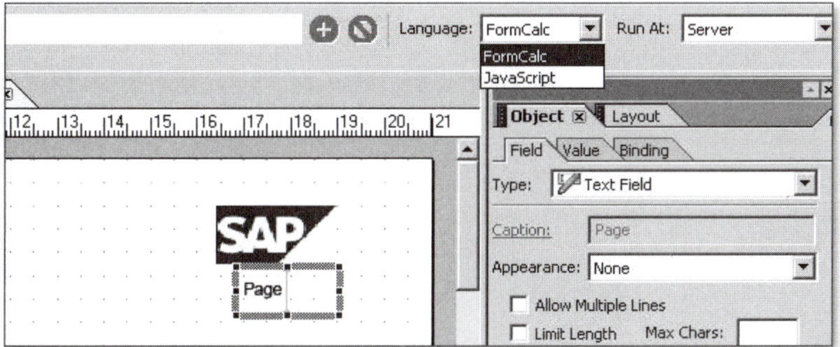

**Figure 3.41** Displaying the Two Scripting Languages in Adobe LiveCycle Designer

By positioning the mouse pointer in any field (e.g., Earnings) in Adobe LiveCycle Designer and navigating to the XML SOURCE tab (see Figure 3.42), you can view the corresponding XML resolution of the data fields (e.g., EARNINGS) and the format in the respective XML code (see Figure 3.43).

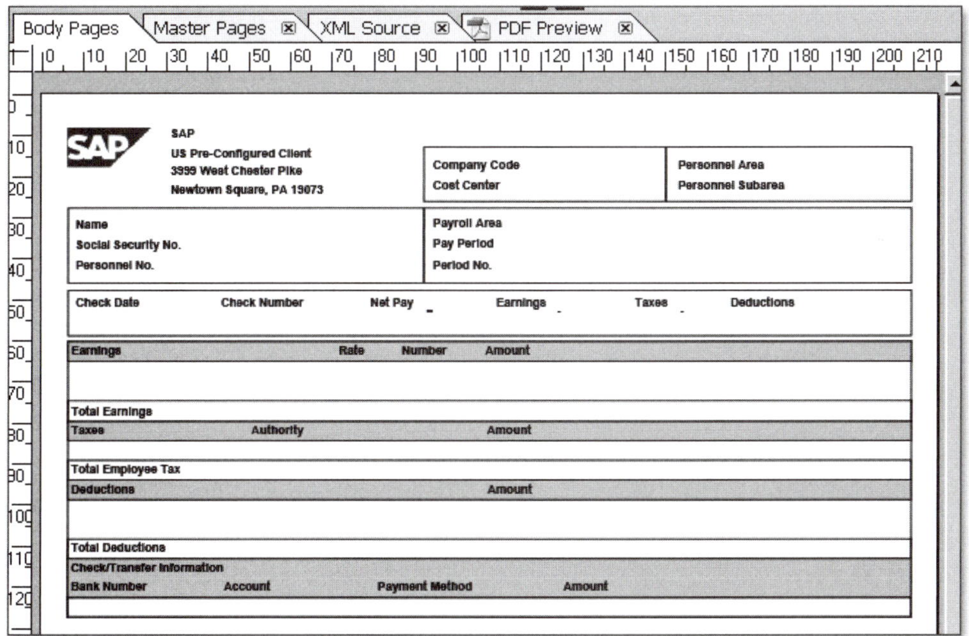

**Figure 3.42** Displaying the Body Page in Adobe LiveCycle Designer (Design Mode)

```
  Body Pages  \  Master Pages  ⊠  \  XML Source  ⊠  \  ⚙ PDF Preview  ⊠  \
          <ui>
              <textEdit>
                  <border presence="hidden">
                      <?templateDesigner StyleID aped0?></border>
                  <margin/>
              </textEdit>
          </ui>
          <font typeface="Arial"/>
          <margin bottomInset="1mm" leftInset="1mm" rightInset="1mm" topInset="1mm"/>
          <para vAlign="middle"/>
          <caption reserve="25mm">
              <font typeface="Arial"/>
              <para vAlign="middle"/>
              <value>
                  <text xmlns:xft-xliff="http://www.xfa.org/schema/xfa-xliff/1.0/" xft-xl
              </value>
          </caption>
          <value>
              <text maxChars="5"/>
          </value>
          <bind match="dataRef" ref="STAR_ITY_PERS_STRUCT.DATA[*].DIM_TIME_ADMIN.DATA[*
          <desc>
              <text xmlns:xft-xliff="http://www.xfa.org/schema/xfa-xliff/1.0/" name="Sch
          </desc>
          <?digestForSAP digest="509ad170640cbb256087069a45eedbb2"?></field>
      <field access="readOnly" h="9mm" id="floatingField018467" name="Name" presence="
          <ui>
              <textEdit>
                  <border presence="hidden">
                      <?templateDesigner StyleID aped0?></border>
                  <margin/>
              </textEdit>
          </ui>
          <font typeface="Arial"/>
          <margin bottomInset="1mm" leftInset="1mm" rightInset="1mm" topInset="1mm"/>
          <para vAlign="middle"/>
          <caption reserve="25mm">
```

**Figure 3.43**  Formatting the Data Fields in XML Code

> **Caution**
>
> Although these XML elements and data can also be changed directly to quickly change a form, this procedure is not recommended because it may damage the form.

Because it is integrated with the SAP development environment, the XML data contains information on the corresponding data schema. Consequently, you shouldn't use the temporary storage to copy forms and content because the XML data and layout might be damaged or become incomplete during the copy process. Instead, use the development environment via Transaction SFP or HRFORMS through the menu. You can download the form locally using the UTILITIES • DOWNLOAD FORM entry (see Figure 3.44).

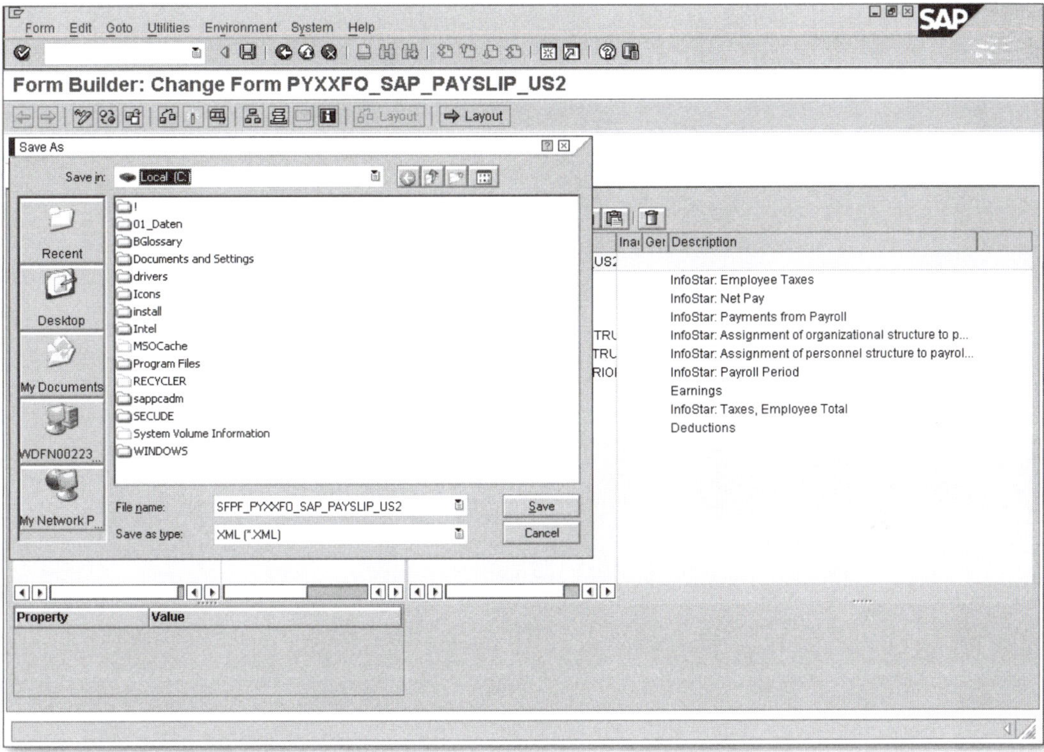

**Figure 3.44** Downloading Forms

You can use the JavaScript und FormCalc elements to implement calculations and checks, but only for fields in the form. This enables you to perform plain validation checks and to form totals.

These elements refer to the form and don't actively interact with the SAP ERP HCM system. So, you should only map simple calculations or checks, and you shouldn't implement complex application developments that lead to an increased maintenance effort.

At this point, you can refer to the documentation of Adobe LiveCycle Designer or the SAP PRESS book *SAP Interactive Forms by Adobe* for more information on the exact scripting functions. Figure 3.45 shows an example of the initial screen. You can navigate to the help via the HELP menu item or by pressing F1.

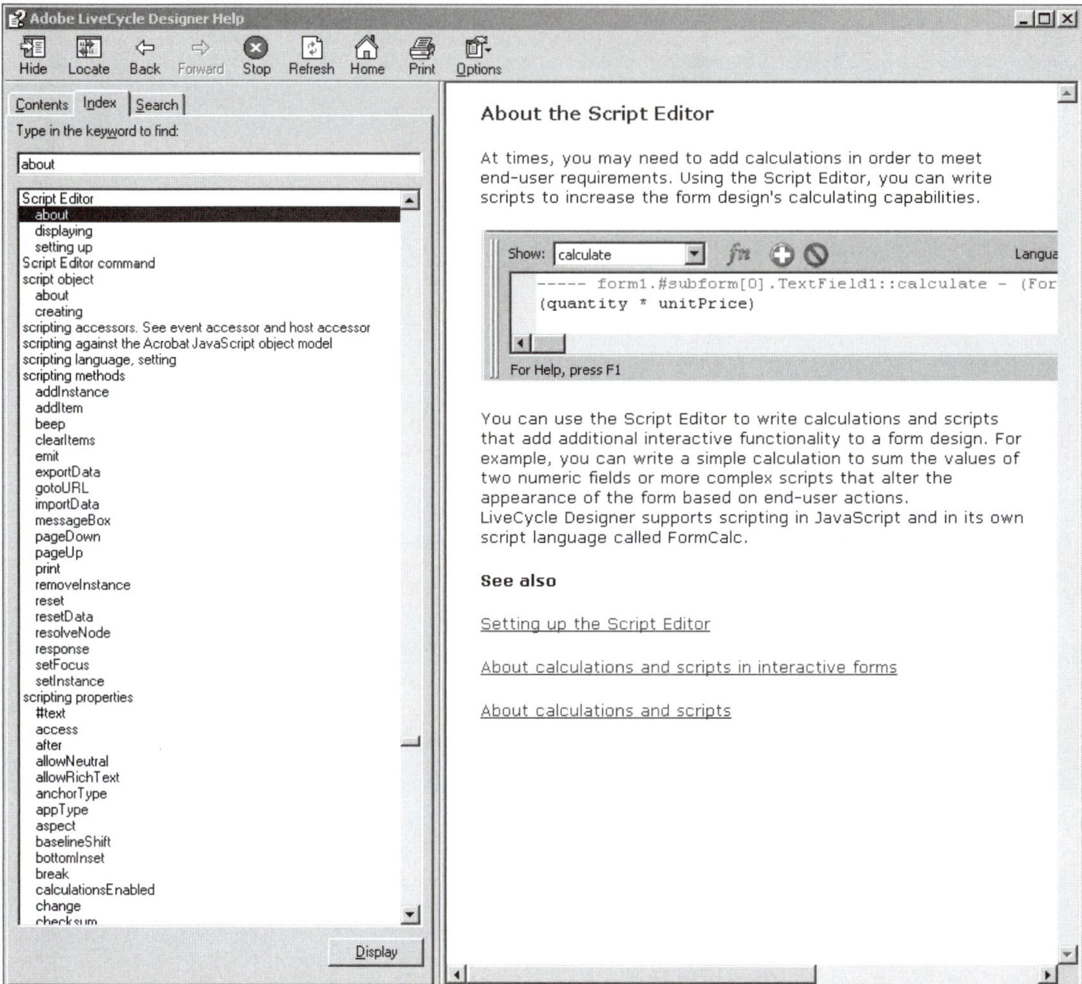

**Figure 3.45** Script Editor Help

All data for the form must be read with ABAP code. This is usually done in the application program but is also possible within the coding in the interface. However, for calculations within the form, you can also use scripting, which is executed at runtime and triggered by ADS. As already mentioned, the two programming languages available for scripting are JavaScript (recommended for interactive scenarios) and FormCalc by Adobe (recommended for printing scenarios).

One of the major advantages of the entire form development is the WYSIWYG (What You See Is What You Get) Editor. After designing the form, you can view it in the design environment via the PDF PREVIEW tab to get a first impression. A preview of the payslip might look like the one displayed in Figure 3.46, for example.

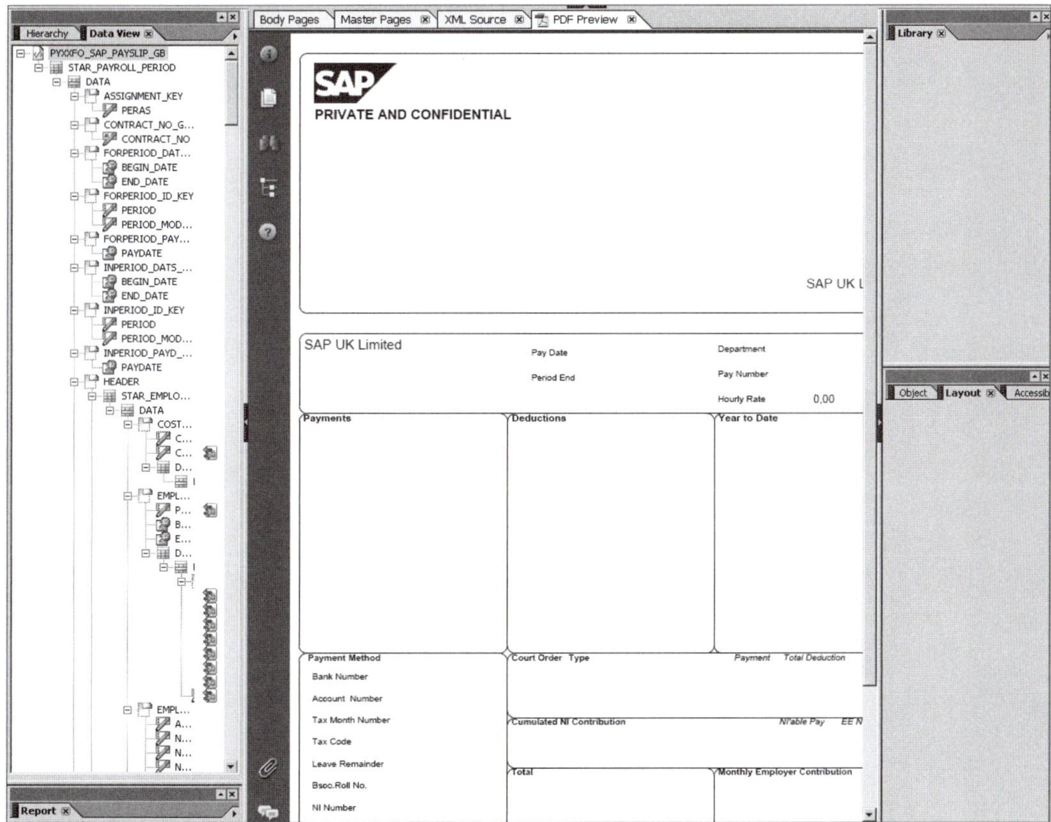


**Figure 3.46**  PDF Preview

If the system doesn't display the PDF PREVIEW tab, you must change the browser plug-in settings for Adobe Reader or maybe re-install Adobe Reader. To change the settings, call Adobe Reader, and select EDIT • DEFAULT SETTINGS • INTERNET in the menu (see Figure 3.47). Then, select the DISPLAY PDF IN BROWSER field.

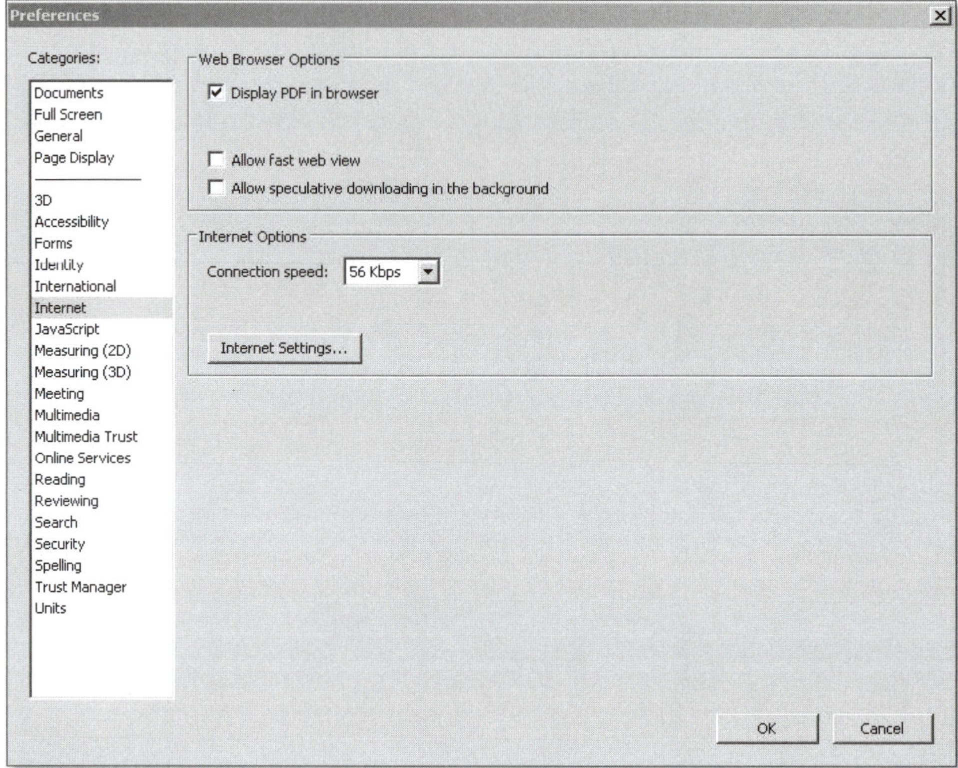

**Figure 3.47**  Browser Plug-In Settings for Adobe Reader

### General Form Properties

Now that you're familiar with the basic functions of Adobe LiveCycle Designer, we'll provide some information on the general form properties and describe the first simple step for testing a form.

The EDIT menu in the menu bar and toolbar of Adobe LiveCycle Designer (see Figure 3.48) includes the FORM PROPERTIES options. You can use these options to change and configure the basic properties of the form when you start your work or at any time later. Let's consider the most interesting settings.

**Figure 3.48**  Menu Bar and Toolbar

The FORM PROPERTIES dialog box provides the INFO, DEFAULTS, PERFORMANCE, VARI-ABLES, and COMPATIBILITY tabs (see Figure 3.49).

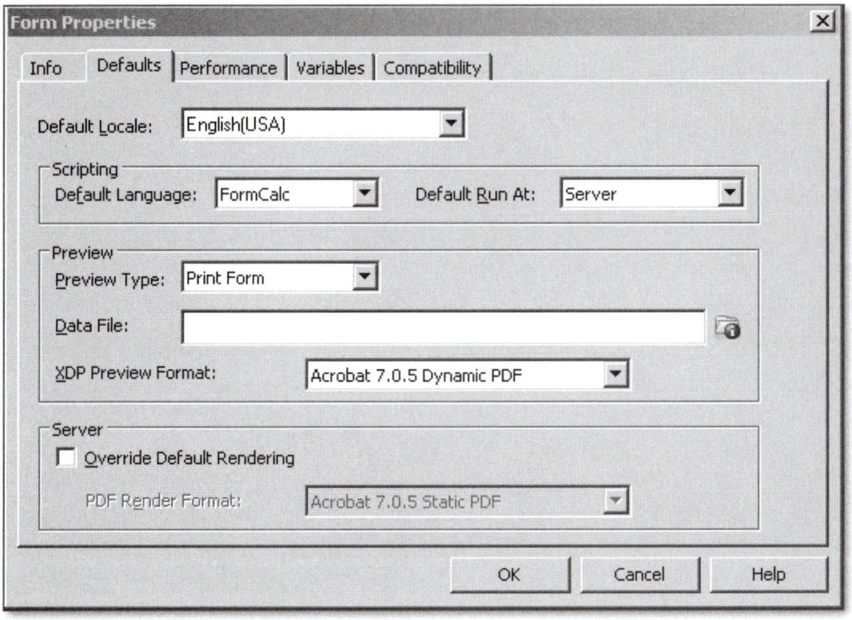

**Figure 3.49** Form Properties Dialog Box

The DEFAULTS tab, which is displayed in Figure 3.49, has the following features:

▶ The settings for the DEFAULT LOCALE field only apply to the already-mentioned local test of the forms. Like the following option, entry of the data file, this field is overridden by the respective SAP application program and so is not relevant.

▶ The entry of a DATA FILE for the PREVIEW enables you to locally test the forms in the development environment without the corresponding application program. You can test the form with some data, but the form isn't activated, and you don't have to enter the data manually each time you run this local test.

The system uses the data file entered here for the preview in Adobe LiveCycle Designer. Remember that it's a local test, so Adobe Document Services are not called. This may also affect the appearance of the forms in that fonts sometimes may appear different in a preview than after rendering by ADS.

▶ The OVERRIDE DEFAULT RENDERING setting doesn't apply to the use of Adobe LiveCycle Designer in SAP environments and shouldn't be selected.

> **Note**
>
> SAP Training BC 480 for PDF-based print forms provides detailed information on using the Adobe LiveCycle Designer. This course is designed for form developers.

**Font Types and Font Formats**

If you want to use more fonts or your own fonts in addition to the available fonts, you can install them retroactively in Adobe LiveCycle Designer. The installation guide describes the installation of additional fonts. However, if you use additional fonts, you must ensure that the fonts are also installed on the Adobe Document Services software component (Document Services Font Manager), so that they can be processed at the runtime of the program. A mere installation in the development environment — Adobe LiveCycle Designer — isn't sufficient.

To change the font type or font style (italics, underlined, bold, colored, etc.), select the corresponding text, and configure the settings in the Font palette. However, in the first step, these settings only refer to the local environment of Adobe LiveCycle Designer (see Figure 3.50).

> **Warning**
>
> The preview of Adobe LiveCycle Designer displays the text with the font types that are installed on the local computer. These font types may completely differ from those that are available at runtime (for ADS). To avoid inconsistencies, you should only use the fonts that are installed in the operating system that runs ADS.

The Times, Arial, and Courier fonts are usually always available. If it isn't required, avoid using too many font types per document because this may affect the processing performance (irrespective of design aspects). Nevertheless, the installation of new fonts has been simplified compared to SAPscript or SAP Smart Forms.

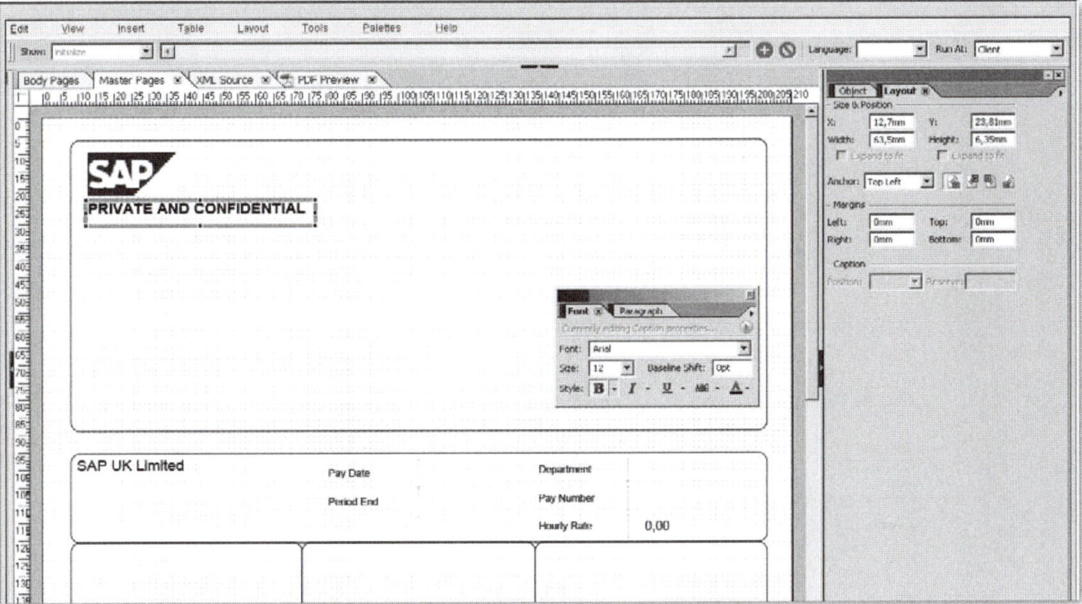

**Figure 3.50** Fonts

## Installation of Fonts

Because common TrueType fonts and bar codes can now also be printed on any PostScript, PCL, or PDF printer, you have the option to install your own fonts in ADS. You can then also use them when calling and converting the program to get the desired result.

At first, you may find it difficult to install new fonts. However, because you can use the J2EE Engine for this task, it's now much easier compared to SAPscript or Smart Forms.

The fonts are installed on ADS, usually by a Basis administrator following these steps:

1. **Call the Font Manager**
   Install the font using the Font Manager.

2. **Create a subdirectory**
   Create a subdirectory with the description *fonts/* in the */usr/sap/<SAPSID>/SYS/gobal/AdobeDocumentServices/FontManagerService* directory.

3. **Create another subdirectory in the subdirectory**
   Create a subdirectory with the description *customer/* under the *fonts/* directory that you created in the previous step.

4. **Copy the required fonts**
   Copy the required fonts to the directory.

Fonts that are not available for ADS at rendering time are replaced according to the substitution rules in the *usr/sap/<SAPSID>/SYS/global/AdobeDocumentServices/lib/xfa.xci* file. A different file may be specified at runtime. This is implemented in the XDCNAME field of the IE_OUTPUTPARAMS parameter of the FP_JOB_OPEN function module.

Don't confuse the font substitution at rendering time in ADS with the font substitution at design time in Adobe LiveCycle Designer. Adobe LiveCycle Designer has its own font substitution mechanism. You can configure the settings via the TOOLS • OPTIONS menu item (see Figure 3.51).

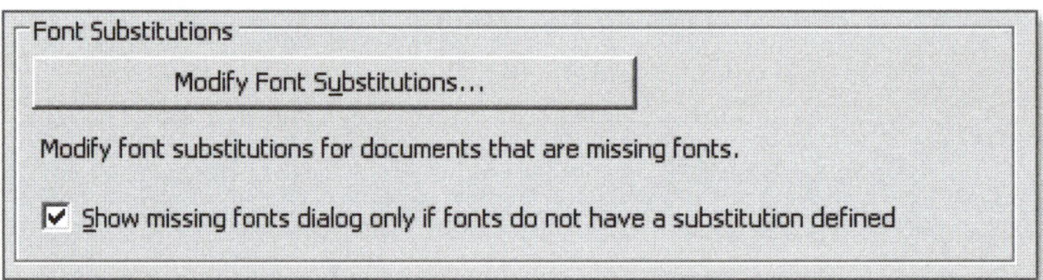

**Figure 3.51** Font Substitution

These additional fonts may be lost during the conversion for PDF/A long-time archiving and may not be suited for long-time archiving and documentation.

> **Note**
>
> PDF/A is an ISO standard for the use of *Portable Document Formats* (PDF) for the long-time archiving of electronic documents. PDF/A's content and structure is thus disclosed and binding.

### 3.2.4 Example of Designing a Form with Adobe LiveCycle Designer

So far, this chapter has provided general information on the options and functions of Adobe LiveCycle Designer. Now let's look at an example of how you can design a form. We can't cover all aspects in detail here, so this example focuses on how to use the main functions.

Before you begin designing the form, you should configure the basic functions in the layout editor, which are defined using the DRAWING AIDS palette. Here, you can select various options; for example, you should display the grid and a horizontal and vertical ruler (see Figures 3.52 and 3.53). These settings will help with the graphical work in the WYSIWYG Editor and the creative design of the form.

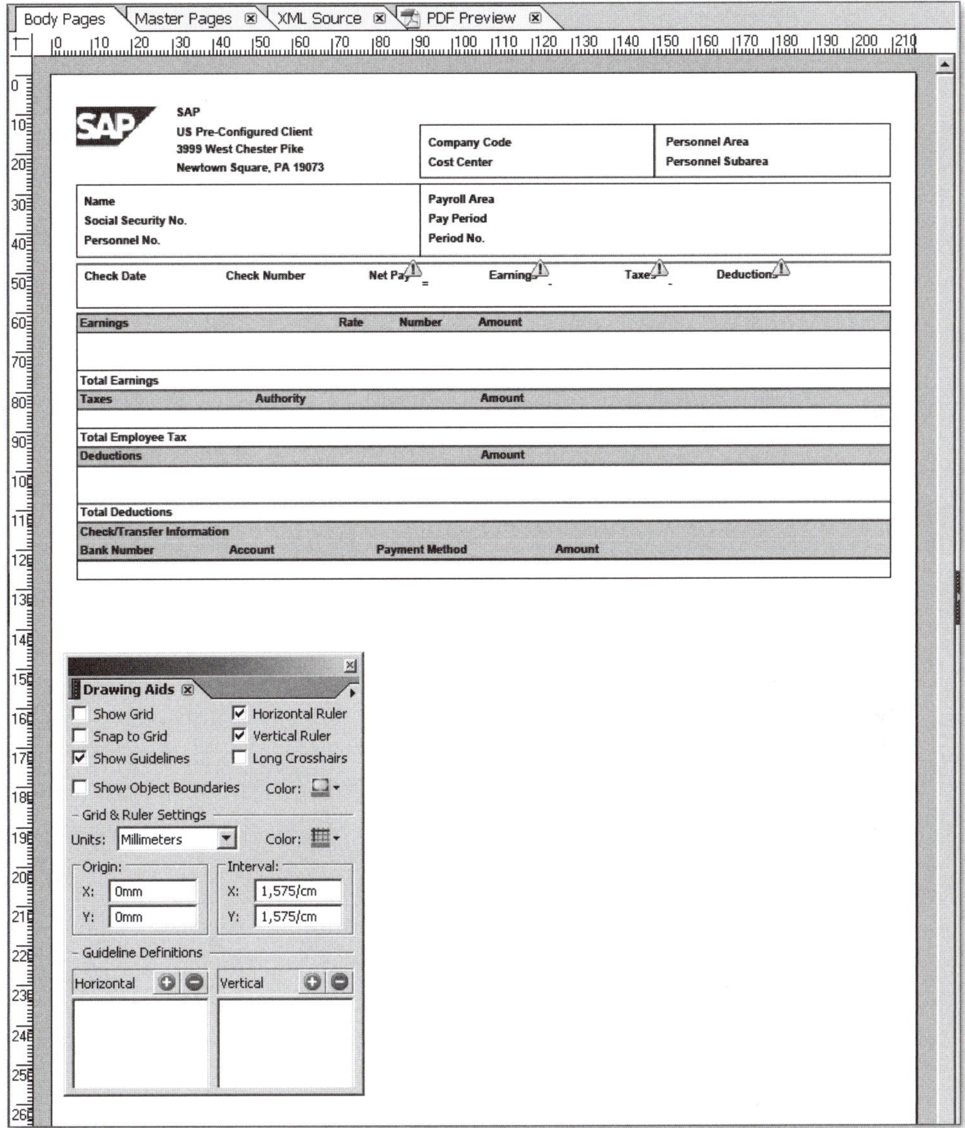

**Figure 3.52** Display Without Drawing Aids

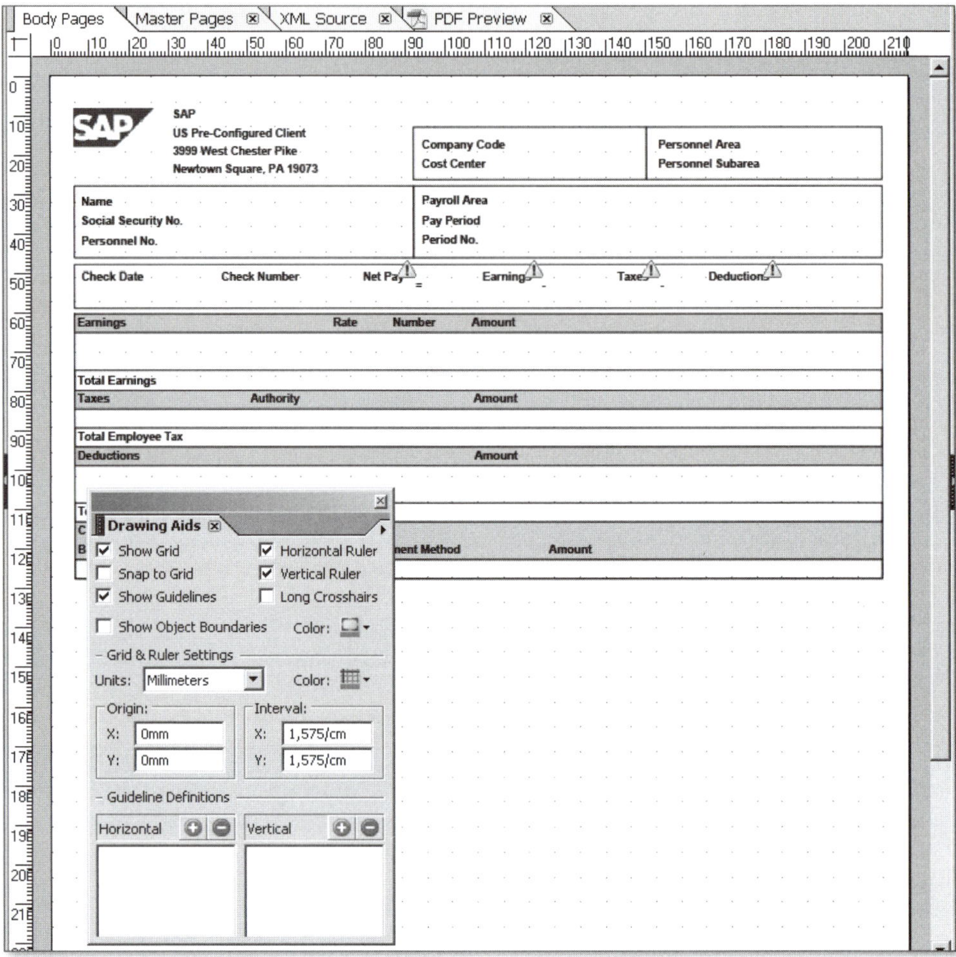



**Figure 3.53**  Display with Drawing Aids

For example, if you want to insert a new body page in the payslip, select the INSERT and INSERT TEXT menu items in the layout editor. The result is a new page in the central workspace (see Figure 3.54).

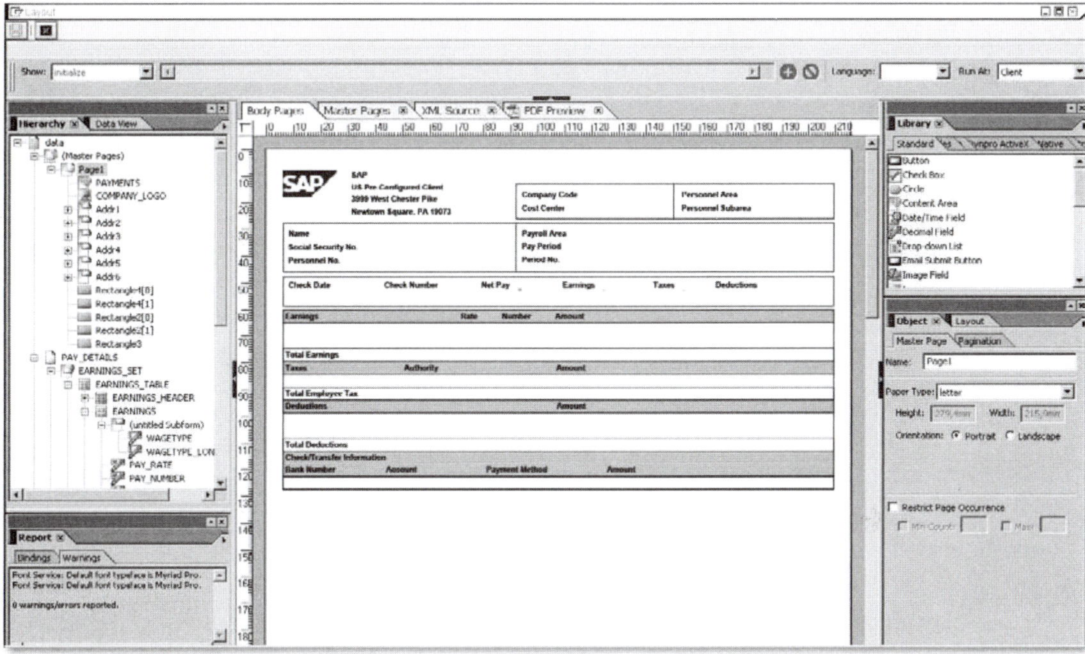

**Figure 3.54**  Inserting a New Page

The grid and the rulers are activated here to better arrange the content in the form. From the general settings of the master form, the header of the payslip with the logo, the address area, and the personal and organizational data of the employee is retrieved.

The left- and right workspaces display the various objects from the palette settings you can use. This enables you to position the cost center from the context, which is provided via the interface in the form. For this purpose, position the mouse in the Data View workspace in the KEY field. Hold the mouse button down, and drag the field to the right in the central workspace; release the mouse button at the required spot and drop the field. The example shows that all fields assigned to the KEY field in the hierarchy are also transferred: COSTCENTER, CTRL_AREA, CATEXT, and CCTEXT (see Figure 3.55). This makes it much easier for you, because you don't have to transfer all fields separately.

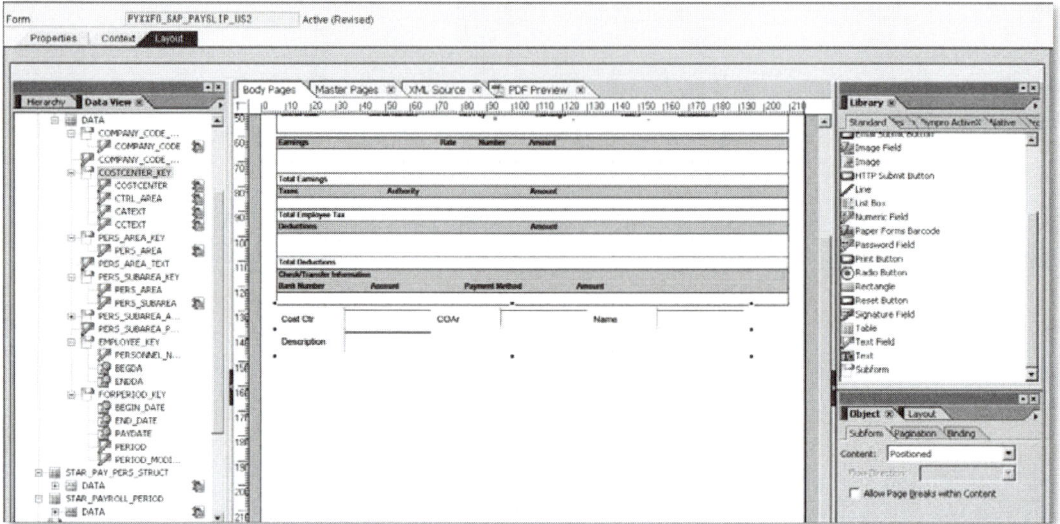

**Figure 3.55** Inserting a New Object

The data has been copied and must now be processed. Because the inserted objects still have the descriptions from the SAP system, you should check and rename them, if required, to ensure that employees and users can understand the field descriptions. The following example of the controlling area illustrates this aspect. Double-click on the COAR field. In the right workspace, you can modify the object description via the CAPTION field. Figure 3.56 displays these fields in their unmodified form.

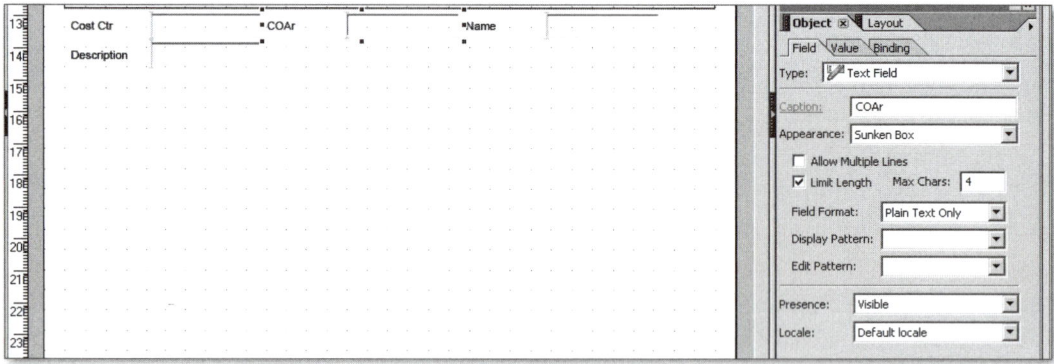

**Figure 3.56** Unmodified Field Description "COAr"

In the CAPTION field, you can make the respective changes by replacing "COAr" with "Controlling Area" (see Figure 3.57).

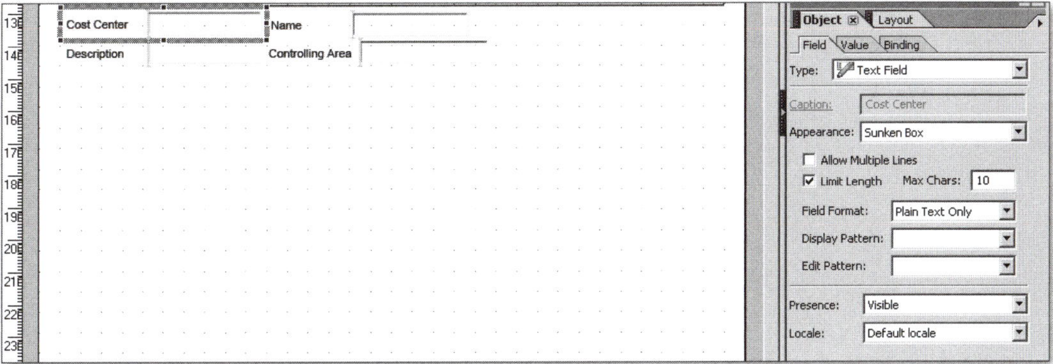

**Figure 3.57** Modified Field Description

However, the result in the central workspace doesn't display the entire new description because it's too long and overlapped by the next field. You can correct this in the next step by adapting the position of the fields accordingly as shown in Figure 3.58.

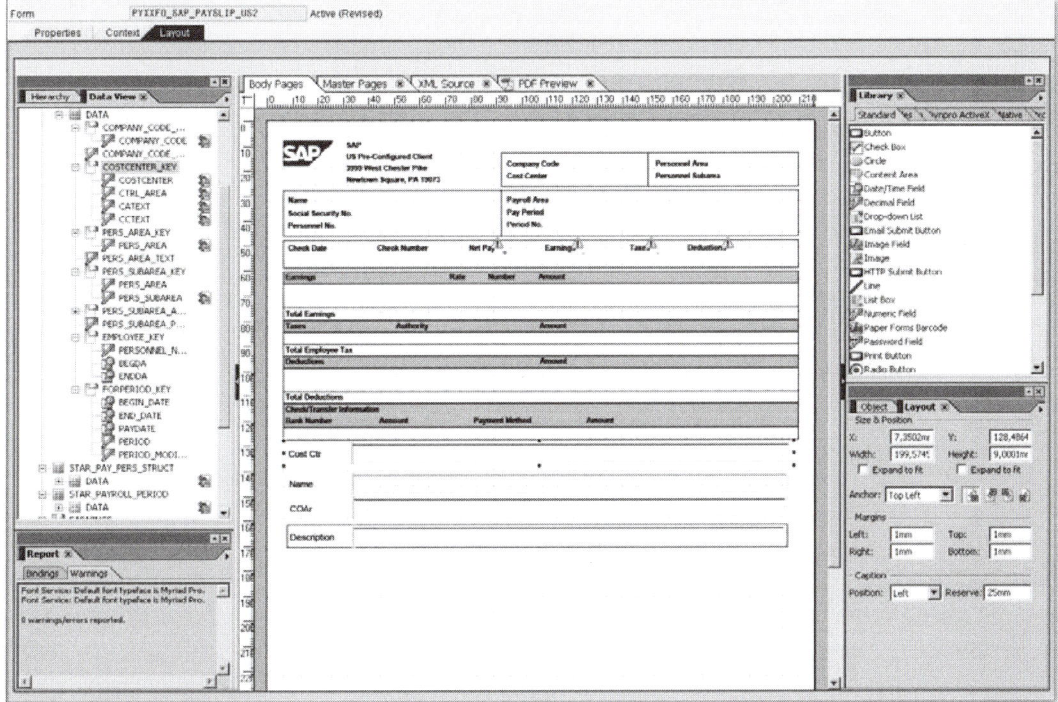

**Figure 3.58** Display with Adapted Field Arrangement

To implement these adaptations in Adobe LiveCycle Designer, you can select and move individual fields using the mouse. If you want to move entire blocks or sections, select the entire area and move it via an action. You'll notice that, with a little practice, Adobe LiveCycle Designer is as easy to use as the Microsoft Office environment, for example.

> **Tip**
>
> You can undo changes anytime by pressing `Ctrl` + `Z` or by choosing EDIT • UNDO.

Changing the description is certainly the first useful step for designing the fields and form in a user-friendly way. You can also customize the form, color, and border of objects and add many additional elements. Figure 3.59 shows some modifications to illustrate these options. APPEARANCE: CUSTOM enables you, for example, to modify the edges, corners, and background fill for the DESCRIPTION field.

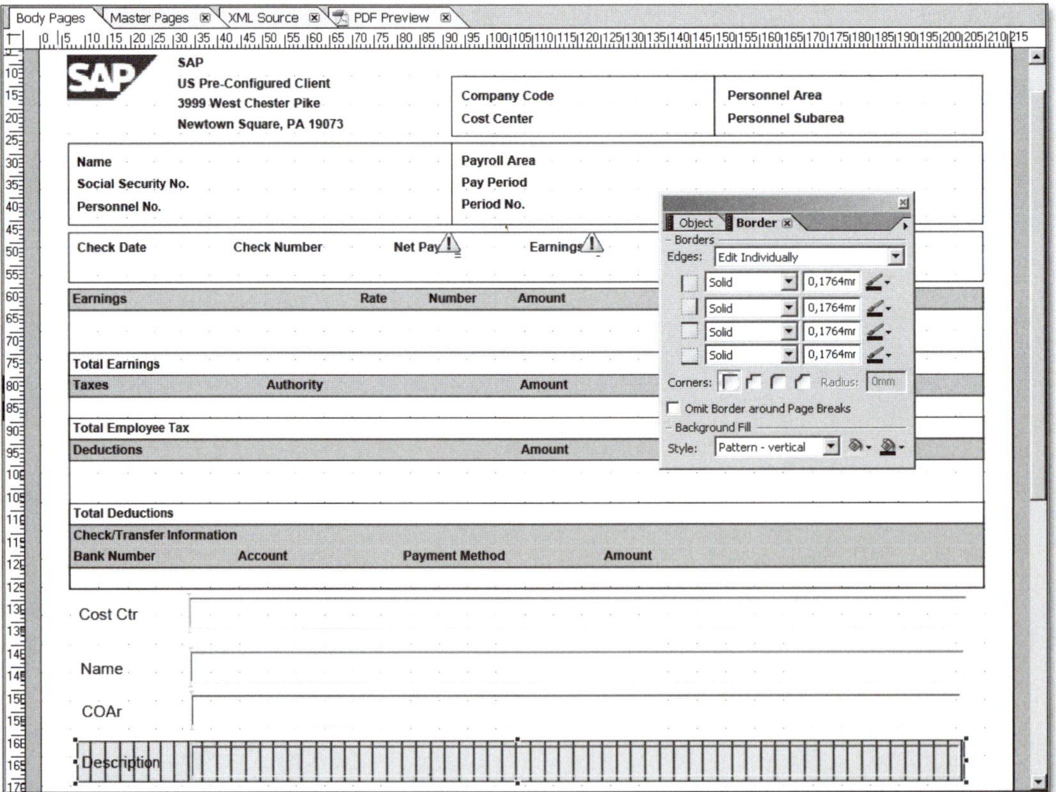

**Figure 3.59** Customizing the Appearance

You can insert additional fields and design elements in the form from the general library, which you can find in the top-right workspace. Select the required fields using the mouse, drag them into the form, and drop them wherever you like. Then, you can customize the appearance via the functions provided. In Figure 3.60, we modified the border, its color, and the background color via the appearance settings.

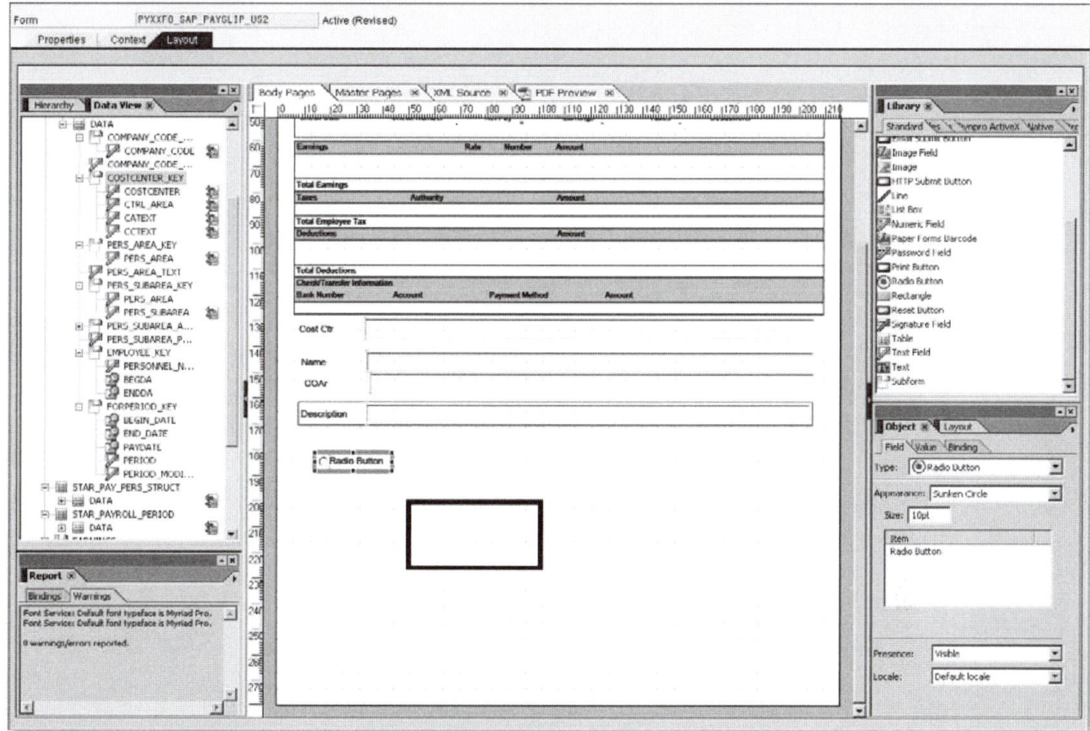

**Figure 3.60** Integrating a Radio Button and a Rectangle

This brief section has provided some examples of the options of Adobe LiveCycle Designer for designing the content and layout of forms. You'll become more acquainted with the options and get more ideas when actually working with this tool. The Adobe LiveCycle Designer documentation (press F1) contains additional information. In particular, refer to the Defining Object Properties chapter.

### 3.2.5    New Process Options with the Integrated Adobe Technology

The new functions of the SAP system and the integration of Adobe technologies provide options to rethink the existing processes and their design. So far, the SAP system has generated the payslip and time statement and printed them in regular intervals. The next step in a process that uses the new options might be to automatically store the payslip in the archive after its creation and link it with the SAP master data or an entry in the electronic personnel file for documentation purposes. (The electronic personnel file is part of the SAP NetWeaver component, *Records Management*.)

The employee or manager can then access the payslip, which is electronically stored in the archive, via the SAP GUI or the respective portal role. The payslip always displays the facts and results at the time of creation. This enables you to generate and archive an electronic payslip that can't be changed, similar to a hardcopy.

As an alternative or as a supplement to the hardcopy, employees can directly call the payslip and then view the result with the current values. In contrast to the previous procedure, the content of the payslip may change when it's called later if the basic principles have changed because the system generates the payslip at runtime; that is, it's called in real time.

In both scenarios, the payslip doesn't have to be printed, which means you can reduce costs. Alternatively, you can also consider whether you want to email the generated payslip to the employee. However, this procedure may raise security-relevant questions, particularly for the payslip.

## 3.3    Conclusion

This chapter described the most important functions of the Form Builder for Smart Forms and Form Builder for SAP Interactive Forms. Both tools are integrated with the Forms Workplace and are used to design the layout of forms.

In the first section we focused on the Form Builder for Smart Forms, and provided a brief overview of the user interface and the elements of the Form Builder. You should now be able to identify them in your form and understand their usage. Then, we covered font formats, their usage, and their maintenance, so you should have no problem when you're prompted to create a new paragraph or character format and use it to format an output text in the form. This chapter also detailed the usage of text modules so that you can now integrate larger text passages with a form using text modules without any problems. We described the output of a company logo, which you can import into your system, as well as the output of the more difficult bar codes. Before you begin implementing a bar code, you need to determine how the bar code digit that is supposed to be converted is structured, whether a system bar code exists and can be used, and where exactly this is supposed to be positioned. You should also start testing at an early stage. These tests should include printing and reading the bar code. The last section on the Form Builder for Smart Forms introduced a simple method to activate and deactivate areas in your form. This function supports you if you have to implement comprehensive changes.

The Form Builder for Smart Forms is a very complex tool that shouldn't be underestimated. If you spend some time with this tool to manage all of its functions and solution options, over time, you'll certainly succeed.

The Form Builder for SAP Interactive Forms also provides many options to create and design (print) forms. Just as we did for the Form Builder for Smart Forms, we introduced the configuration options of this new development environment. You probably noticed that it has a lot in common with Smart Forms, for example, the definition of the form interface and the text modules. This chapter also covered the structure of a form, the layout options, and the WYSIWYG Editor. We explained the separation between design tool and runtime environment (rendering) with regard to the form functions. However, when working intensively with Adobe LiveCycle Designer, you'll certainly explore many more functions that the existing form environment of the SAP system doesn't provide.

The Form Builder is a flexible design tool in the SAP development environment that you definitely should be involved with. The next chapter deals with the detailed design of the payslip using both tools.

# 4    Payslip — Creation and Customizing

This chapter explains how you can create a payslip in the design environment with Smart Forms or Adobe LiveCycle Designer.

To create a payslip with the Form Builder for SAP Interactive Forms, Adobe Live-Cycle Designer must be installed as the design tool and Adobe Document Services (ADS) as the basis component. Chapter 3, section 3.2.2, Prerequisites for Using SAP Interactive Forms, discussed these prerequisites, so you can refer back if you need a refresher. The procedure for providing the data is the same for both Smart Forms and Adobe LiveCycle Designer.

## 4.1    Creating the Form

The new sample form SAP_PAYSLIP_US2, delivered with SAP ERP HCM 6.0, uses the Form Builder for SAP Interactive Forms to design the layout. In contrast, the SAP_PAYSLIP_DE sample form still uses Smart Forms for the layout design.

In the following sections, we will use the functions that were described in Chapter 2, section 2.1, The SAP Standard MetaNet. You can navigate to the Forms Workplace and then directly to Customizing via Transaction HRFORMS or the following IMG path: PAYROLL • PAYROLL INTERNATIONAL (or the respective country) • FORMS USING HR FORMS WORKPLACE • EDIT HR FORMS USING FORMS WORKPLACE (see Figures 4.1 and 4.2).

> **Tip**
>
> You can call the forms using Development Transaction SFP. However, for HCM forms, you should use the IMG path or Transaction HRFORMS to ensure that the form is always correctly integrated with the application.

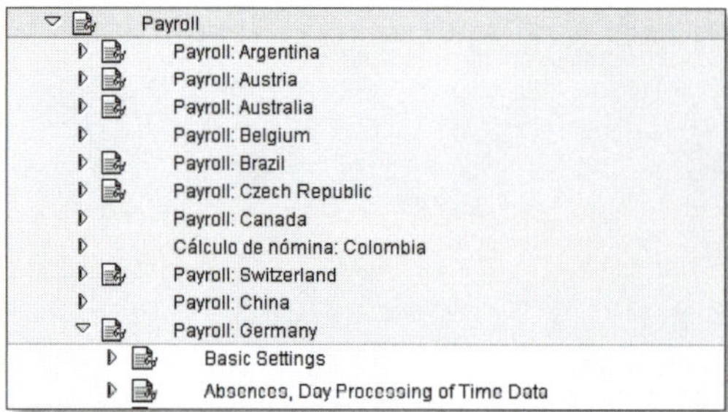



**Figure 4.1** Payroll IMG Path

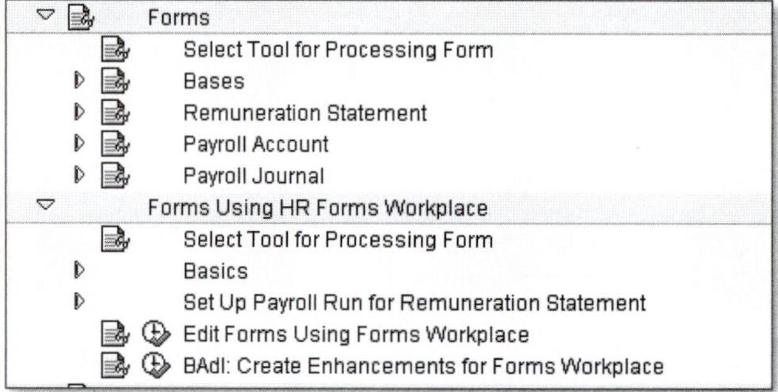



**Figure 4.2** Forms Using HR Forms Workplace IMG Path

HR Forms Workplace

HR Forms: Overview

| St | CGrpg | HR Form Name | Changed by | Changed on | Last changed at | Structu | Form | Progra | Form Class | Layout Editor | Structuring Stars |
|---|---|---|---|---|---|---|---|---|---|---|---|
| ⊙ | 01 | SAP_IW_WOSTT | JUSCHKA | 08.02.2006 | 08:45:01 | 1 | 1 | 1 | NONE | Form Builder | Flat Structure |
| ⊙ | | SAP_IW_WSTT_DE | JUSCHKA | 08.02.2006 | 10:30:25 | 1 | 1 | 1 | PAYSLIP | Form Builder | Flat Structure |
| ⊙ | | SAP_PAYRACC_DE | SAP | 04.11.2000 | 16:22:55 | 1 | 1 | 1 | PAYRACC | Form Builder | Flat Structure |
| □ | | SAP_PAYSLIP_DE | MUELLERVO | 04.01.2008 | 10:45:21 | 3 | 3 | 3 | PAYSLIP | SAP Smart Forms | Nested Structure |
| □ | | SAP_PAYSLIP_DE_P | SAP | 19.09.2000 | 10:44:11 | 3 | 3 | 3 | PAYSLIP | Form Builder | Flat Structure |
| ⊙ | | SAP_PAYSLIP_DE3 | SAP | 24.06.2004 | 13:13:08 | 1 | 3 | 1 | PAYSLIP | Form Builder | Nested Structure |
| ⊙ | | SAP_PAYSLIP_DE4 | SAP | 13.09.2004 | 14:16:13 | 1 | 3 | 1 | PAYSLIP | Form Builder | Flat Structure |
| ⊙ | | ZHRDE70_GRP00 | RODEIKE | 20.06.2003 | 19:38:12 | 1 | 3 | 1 | PAYSLIP | SAP Smart Forms | Nested Structure |
| ⊙ | | ZIDES_ENTGELT_NW | MUELLERV | 22.02.2005 | 16:05:26 | 1 | 3 | 1 | PAYSLIP | SAP Smart Forms | Nested Structure |
| ⊙ | 02 | SAP_PAYJNAL_CH | SAP | 16.05.2007 | 17:50:09 | 1 | 1 | 1 | PAYJNAL | Form Builder | Flat Structure |
| ⊙ | | SAP_PAYRACC_CH01 | SAP | 04.12.2006 | 01:40:27 | 1 | 1 | 1 | PAYRACC | Form Builder | Flat Structure |
| ⊙ | | SAP_PAYSLIP_CH | SAP | 13.07.2004 | 11:10:06 | 1 | 1 | 1 | PAYSLIP | Form Builder | Nested Structure |
| ⊙ | 03 | SAP_PAYJNAL_AT | SAP | 19.09.2008 | 16:30:29 | 1 | 1 | 1 | PAYJNAL | Form Builder | Flat Structure |
| ⊙ | | SAP_PAYRACC_AT | DINGLU | 21.11.2006 | 00:20:37 | 1 | 1 | 1 | PAYRACC | Form Builder | Flat Structure |
| ⊙ | | SAP_PAYSLIP_AT | SAP | 13.07.2004 | 13:15:06 | 1 | 1 | 1 | PAYSLIP | Form Builder | Nested Structure |
| ⊙ | | SAP_PAYSLIP_AT01 | LIURIC | 29.11.2006 | 05:46:40 | 1 | 1 | 1 | PAYSLIP | Form Builder | Flat Structure |
| ⊙ | | SAP_PAYSLIP_AT02 | SAP | 28.08.2008 | 22:45:23 | 1 | 1 | 1 | PAYSLIP | Form Builder | Flat Structure |
| ⊙ | | SAP_PAYSLIP_AT03 | LIURIC | 20.11.2006 | 06:55:49 | 1 | 1 | 1 | PAYSLIP | Form Builder | Flat Structure |
| ⊙ | | SAP_PAYSLIP_AT04 | LIURIC | 04.12.2006 | 09:44:15 | 1 | 1 | 1 | PAYSLIP | Form Builder | Flat Structure |
| ⊙ | | SAP_PAYSLIP_AT05 | LIURIC | 04.12.2006 | 09:45:44 | 1 | 1 | 1 | PAYSLIP | Form Builder | Flat Structure |
| ⊙ | 04 | SAP_PAYJNAL_ES | C5113016 | 29.04.2000 | 20:11:19 | 1 | 1 | 1 | PAYJNAL | Form Builder | Flat Structure |
| ⊙ | | SAP_PAYRACC_ES | SAP | 04.12.2007 | 17:17:05 | 1 | 1 | 1 | PAYRACC | Form Builder | Flat Structure |
| ⊙ | | SAP_PAYSLIP_ES_1 | SAP | 28.08.2000 | 19:05:44 | 1 | 1 | 1 | PAYSLIP | Form Builder | Flat Structure |
| ⊙ | | SAP_PAYSLIP_ES1 | SAP | 27.08.2008 | 21:13:41 | 1 | 1 | 1 | PAYSLIP | Form Builder | Flat Structure |
| ⊙ | 05 | SAP_FLEX_PAYMNT | SAP | 14.11.2000 | 22:31:50 | 1 | 1 | 1 | PAYSLIP | Form Builder | Flat Structure |

**Figure 4.3** HR Forms Workplace — Form Overview

Figure 4.3 displays the Smart Forms and Form Builder forms in the LAYOUT EDI-
TOR column. When the form is called, the system calls the corresponding layout
editor.

### 4.1.1    SAP_PAYSLIP_DE

This section describes the creation of a form with Smart Forms. The SAP_PAYSLIP_
DE form is a payslip that the SAP system supplies with respective data and whose
design you can create or customize using the Form Builder for Smart Forms.

You must first select and copy the provided form to customize it according to your
requirements. For this purpose, select the respective row, and copy the form using
the COPY function or by pressing ⎡Ctrl⎤ + ⎡F5⎤ (see Figure 4.4).

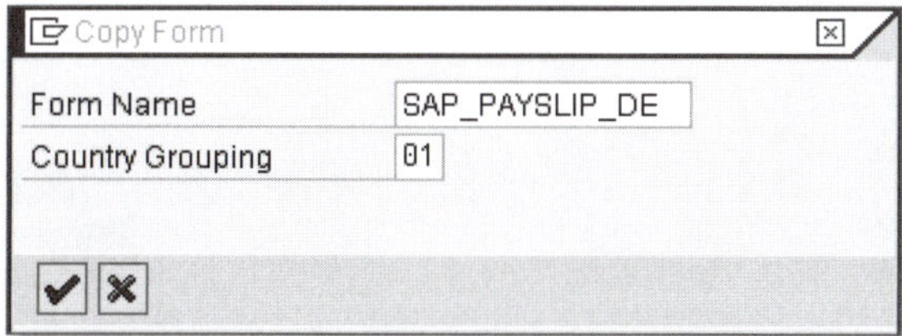


**Figure 4.4**    Copying a Form

After copying the form, you can assign a new form name to it in the dialog box
according to the corresponding naming conventions. The system automatically
generates a transport request, which documents the new form and all changes.
Table HRFORMS is updated to the new entry, and the new form is displayed in the
complete view with the corresponding MetaNet and InfoNet.

By double-clicking the form, you navigate to the overview of the MetaNet (see
Figure 4.5).

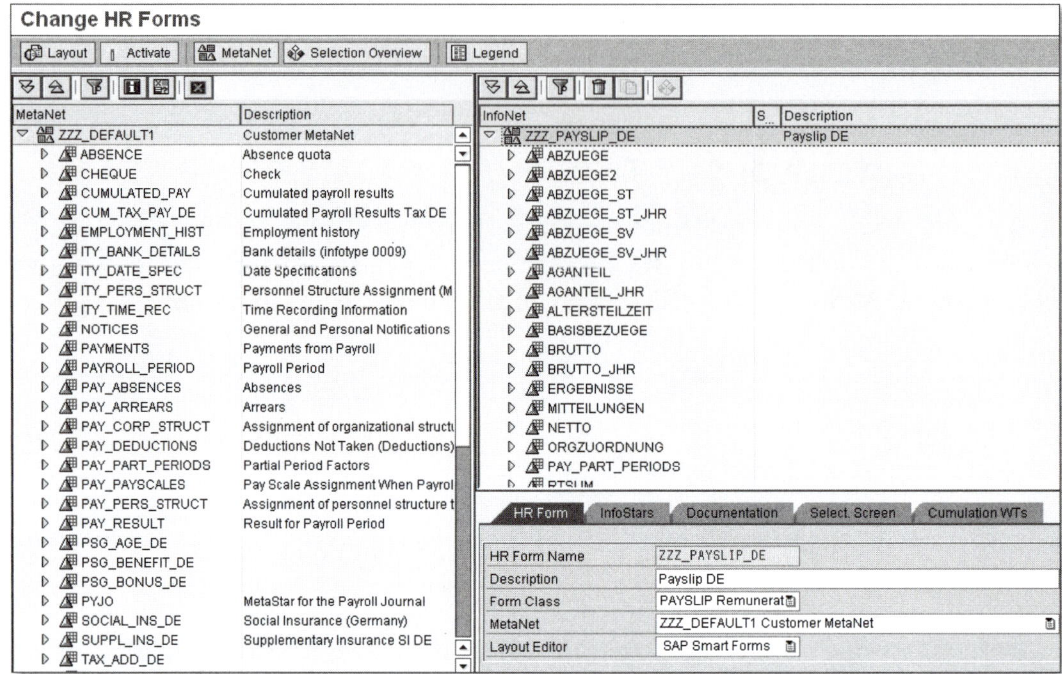

**Figure 4.5** Data Retrieval in the HR Forms Workplace

The right bottom area of Figure 4.5 displays the details of the form, such as the form data, form name, and form class (see Figure 4.6).

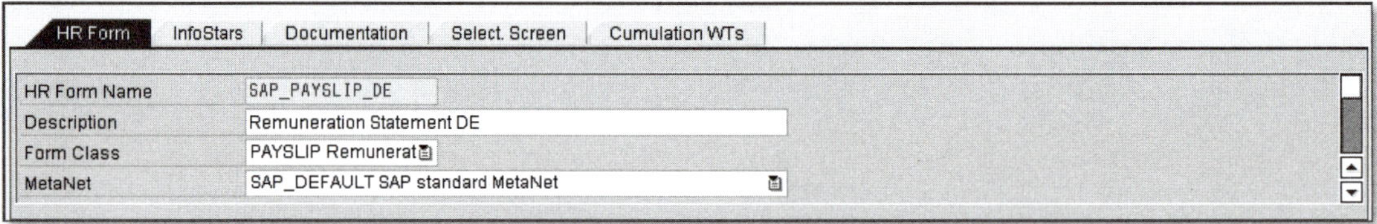

**Figure 4.6** Properties of the HR Form

You can navigate to the layout editor via the LAYOUT button. The system first displays the message FORM STRUCTURE IS BEING GENERATED IN THE DATA DICTIONARY and then the screen shown in Figure 4.7 with the integrated Form Builder for the form.

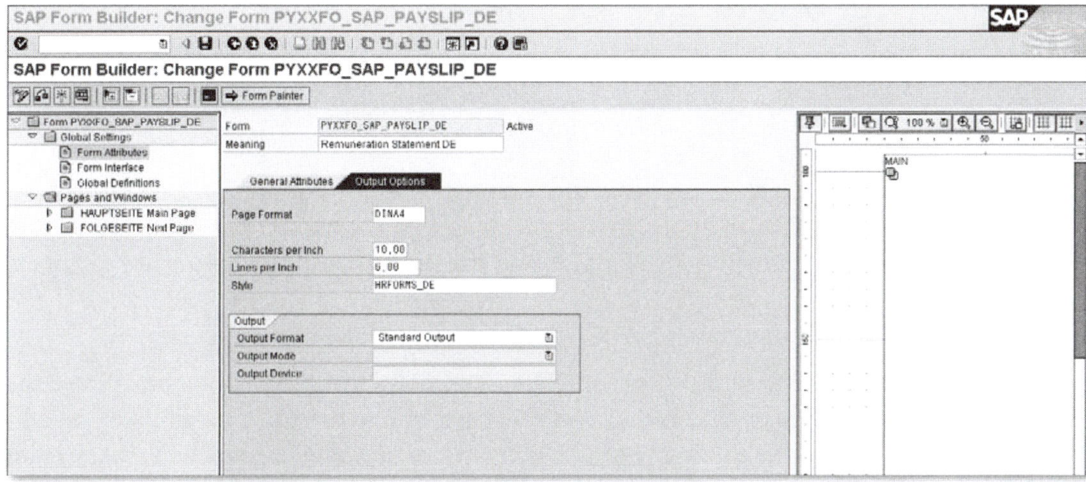

**Figure 4.7**  Payslip in the Form Builder for Smart Forms

For the SAP_PAYSLIP_DE standard form, this looks like Figure 4.8.

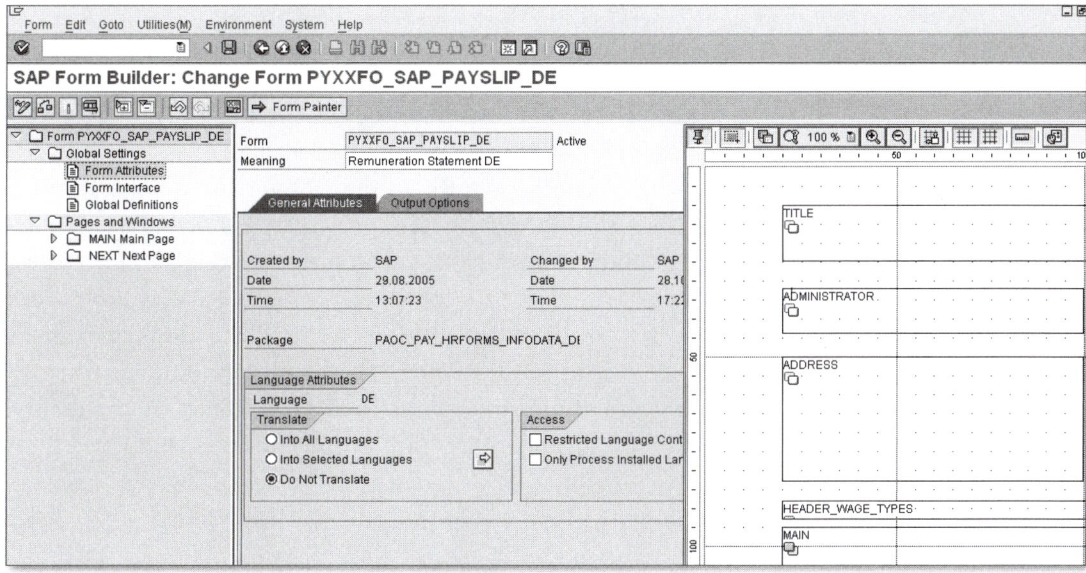

**Figure 4.8**  SAP_PAYSLIP_DE Standard Form in the Form Builder for Smart Forms

To create a new form, follow these steps:

1. Choose CREATE. The system inserts a new line in the list of the existing HR forms. The NAME, COUNTRY GROUPING, and FORM CLASS columns are ready for input.

2. Enter the name of the HR form. Select the country grouping and form class. The name (less than 16 characters, no special characters) must not yet exist in the system and should comply with the corresponding naming conventions. The system creates the HR form when all specifications are free of errors. If you want to continue with the structuring of the InfoNet, press Enter.

3. The system then displays the Create Object Catalog Entry dialog box. Enter the required values, and select SAVE. This takes you to the editor where you can edit the InfoNet. The left area of the editor (refer to Figure 4.5) includes a selection tree that contains the MetaNet with all HR data that is available. The right area displays the InfoNet, which is still empty and doesn't contain any objects.

4. Insert the required InfoStars, InfoDimensions, and InfoFigures in the InfoNet via drag-and-drop.

5. Specify the necessary information in the tabs of the individual objects.

6. Create the selections that you require in your form.

7. Select LAYOUT to continue with the Customizing for the form in the graphical tool. Use the Form Builder for Smart Forms. You can display or hide it with the FORM PAINTER button (refer to Figure 4.8). This facilitates the work with various windows and enables you to enlarge the individual windows. By double-clicking on the respective fields on the left, you can easily navigate in the Form Painter in the right area, and select the proper fields. This makes your work much easier, and you always have the connection between the proper fields and their definition. Here, you can customize the form definition of your HR form and use specific formatting options for each form value. In the central area, you can configure the general attributes, output options, and conditions (see Figure 4.9).

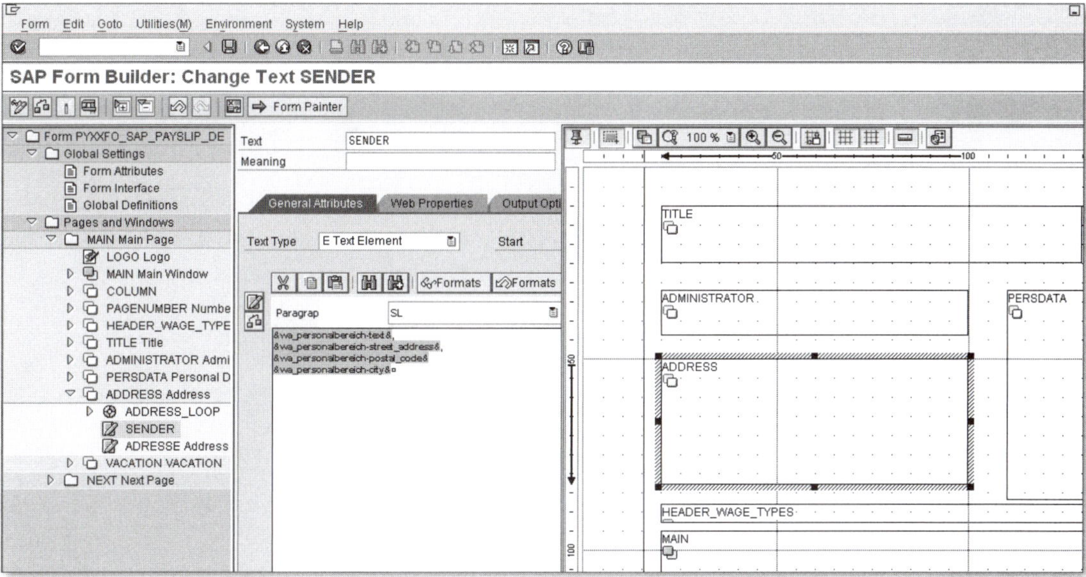

**Figure 4.9**  Form Painter

8. After making the necessary changes, save the form by clicking on the Save button.

9. Activate the form by pressing `Ctrl` + `F3`. The corresponding print program for this form is generated and can be used.

You now know how you can use a Smart Forms form and customize it if required. The next section describes the necessary steps for the corresponding Adobe form.

### 4.1.2  SAP_PAYSLIP_US2

This section discusses the design process of the payslip with the Form Builder for SAP Interactive Forms. As an alternative to the procedure described in Section 4.1.1, SAP_PAYSLIP_DE, you can directly generate a PDF form in the SAP development environment using Adobe LiveCycle Designer. The steps up to calling the layout editor are identical to the steps used in the previous section. This also means that the data is retrieved in the same way for both form developments.

1. In the HR Forms Workplace, select the SAP_PAYSLIP_US2 form. The data is retrieved via the interface in the same ways as for Smart Forms (as described in the previous section), which means that the data retrieval is controlled via the MetaNet and InfoNet (see Figure 4.10).

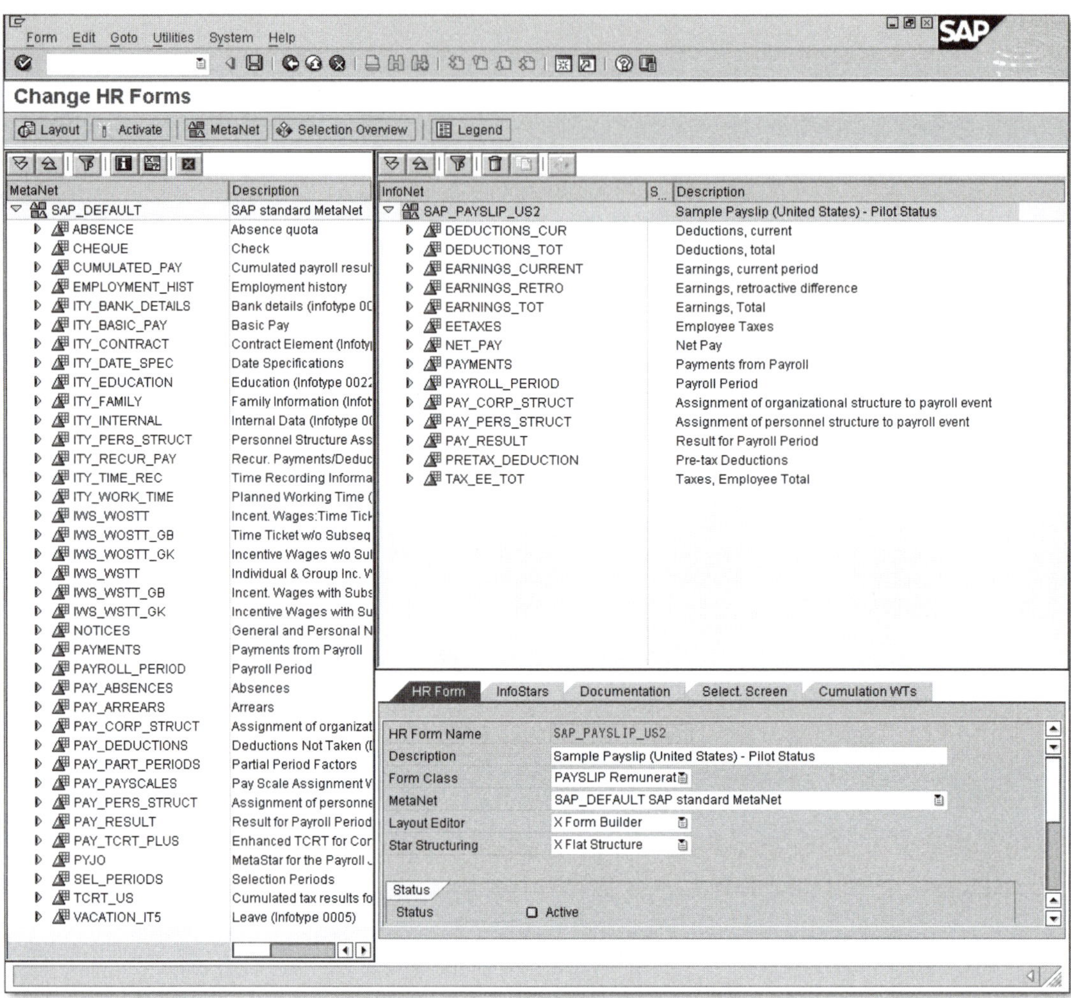

**Figure 4.10** MetaNet, InfoNet, and Properties of the Form

2. Click the LAYOUT button to go to the Form Builder environment. The Form Builder is displayed with the generated interface and context for the Adobe form. You can view the payslip with the fields from the SAP Data Dictionary. The left area of Adobe LiveCycle Designer contains the DATA VIEW (see Figure 4.11).

In the center of Figure 4.11, you can see the form for the payslip. This is a template for which you can customize the design and logo. The example also includes a master page and several body pages.

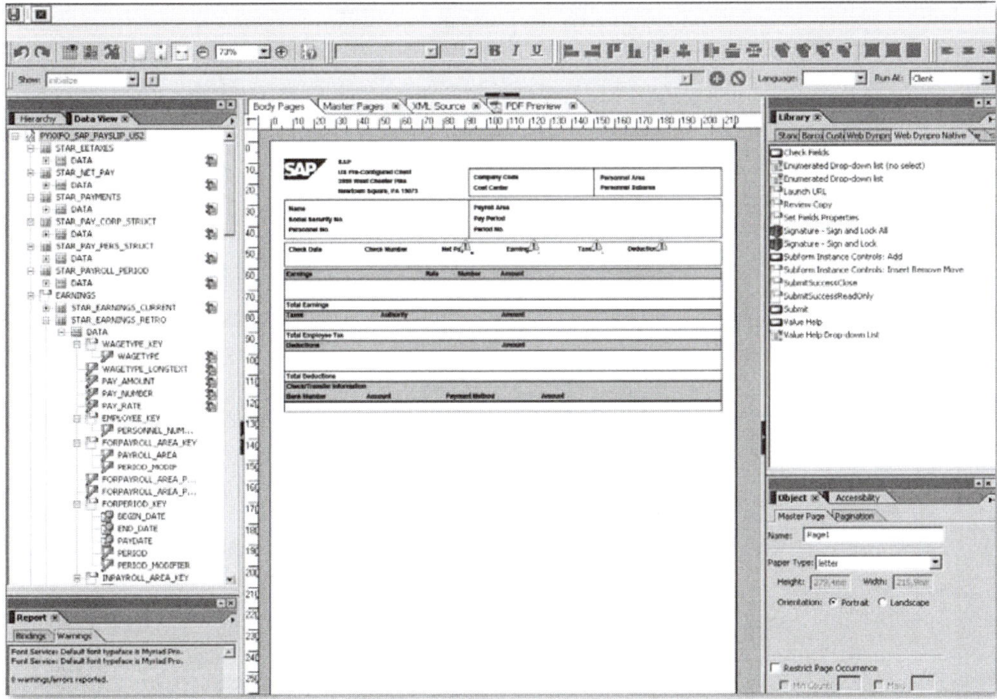

**Figure 4.11**  Form in Adobe LiveCycle Designer with SAP Data Dictionary Fields on the Left

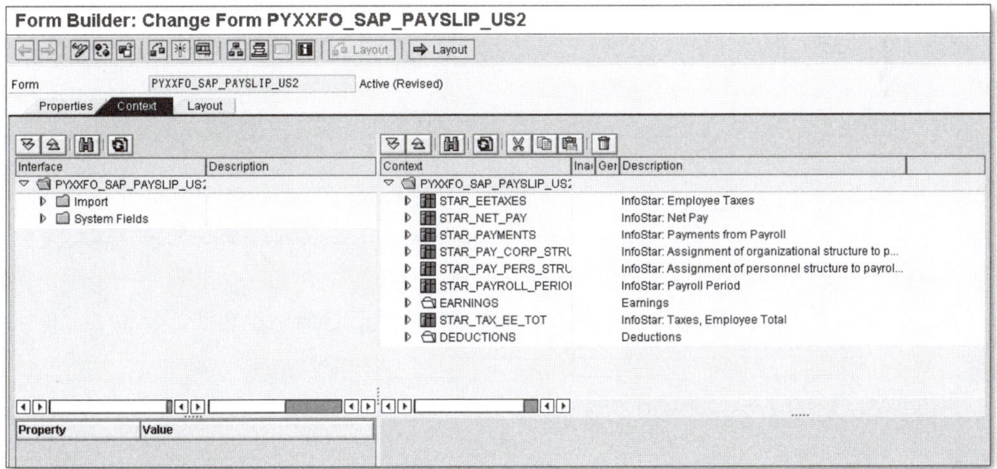

**Figure 4.12**  Form Context of the Form for the Interface

This form context shown in Figure 4.12 serves to define the fields that are available in the form design. All fields that have been provided via this data retrieval method can afterwards be used in Adobe LiveCycle Designer, so you need to define all fields here to access them in the design environment. Adobe LiveCycle Designer is called by double-clicking on LAYOUT. Figure 4.13 shows the central workspace.

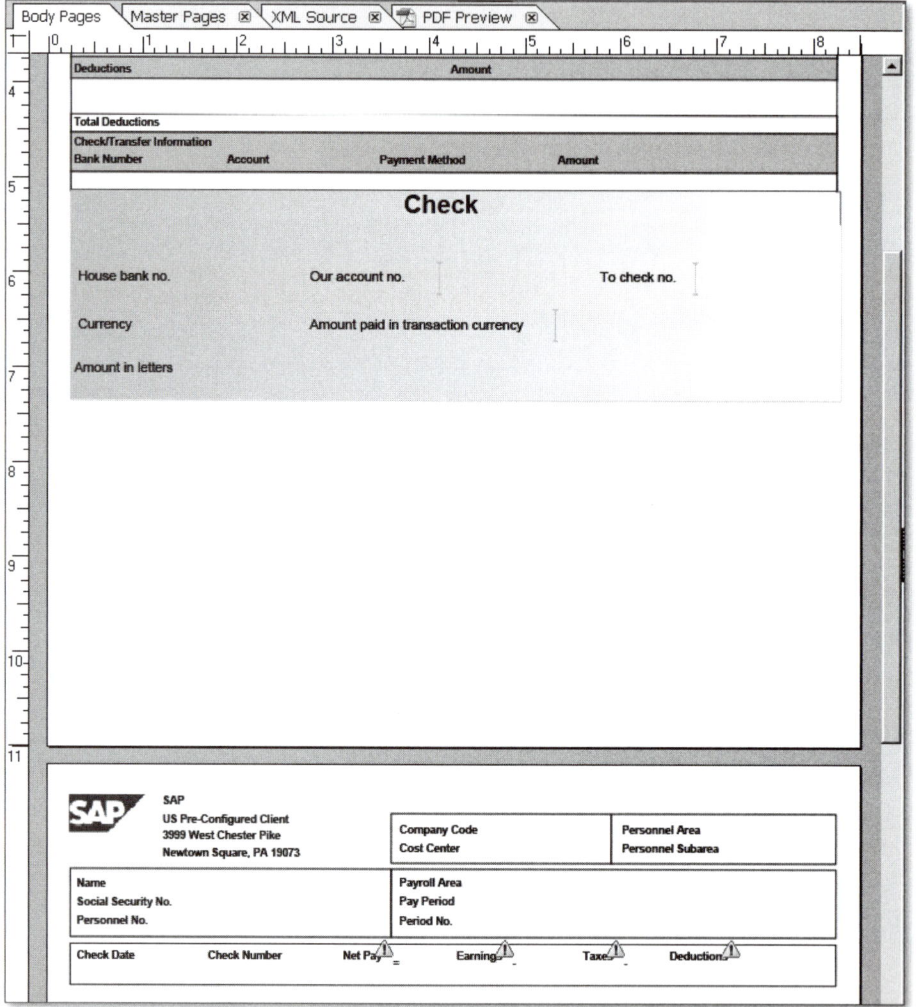

**Figure 4.13** Central Area of the Payslip in Adobe LiveCycle Designer — Body Pages with Page Break

Let's suppose you want to output the bank details of an employee on a page. In this case, you can select the BANK_KEY field group in the left workspace, that is, the DATA VIEW. Keep the mouse button pressed, and drag the entire group to the right in the central workspace. The system automatically copies the BANK_NUM-BER, CONTROL_KEY, and COUNTRY fields. You can now arrange them in the form. You can see part of the result in Figure 4.14.

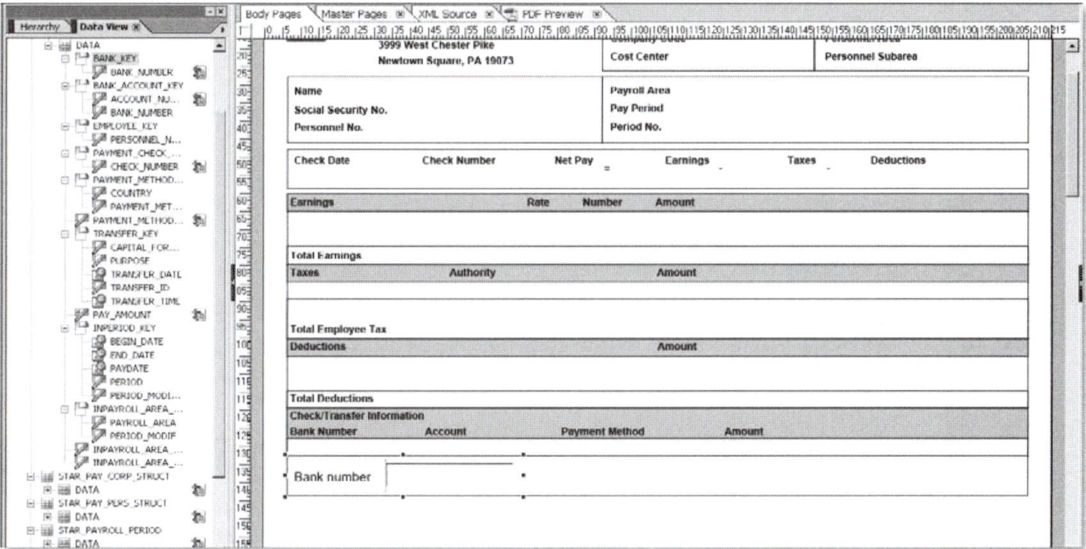

**Figure 4.14**  Example of the Transfer and Arrangement of Fields

After customizing and modifying the form, you can view it in the PDF preview. At this stage, the PDF preview displays the form and its layout but not yet the corresponding data. If the design looks good, you can store it, and the form is then logged in a transport request (see Figure 4.15).

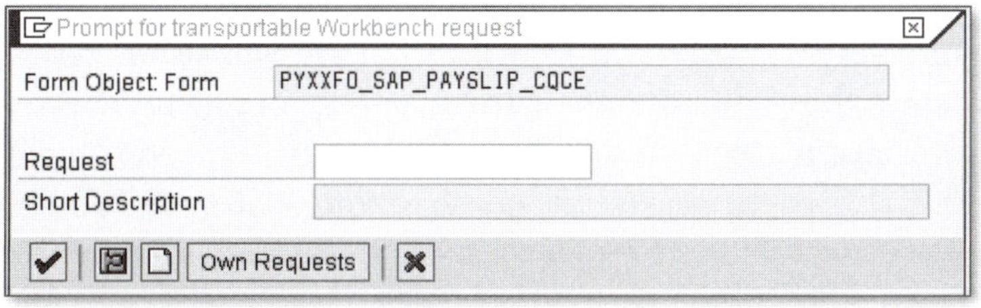

**Figure 4.15**  Dialog Box for a Transport Request

You now return to the Form Builder in the SAP system. Here, you can test the form by pressing F8 or Shift + F5 (PRINT PROGRAM [TEST]) alternatively (see Figure 4.16).

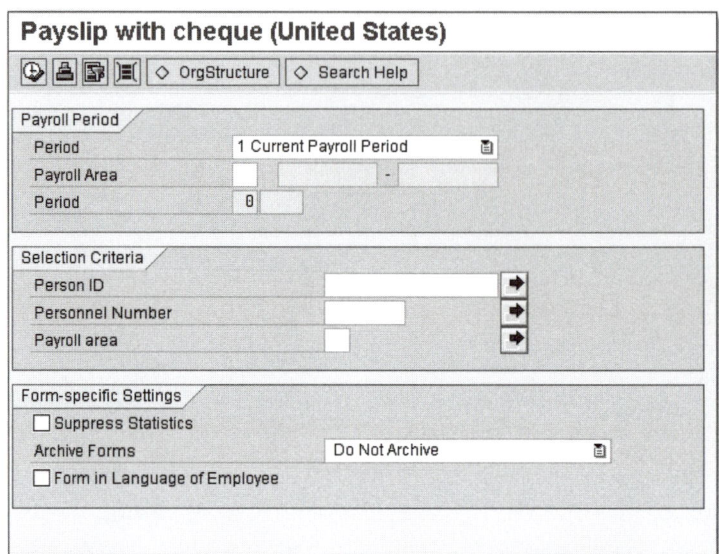


**Figure 4.16**  Selection Screen with the Parameters of the Print Program

## 4.2  Customizing

In addition to creating the form in the Forms Workplace and designing the layout in the Form Builder, you have more customizing options that enable you to modify the form and output. In this section, we describe how you can modify the selection screen of the print program, which effects the available parameters you have. You will also see how to identify and group the wage types that you want to output in your payslip. In addition to using and outputting wage types, which you maintain in Table T512W, you can define cumulation wage types, which you can also provide in your InfoNet and position in your payslip. We will also describe how to specifically suppress the output of retroactive accounting results. However, this aspect cannot be considered a mere Customizing step because it involves more development work. This also applies if you include Infotype 0655 (ESS Settings Remuneration Statement) for providing employees with the payslip in Employee Self-Service (ESS).

> **Note**
>
> If Customizing varies depending on the layout editor you use (Form Builder for Smart Forms or Form Builder for SAP Interactive Forms), the respective section explicitly indicates this.

### 4.2.1 The Selection Screen

The selection screen of your print program enables you to choose the data and the personnel numbers for the people you want to create the payslips for. You decide whose payroll results will be evaluated. You can modify the selection screen of your form via the maintenance of the InfoNet properties in the Forms Workplace in the SELECTION SCREEN tab. The maintenance doesn't depend on the selected layout editor (Form Builder for Smart Forms or for SAP Interactive Forms). The following *report categories* arc available to define the number and visibility of the fields in the selection screen:

- HRF_PACE (Remuneration Statements — With Off-cycle and CE)
- HRF_PNOC (Remuneration Statements — Without Off-cycle and CE)
- HRF_PAYS (Remuneration Statements — With Off-cycle)

> **Note**
>
> The logical database, PNPCE, is similar to the logical database, PNP, but can process the concurrent employment concept. The logical databases, PNP and PNPCE, allow for quick access to personnel master data and are used for its evaluation. For the logical database, PNPCE, all report categories are valid.

CE (*Concurrent Employment*) in the description of the two report categories, HRF_PACE and HRF_PNOC, indicates that the field for the entry of external person IDs can be used in the selection screen. This ID is relevant for concurrent employment and is used as a unique number for identifying a person in the SAP system. The difference between the report categories with or without *off-cycle* (special run) is that the possible input values for the period include the special run in the selection screen. If you select this period, the selection screen changes, and you can enter the reason and time for the special run (see Figure 4.17).

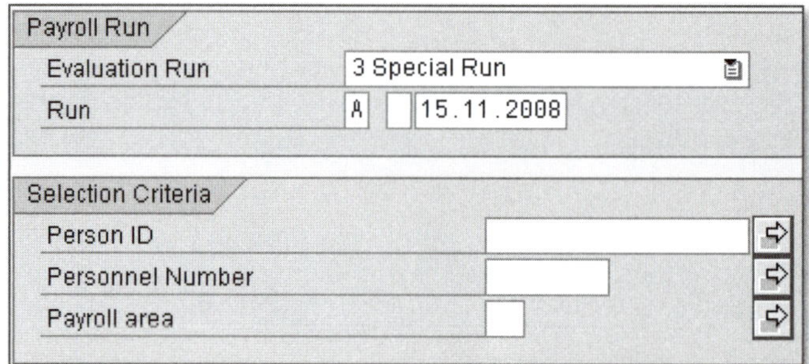

**Figure 4.17** Special Run and Person ID in the Selection Screen

You can use the report categories as templates for your own categories. You can navigate to the maintenance of a report category by double-clicking on it. Select the change mode, and copy the report category to customize it accordingly.

Besides the report category, you can predefine default values for optional fields for your selection screen (see Figure 4.18).

| HR Form | InfoStars | Documentation | Select. Screen | Cumulation WTs |
|---------|-----------|---------------|----------------|----------------|

Report category      HRF_PAYS    HRFORMS: Remuneration Statements - With Off-cycle

Optional fields in the selection screen

| Show | Selection Field | Set Default Value | Default Value |
|------|-----------------|-------------------|---------------|
| ☑ | Include retroactive accounting: no, yes, also retr accg runs | ☑ | X |
| ☑ | Consider and Display Archived Payroll Results | ☐ | |
| ☑ | Currency conversion | ☐ | |
| ☑ | Only Read Infotype Records in the Time Interval | ☐ | |
| ☑ | In-view payroll periods | ☑ | X |
| ☑ | Alternative Currency | ☐ | |
| ☑ | Number of Employees per Form (0= All) | ☑ | 1 |
| ☑ | Simulate multiple payroll | ☐ | |

**Figure 4.18** Select. Screen Tab

By selecting the SHOW column, you specify whether the field in the selection field of the print program is visible when the print program is executed (see Figure 4.19).

> **Note**
>
> The visibility of selection fields is managed independently of the definition of the default values. A default value remains valid even if the field isn't displayed in the selection screen.

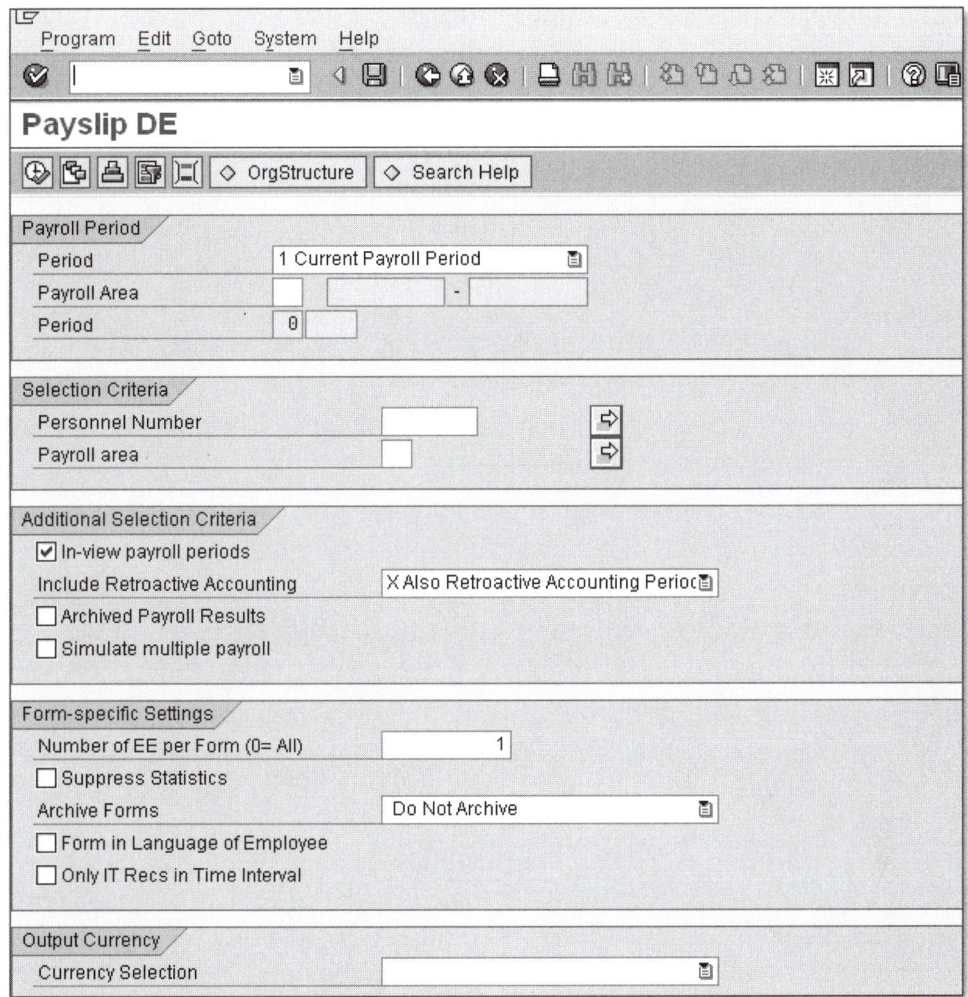



**Figure 4.19** Selection Screen of the Print Program

The following list describes the selection screen parameters (see Figure 4.19):

▶ By entering the payroll PERIOD or a special run and further selection criteria, such as the PERSONNEL NUMBER or PAYROLL AREA, you define when and for whom the system is supposed to create the payslip.

- Select the IN-VIEW PAYROLL PERIODS checkbox if you want to select the payroll results according to their *in-period*. If this flag isn't set, the system selects the data according to the *for-period*. You can have the system consider retroactive accounting by using the INCLUDE RETROACTIVE ACCOUNTING option. The system includes retroactive accounting based on the following options:

  - O: No other results are included besides original results.

  - X: Retroactive accounting and current results are included so that differences may be displayed.

  - Blank: The system includes retroactive accounting but not the related retroactive periods so that no differences are displayed.

    If you want to display the differences, select the in-period view, and enter X for the display of retroactive accounting.

- The ARCHIVED PAYROLL RESULTS checkbox is used for the *payroll account* and includes archived results if set.

- Select the SIMULATE MULTIPLE PAYROLL checkbox if you want to run the payroll for multiple reference personnel numbers of an employee or if you want to simulate multiple payroll. If this isn't the case, you can neglect this parameter.

- The NUMBER OF EE PER FORM parameter defines how many personnel numbers are processed in one form. If you enter "0," the form is called only once, and all personnel numbers are processed in the same form. If you enter a value that is greater than "0," the system completes the form as soon as the value is reached and then calls it again. If you process multiple personnel numbers in one form, you must ensure that the person-dependent InfoStars contain at least one of the EMPLOYEE or ASSIGNMENT InfoDimensions. If you set the value to "1," the system calls the form for each selected personnel number. For SAP Interactive Forms, this means that the greater this value, the faster the processing. However, if the value is too large, this may lead to overflow errors. For Smart Forms-based forms, the system only distinguishes between "0" and "not equal to 0"; that is, either a form is called for each personnel number or for all personnel numbers. If you want to provide cross-person data in your form, specify the value "0." Note that this may lead to an overflow error. This applies to both SAP Interactive Forms and Smart Forms.

▸ As the name of the SUPPRESS STATISTICS checkbox already implies, select it if you want to avoid outputting the statistics that contain the number of processed and rejected personnel numbers as well as the number of printed pages and processed payroll results. The system still outputs error messages if you set this parameter.

▸ The next parameter, ARCHIVE FORMS, includes the following definitions:

  ▸ P: Archive and print

  ▸ X: Archive

  ▸ Blank: Do Not Archive

  The form is transferred into the archive if you select P or X. If you set the P parameter, the system also prints the form. You can change the key for archiving in the HRFORM_HRF02 Business Add-In in the SET_ARCHIVE_INDEX method as described in Section 6.3.3, SET_ARCHIVE_INDEX Method. If you want to archive the form, you must generate the form for each employee. Set the NUMBER OF EE PER FORM parameter accordingly. More information about archiving in SAP ERP HCM is available in the SAP PRESS book, *Archiving Your SAP Data* (see Appendix H, Additional Information).

▸ If you want to output the form in the employee's language, use the FORM IN LANGUAGE OF EMPLOYEE parameter. If you start the form from ESS, it's output in the logon language of the employee. Otherwise, the form is output in the language that is defined in Infotype 0002 (Personal Data).

▸ The ONLY IT RECS IN TIME INTERVAL option enables you to restrict the time interval for the selection of the infotypes that are supposed to be output to the start and end date. This only makes sense if you want to solely use current infotype records and don't need data from the past for retroactive accounting.

▸ The CURRENCY SELECTION parameter can be used to define the conversion of the currency. The following values are available:

  ▸ A: Use alternative currency

  ▸ F: Use currency of the for-period

  ▸ I: Use currency of the in-period

  ▸ N: No currency conversion

When you select the alternative currency, the selection screen displays an additional field in which you can enter the alternative currency (see Figure 4.20).

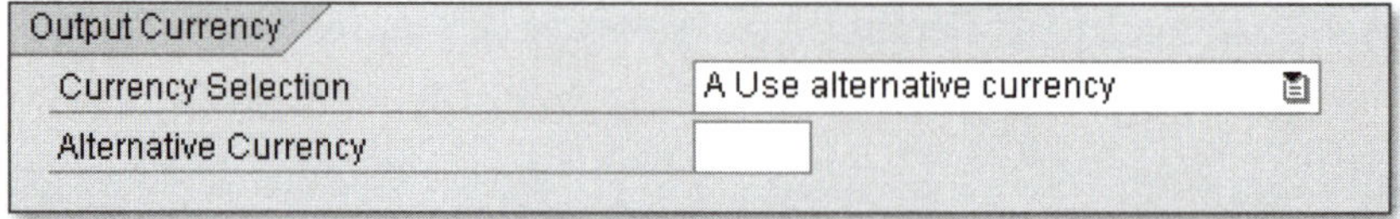

**Figure 4.20** Defining the Alternative Currency

With the F and I indicators, you select the currency of the for-period or in-period. If the output currencies within the periods vary, and you want to output only one currency, you need to select one of these indicators. If you don't want to convert the currency, select K.

### 4.2.2 Selecting and Grouping Wage Types

You can control the output of wage types in the payslip by grouping wage types via Evaluation Classes 02 (Assigning Wage Types for Form Printout) and 03 (Assigning Wage Types for Payroll Account). Customizing for grouping wage types via evaluation classes is carried out in the same way for both layout editors.

Evaluation classes and their characteristics belong to the properties of a wage type and control the processing of a wage type for the evaluation and mapping of the payroll results. You use Evaluation Class 02 to group wage types by their characteristics. Table 4.1 lists the default characteristics of this evaluation class to which you can add your own characteristics.

| Characteristic | Description |
| --- | --- |
| – | Printout in the form without specific assignment |
| 00 | No printout in the form |
| 01 | Print control for personal payments and deductions |
| 02 | Print control for wage types that are included in gross (/101) |

**Table 4.1** Characteristics of Evaluation Class 02

| Characteristic | Description |
| --- | --- |
| 03 | Print control for wage types from time-based payments that are included in gross (/101) |
| 06 | Print control for wage types from month of origin PS (Public Sector) |
| 07 | PS (Public Sector): specific printout of loans |
| 08 | PS: specific printout of loan deduction |
| 09 | PS: specific printout of flat-rate reduction |

**Table 4.1**  Characteristics of Evaluation Class 02 (Cont.)

You create some characteristics by processing the MAINTAIN EVALUATION CLASSES AND THEIR CHARACTERISTICS activity in the IMG. The corresponding path is as follows: PAYROLL • PAYROLL INTERNATIONAL (or the respective country) • GENERAL SETTINGS • WAGE TYPE MAINTENANCE ENVIRONMENT • PROCESSING CLASSES AND EVALUATION CLASSES. You can also call the two views, V_T52D3 (EVALUATION CLASSES) and V_T52D4 (VALUES OF THE EVALUATION CLASS), directly using Transaction SM30. If you need additional characteristics, create them, and then proceed with the next step; that is, assign the characteristics to the wage types. For this purpose, call the MAINTAIN EVALUATION CLASSES AND THEIR CHARACTERISTICS activity via the following IMG path: PAYROLL • PAYROLL INTERNATIONAL (or the respective country) • FORMS USING HR FORMS WORKPLACE • GENERAL PRINCIPLES. You can also call View V_512W_D directly with Transaction SM30.

If you want to check the appearance of the assignment of your wage types to the characteristics of an evaluation class, call the report for the wage type utilization. You can find this report in the SAP menu via PERSONNEL • PAYROLL • INTERNATIONAL (or the respective country) • TOOLS • CUSTOMIZING TOOLS or Transaction PC00_M99_DLGA20. Specify the country grouping, and run the report. Depending on the selected output format, the system provides an overview of the properties of the wage types. Select the evaluation class that you used to group your wage types for the payslip. Figure 4.21 maps the wage type properties in a tree structure.

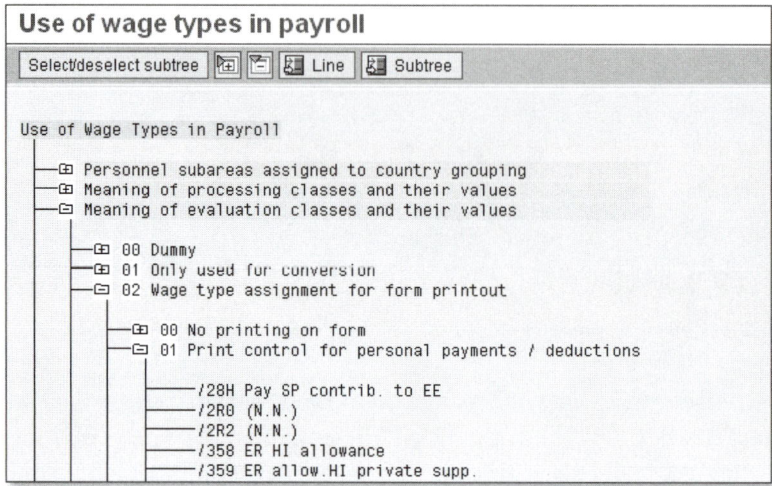



**Figure 4.21** Wage Type Utilization Statement as a Tree Structure

After grouping your wage types according to your requirements for the output in the form, you can proceed with customizing the InfoNet. Call your form in the Forms Workplace. Copy the grouping that you implemented in Evaluation Class 02 to your form. Now, create InfoStars in which you use the EVALCLASS02 Info-Dimension, and restrict the selection of the characteristics of Evaluation Class 02, as shown in Figure 4.22.

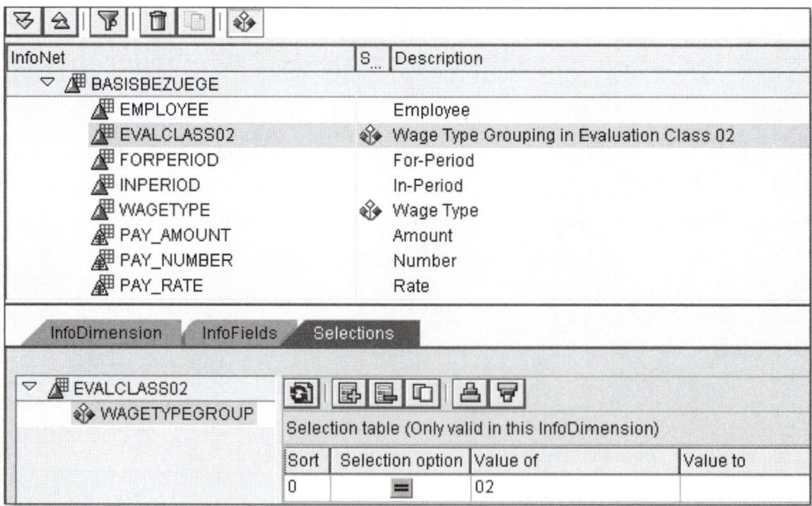



**Figure 4.22** Using Evaluation Class 02 in the InfoStar

The Basisbezuege InfoStar contains a selection of the EVALCLASS02 InfoDimension in which you can select all wage types whose properties include Evaluation Class 02. You can also limit the wage types via the Wagetype InfoDimension, which means that only wage types that meet this condition are provided in the InfoStar. In the Form Builder, you can integrate the InfoStar and output all included wage types without further checks or restrictions.

You can also categorize wage types with different characteristics in an InfoDimension by specifying several characteristics in the selection table of the InfoDimension. You can change the order of the wage types in the Sort column. As a maximum, two-digit numerical sort criteria are permitted. Instead of making your selection via the characteristic of an evaluation class, you can also select wage types directly by specifying the complete key or a part of it in the selection table (see Figure 4.23). You use the Selection Option field to define whether you want to exclude or integrate one or several wage types. You can also decide whether the entered key, for example, 5*, is a pattern that should be used to compare and select the available wage types. By grouping and selecting wage types, you can limit the data that is output in your form.

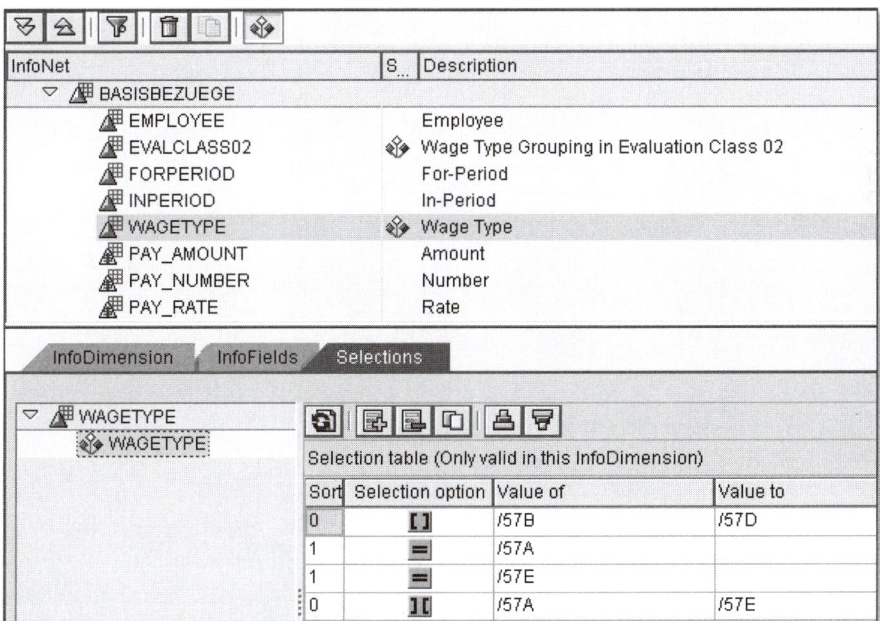

**Figure 4.23** Directly Selecting Wage Types in the WAGETYPE InfoDimension

| Sort | Selection option | Value of | Value to |
|---|---|---|---|
| 0 | [] | /57B | /57D |
| 1 | = | /57A | |
| 1 | = | /57E | |
| 0 | ][ | /57A | /57E |

If you already use Evaluation Class 02 for the old mapping of the payslip and don't want to change it, you can also use an evaluation class that isn't used. However, for this procedure, you need to take further steps in the MetaNet. To use an evaluation class that isn't yet used in your InfoNet, you have to create the class in your MetaNet:

1. If you want to use the evaluation class for several country groupings and you've copied the international MetaNet, you must decide which country grouping you want to use to create the new MetaDimension. Select the international MetaNet (Country Grouping 99) if the MetaDimension is to be available for all country-dependent MetaNets.

2. Copy the EVALCLASS02A MetaDimension as shown in Figure 4.24. In our example, we used Evaluation Class 20 and Country Grouping 99. The naming conventions for evaluation classes and their characteristics are provided in the country-dependent view, V_T52DN (Namespace for Processing and Evaluation Classes). We created the new MetaDimension with the name ZEVALCLASS20.

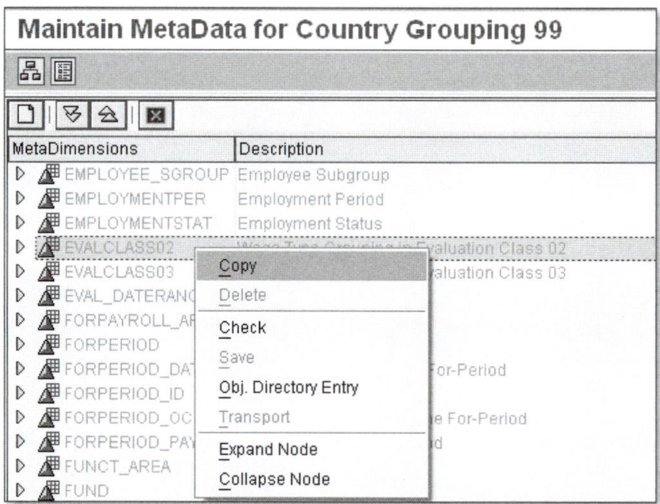



**Figure 4.24** Copying the EVALCLASS02 MetaDimension

3. In the attributes of the new ZEVALCLASS20 MetaDimension, select the TAB. FLD.VALS. (Tab Field Values) tab. Change the fixed value to the evaluation class that you selected. The system uses this value to read Tables T52D4 and T52D3 in which the characteristics and descriptions of the evaluation class are defined (see Figure 4.25).

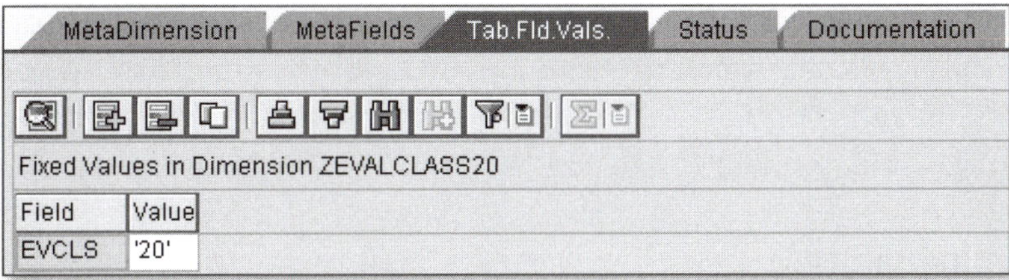

**Figure 4.25** Customizing the Field Values

4. To limit and select the payroll results with the new evaluation class, you need to include the MetaDimension in the PAY_RESULT MetaStar. Because you can't change the PAY_RESULT MetaStar, instead copy it, and add the ZEVALCLASS20 MetaDimension (see Figure 4.26).

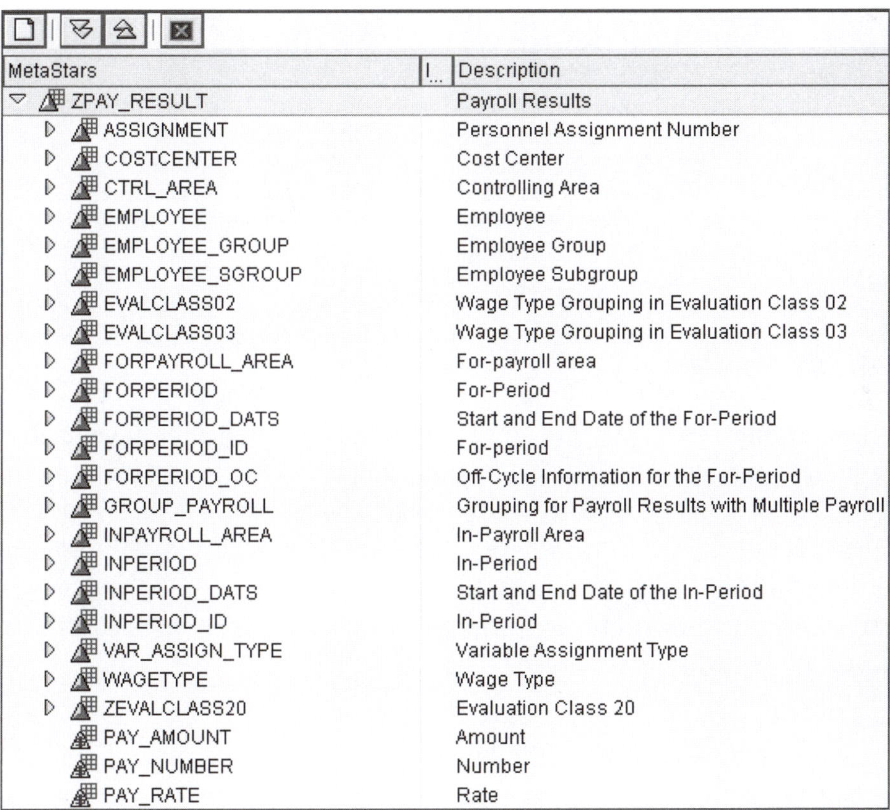

| MetaStars | I... | Description |
|---|---|---|
| ▽ ZPAY_RESULT | | Payroll Results |
| ▷ ASSIGNMENT | | Personnel Assignment Number |
| ▷ COSTCENTER | | Cost Center |
| ▷ CTRL_AREA | | Controlling Area |
| ▷ EMPLOYEE | | Employee |
| ▷ EMPLOYEE_GROUP | | Employee Group |
| ▷ EMPLOYEE_SGROUP | | Employee Subgroup |
| ▷ EVALCLASS02 | | Wage Type Grouping in Evaluation Class 02 |
| ▷ EVALCLASS03 | | Wage Type Grouping in Evaluation Class 03 |
| ▷ FORPAYROLL_AREA | | For-payroll area |
| ▷ FORPERIOD | | For-Period |
| ▷ FORPERIOD_DATS | | Start and End Date of the For-Period |
| ▷ FORPERIOD_ID | | For-period |
| ▷ FORPERIOD_OC | | Off-Cycle Information for the For-Period |
| ▷ GROUP_PAYROLL | | Grouping for Payroll Results with Multiple Payroll |
| ▷ INPAYROLL_AREA | | In-Payroll Area |
| ▷ INPERIOD | | In-Period |
| ▷ INPERIOD_DATS | | Start and End Date of the In-Period |
| ▷ INPERIOD_ID | | In-Period |
| ▷ VAR_ASSIGN_TYPE | | Variable Assignment Type |
| ▷ WAGETYPE | | Wage Type |
| ▷ ZEVALCLASS20 | | Evaluation Class 20 |
| PAY_AMOUNT | | Amount |
| PAY_NUMBER | | Number |
| PAY_RATE | | Rate |

**Figure 4.26** Customer-Specific ZPAY_RESULT MetaStar

5. After adding the MetaDimension via drag and drop, call the METADIMENSION tab in the attributes. Function modules assume the task of reading the data for the EVALCLASS02 and EVALCLASS03 MetaDimensions. Enter an appropriate name for the function module for the ZEVALCLASS20 MetaDimension. We decided to use the name `Z_HRF_READ_EVALCLASS20`. Click on the CREATE button to create the function module (see Figure 4.27). You should create your own function group for the function modules that you create within the scope of the MetaNet extension.

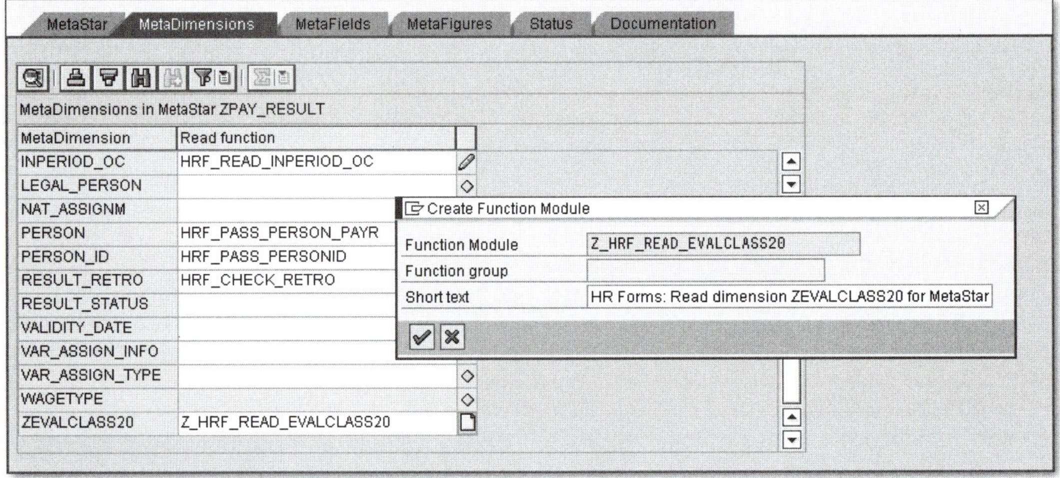


**Figure 4.27**   Creating a Function Module for the MetaDimension

6. Use the program lines from the `HRF_READ_EVALCLASS02` function module, and copy it into your customer-specific function module (see Listing 4.1). Customize the program lines as described in the following section. You also need to copy and customize the `HRF_GET_EVCLS_FROM_WAGETYPE` function module (see Listing 4.2).

7. Add the following constant to the global definitions of your function group so that the constant can also be used in the second function module: `CONSTANTS c_evcls_20 TYPE t52d4-evcls VALUE '20'`.

```
FIELD-SYMBOLS:  <lgart> TYPE lgart.
country = payroll_inter-versc-molga.
```

```
CLEAR wagetypegroup.
ASSIGN COMPONENT 'LGART'
OF STRUCTURE ms_data TO <lgart>.
CHECK sy-subrc EQ 0.

CALL FUNCTION 'Z_HRF_GET_EVCLS_FROM_WAGETYPE'
  EXPORTING
    molga = payroll_inter-versc-molga
    lgart = <lgart>
    endda = payroll_evp-fpend
    evcls = c_evcls_20
  IMPORTING
    evclv = wagetypegroup.
```

**Listing 4.1** Customized Source Code of the Z_HRF_READ_EVALCLASS02 Module

8. Before the `ENDIF` of the last line, add the following program lines to include Evaluation Class 02 in the custom-specific function module, `Z_HRF_GET_EVCLS_FROM_WAGETYPE`. The module reads the characteristic of Evaluation Class 20 of the wage types to be included.

```
CLEAR vwa.
 vwa-molga = molga.
 vwa-lgart = lgart.
 vwa-evcls = c_evcls_20.

 LOOP AT tabw ASSIGNING <wwa>.
   dwa-endda = <wwa>-endda.
   dwa-evclv = <wwa>-aklas+38(2).
   INSERT dwa INTO TABLE vwa-enddatab.

   IF  evcls     EQ c_evcls_20
   AND dwa-endda GE endda
   AND found     EQ space.
     evclv = dwa-evclv.
     found = 'X'.
   ENDIF.
 ENDLOOP.
 INSERT vwa INTO TABLE evcls_tab.
```

**Listing 4.2** Extension for the Source Code of the Z_HRF_GET_EVCLS_FROM_WAGETYPE Module

After you've implemented the extensions and changes described, you can add the MetaStar to your MetaNet and use it in the InfoNet. If you've used the MetaStar with Country Grouping 99, you need to call the MetaNet with the required country grouping in which you want to use the new MetaStar and assign this MetaStar to the MetaNet. Create your own InfoStar tables as described in Figure 4.28. They now include the evaluation class you created as well as its characteristics.

Insert a selection in the ZEVALCLAS20 InfoDimension, and enter the required characteristics into the selection table. Test the print program of the form to make sure that the InfoStar is populated with the required wage types. For this purpose, the attributes of the wage types should have been customized so that the wage types for the selected period are determined and displayed based on the characteristic of the required Evaluation Class 20.

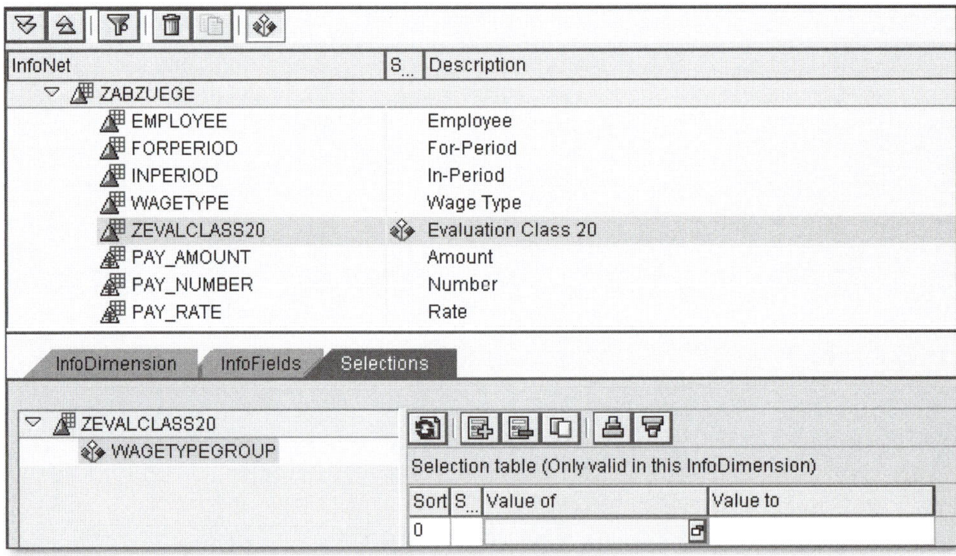

**Figure 4.28**  Integrating Your Own Evaluation Class with an InfoStar

### 4.2.3  Defining and Outputting Cumulation Wage Types

If you want to combine several wage types, you need to define and use cumulation wage types, which you can print in your form afterward. Wage types can be included in a cumulation wage type either positively or negatively. Because multiple groups of cumulation wage types may exist and can be used in different forms, a group of related cumulation wage types is identified by a unique subapplication. Based on this subapplication, you define your cumulation wage types and assign the wage types to them. To forward the information to the payslip, the relevant subapplication is specified in the attributes of the payslip in the Forms Workplace. The definition and output of cumulation wage types is implemented in the same way for both layout editors.

Follow these steps to create your own subapplication and cumulation wage types:

1. Call the table view maintenance (Transaction SM30).

2. Call View V_T596A (Subapplications) with the required country grouping (see Figure 4.29).

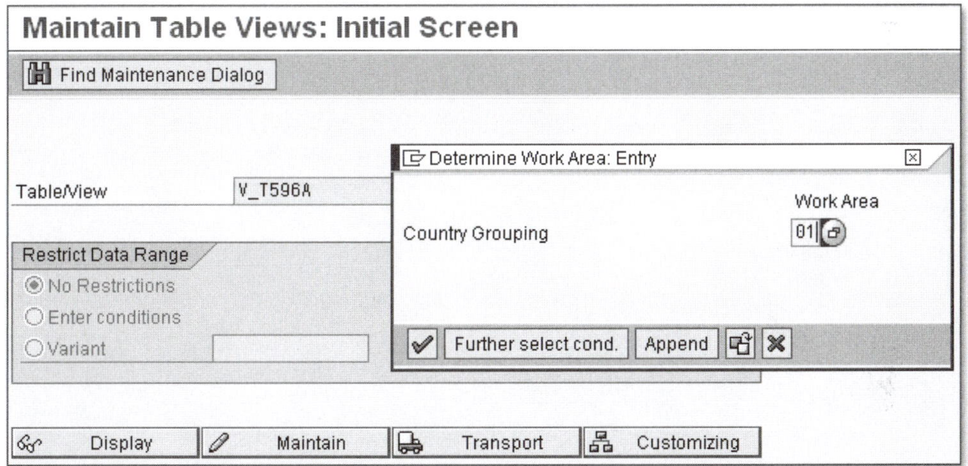

**Figure 4.29**  Creating a Subapplication

3. Copy the existing standard subapplication, CEDT (see Figure 4.30).

**Change View "Subapplications": Overview**

| | Subapp. | Info | Subapplication text | Year | Month | Day | Stat |
|---|---|---|---|---|---|---|---|
| | CEDT | | Payslip - Cumulation Wage Types | O | O | ● | |
| | CIBN | | Contribution statement SI fund procedure | O | ● | O | |
| | CIMV | | Values to reported in SI fund procedure | O | ● | O | |

**Figure 4.30**  Copying Subapplication CEDT

> **Note**
>
> The namespace for customer-specific subapplications states that they must start with a digit between 0 and 9.

4. Create your own cumulation wage types in View V_T596G. Note that the wage types are only defined here. You assign the wage types to the cumulation wage types in the next step in another view. Figure 4.31 displays the standard cumulation wage types that have been defined for the CEDT subapplication.

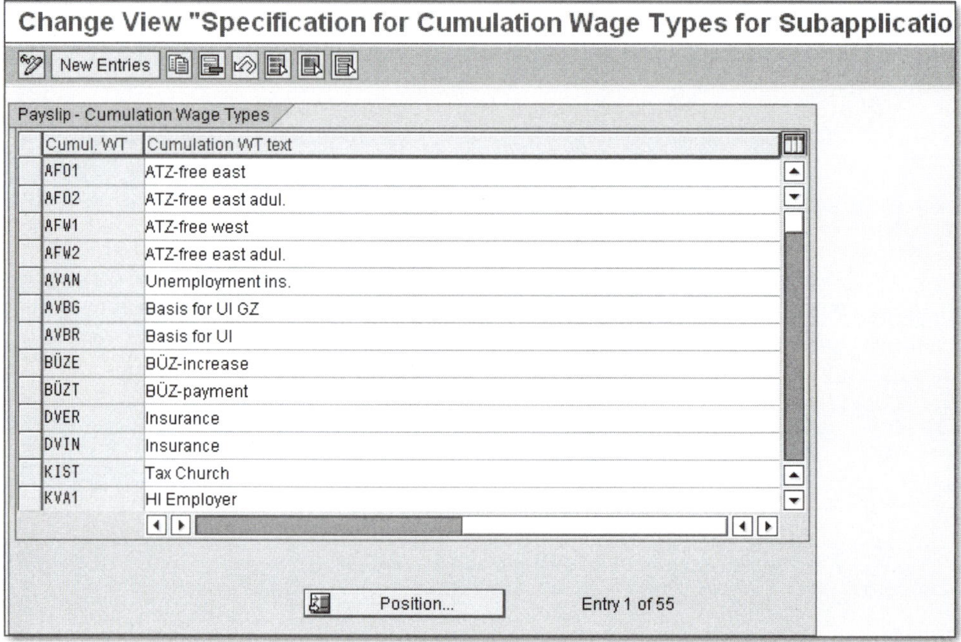

Figure 4.31 Definition of the Cumulation Wage Types

5. After defining the cumulation wage types, you can assign the required wage types to them. The assignment takes place in View V_T596J (Assignment of Wage Types to Cumulation Wage Types) as shown in Figure 4.32.

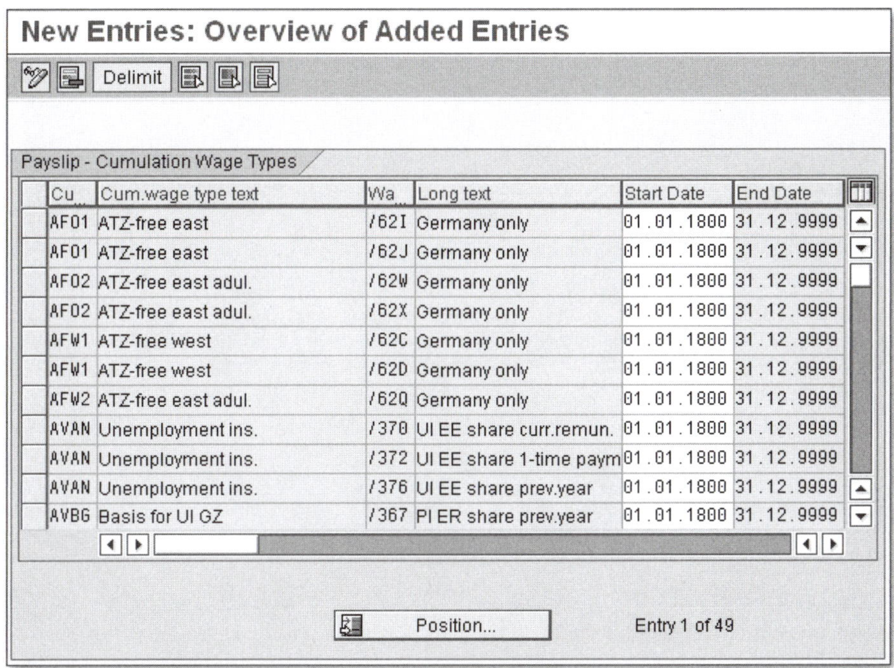

**Figure 4.32** Assigning Wage Types to Cumulation Wage Types

In the AO (Arithmetic Operator) column, you specify whether a wage type is supposed to be included in the cumulation wage type either positively or negatively (see Figure 4.32). If no operator is specified, the wage type is added.

Cumulation wage types are defined in Tables RT (Result Table), CRT (Cumulated Result Table), and SCRT (Cumulated Tax Results) at runtime. As soon as one of the wage types that is assigned to a cumulation wage type is available in one of the mentioned tables, the cumulation wage type is defined. In your InfoNet, you define InfoStars that are either not restricted to specific wage types/cumulation wage types or include the required cumulation wage types. The InfoStars must be based on MetaStars that correspond to Tables RT, CRT, and SCRT. The InfoStar illustrated in Figure 4.33 contains an explicit selection of cumulation wage types.

The ABZUEGE2 InfoStar is based on the PAY_RESULT MetaStar. It contains all payroll results (Cluster Table RT) for the selected period. In the SELECTIONS tab, an explicit sorting was selected via the SORT column and specific cumulation wage types.

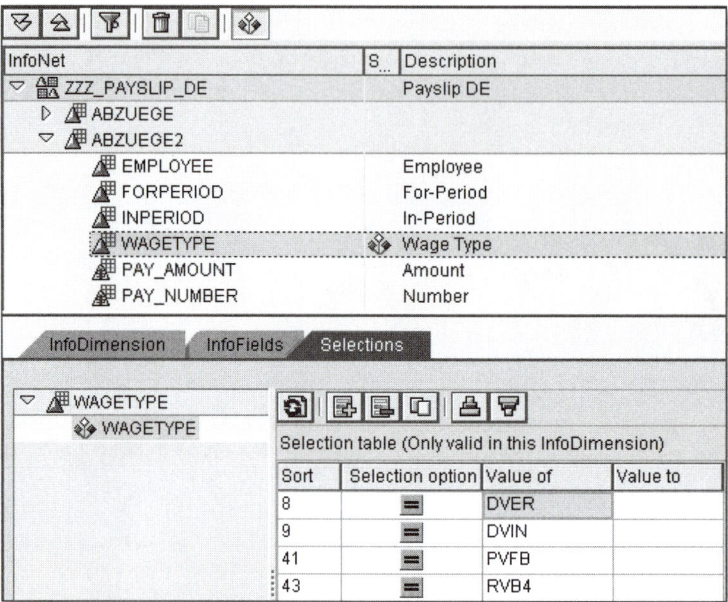

**Figure 4.33**  InfoStar for Cumulation Wage Types

To simplify the selection of cumulation wage types in your InfoNet as much as possible, select a letter or digit, for example, with which all of your cumulation wage types begin. The advantage of this is that you can uniquely identify the cumulation wage types and provide them in an InfoStar by only specifying the first character (see Figure 4.34).

> **Tip**
>
> You don't have to create your own table with cumulation wage types. However, it can be used as an overview and is useful if you want to quickly determine whether the required cumulation wage types are defined.

A prerequisite for using your own wage types that you assigned to your own subapplication is the notification of this subapplication in your form. For this purpose, maintain the subapplication in the CUMULATION WAGE TYPES tab. Call the form via the Forms Workplace. You can find the corresponding tab in the properties of the InfoNet (see Figure 4.35). Enter the subapplication for your cumulation wage types into the CUSTOMER field.

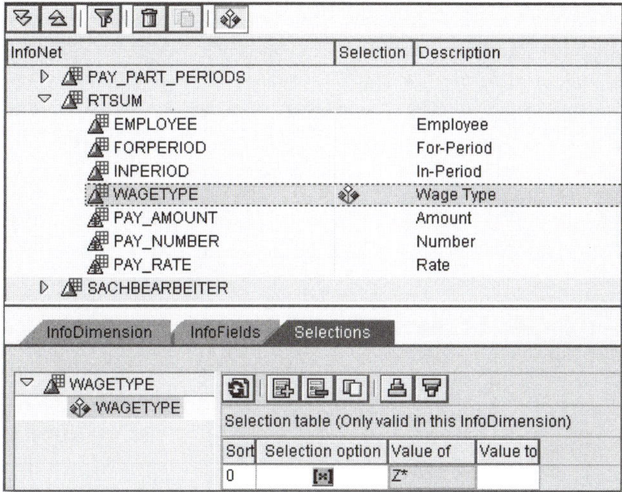

**Figure 4.34**  Restricting Wage Types

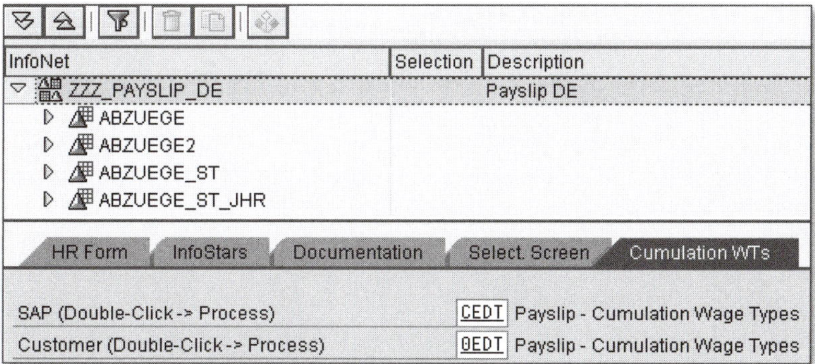

**Figure 4.35**  Cumulation Wage Types Tab

> **Tip**
>
> If you don't want to use the SAP cumulation wage types, delete the CEDT subapplication. The cumulation wage types are now no longer defined and provided, which increases the readability.

### 4.2.4  Controlling the Printing of Retroactive Accounting

In real-world situations, retroactive accounting is usually suppressed if particular conditions are met. This may be the case, for example, if specific wage types haven't changed through retroactive accounting. You can specifically suppress retroactive accounting results in the SAP system so that the employees are only provided with results that are relevant for them. There are two ways to exclude specific For-Periods. However, both methods have the same result. Before these methods are described in detail, this section provides a brief overview.

In the SAP standard, the HRFORM_HRF02 BAdI (Enhancements for HR Forms, see Section 6.3, Enhancements for HR Forms [HRFORM_HRF02]), the INIT program node in the Smart Forms, forms that corresponds to the code initialization in the interface of the PDF-based form, and the XSKIF payroll function (Compare Results with Earlier Periods) are available to check and limit the processing payroll results. You should use either the BAdI, the program node, or the code initialization in combination with the payroll function. This makes the maintenance of modifications much easier and transparent. If possible, avoid a combination of all objects (BAdI, program node, or code initialization in the form and payroll function). Try to keep an overview of everything with regard to the solution for the display of the retroactive accounting. If you select the BAdI, you're prompted in the sample implementation to also use the XSKIF payroll function. This isn't the case for the INIT program node, which enables you to freely decide whether you want to use the function. The same applies to the code initialization in the PDF-based form.

The XSKIF function helps you decide when a retroactive accounting result can be suppressed by comparing the wage types of Result Table RT of the period for which retroactive accounting has to be implemented with the wage types of Result Table RT that have been created in payroll processes from earlier periods. If there are no differences between the wage types that are to be compared (i.e., the wage type or types have not changed), the system generates a *switch wage type*. This switch wage type can then be queried and indicates whether retroactive accounting has to be printed or suppressed. The switch wage type is provided in Result Table RT and has the value "1" in the NUMBER field.

The integration of this function with your payroll schema isn't mandatory. Alternatively, you can check the wage types that have been selected in your Smart Forms form. The current version of the template for the payslip with Smart Forms includes an implementation in the INIT program node in the main window (see Figure 4.36). If required, you can customize and use this implementation.

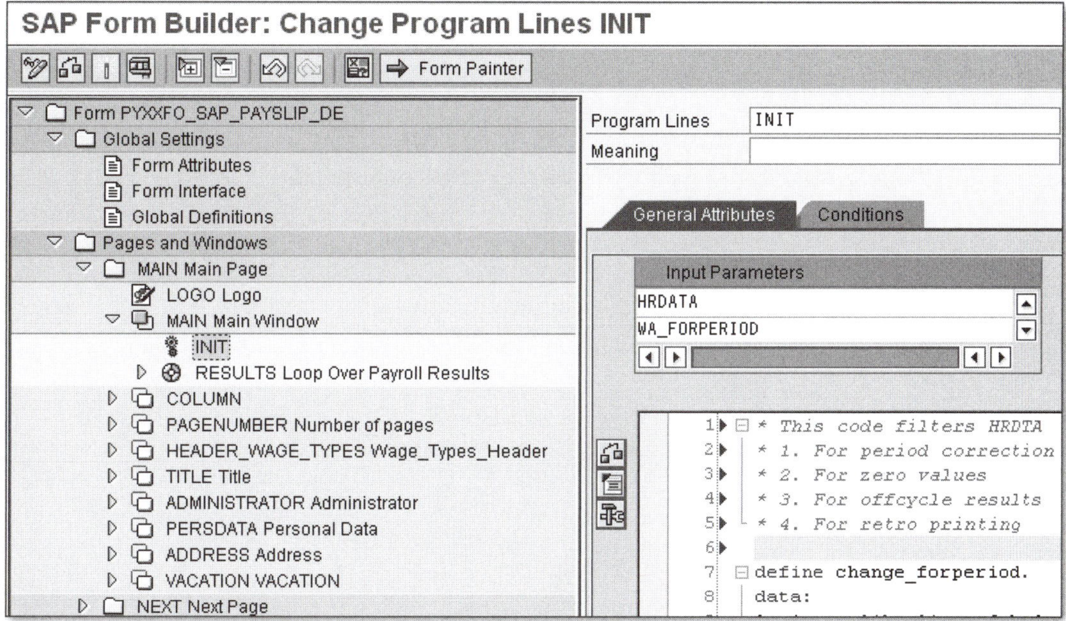

**Figure 4.36**  INIT Program Node

The PYXXFO_SAP_PAYSLIP_US2 form interface of the SAP_PAYSLIP_US2 template also contains the sample implementation for suppressing retroactive accounting results (see Figure 4.37).

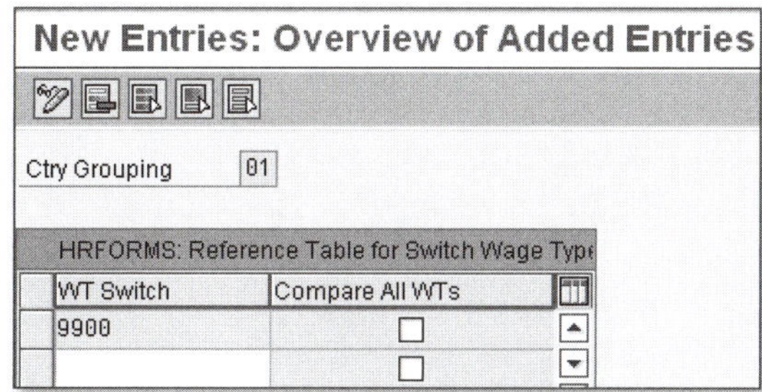

**Figure 4.37**  Code Initialization of the Form Interface

If you want to use the XSKIF function to generate a switch wage type that helps you decide whether retroactive accounting is supposed to be suppressed, follow the steps listed next. You can find all activities and steps in the Customizing IMG via the PAYROLL • PAYROLL INTERNATIONAL • FORMS USING HR FORMS WORKPLACE • CONFIGURE THE PAYROLL RUN FOR THE PAYSLIP path.

1. Carry out the MAINTAIN SWITCH WAGE TYPES activity, and select CREATE WAGE TYPES. The system calls the wage type copier, which enables you to copy a sample wage type. As an alternative, you can also call Table View V_512W_O (Overview of T512W) and create a new wage type or just copy a wage type.

2. Choose EDIT THE TEXT OF THE WAGE TYPE to modify the long and short text.

3. As illustrated in Figure 4.38, define the previously created switch wage type in a further step, DEFINE WAGE TYPE AS THE SWITCH WAGE TYPE.

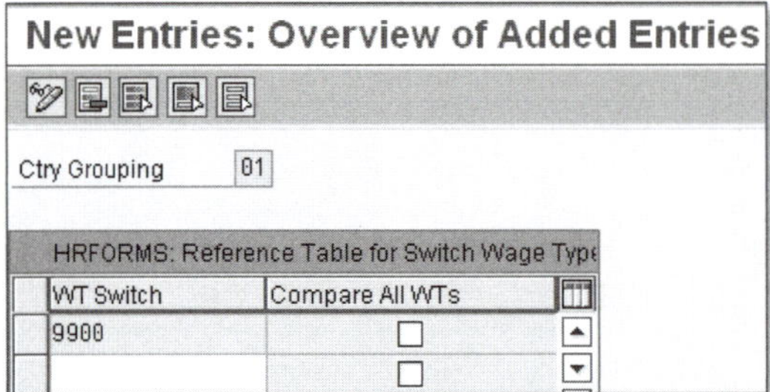

**Figure 4.38**  Defining a Wage Type as the Switch Wage Type

Only select the COMPARE ALL WAGE TYPES field if you want to include all wage types of Result Table RT in the comparison of the payroll results. The result tables are identical only if all wage types match in the periods that are supposed to be compared.

4. If you only want to compare particular wage types, perform the next step, ASSIGN THE SWITCH WAGE TYPE TO THE WAGE TYPES TO BE COMPARED, in which you define the wage types that are supposed to be compared (see Figure 4.39).

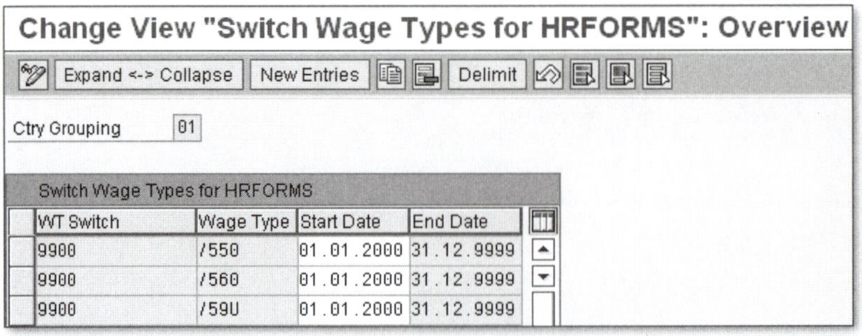

**Figure 4.39**  Assigning the Wage Types to the Switch Wage Type

You can also call the tables illustrated in Figures 4.38 and 4.39 directly using Transaction SM30. These are the following views: V_THRFORMS_FLWTR (HRFORMS: Reference Table for Switch Wage Types) and V_THRFORMS_FLWTS (Switch Wage Types for HRFORMS).

The system generates the switch wage type if the wage types that are to be compared in the payroll period correspond to those of the earlier payroll period. The switch wage type isn't generated if there's a deviation.

5. In the last step — Use FUNCTION FOR SWITCH WAGE TYPES IN THE SCHEMA — include the XSKIF function in your customer-specific payroll schema immediately at the beginning of the final processing (see Figure 4.40).

**Edit Schema: ZEN1**

| Line | Func. | Par1 | Par2 | Par3 | Par4 | D | Text |
|---|---|---|---|---|---|---|---|
| 000010 | BLOCK | BEG | | | | | Final processing |
| 000020 | XCODI | XCD0 | | | | * | Cost Distribution |
| 000030 | XSKIF | | | | | | Compare Payroll Results |

**Figure 4.40** Integrating XSKIF with the Final Processing

The XSKIF function includes all fields of the wage types in the comparison. However, in real-world scenarios, you may only want to check the AMOUNT OF RESULT TABLE RT field, and the NUMBER and AMOUNT PER UNIT fields are not relevant. In this case, copy and enhance the XSKIF function. Insert a parameter in the function, for example, that enables you to decide whether you want to include all fields or only particular fields in a comparison as described next.

Figure 4.41 displays a copy of the XSKIF function and its enhancement, the VAR parameter (Variant). As in the standard function, the possible values of this parameter define whether all fields or only particular fields of a record in Result Table RT of the respective periods are compared. Of course, you can freely define the values. At this point, the comparison is limited to ALL FIELDS or to the RELEVANT FIELDS of Table RT.

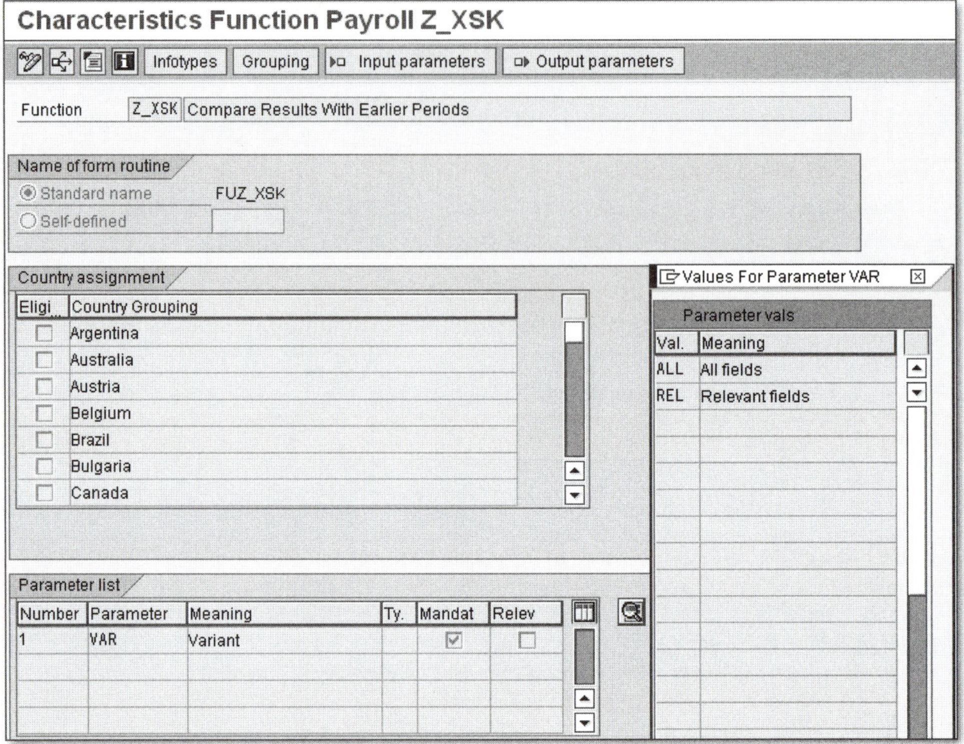

**Figure 4.41** Customizing the XSKIF Function

For our example, the following fields are to be compared:

▶ ABART (grouping of the employee subgroups for the personnel calculation rule)

▶ LGART (wage type)

▶ BETPE (payroll: amount per unit)

▶ ANZHL (payroll: number)

▶ BETRG (payroll: amount)

In Appendix D, Source Code for the Function XSKIF Program, you can see how to copy and enhance the program of the function so that the parameter and its values are included.

After integrating the XSKIF function with your payroll schema, the switch wage type is generated in the next payroll run if required and thus is available in Result Table RT. To query it, independent of whether you use the BAdI or program node, create an InfoStar in your InfoNet in which you limit the content to the switch wage type. Use the PAY_RESULT MetaStar as the basis, or copy an existing InfoStar. Finally, limit the selection of the wage types for the InfoStar to the switch wage type and the RESULT_STATUS InfoDimension to the value "A" by selecting the WAGETYPE InfoDimension. Consequently, the InfoStar contains only the switch wage type that is relevant for the retroactive accounting printout. This switch wage type can be read separately.

In the INIT program node and in the code initialization, irrelevant retroactive accounting periods are eliminated using the `check_betrg` macro. A loop over the for-period checks InfoStar tables, which you may have to customize if you don't use the InfoStars of the standard InfoNet. The macro checks whether there are further wage types with an amount that isn't equal to zero in addition to wage type /553 (Recalculation Difference to the Last Payroll). If this isn't the case, the For-Period is eliminated. At this point, you can define a macro that checks the existence of your switch wage type, for example. This enables you to decide flexibly via Customizing which wage types are relevant for the printout of a retroactive accounting result without having to define them in the program.

The HRFORM_HRF02 BAdI (see Section 6.3, Enhancements for HR Forms [HRFORM_HRF0]) provides a sample implementation of the CHECK_PERNR_LATE method, which describes exactly how to check the InfoStar in which the switch wage type may exist. If you want to use the sample implementation without major modifications, you must check whether you meet the prerequisites that are mentioned in the implementation. You may not be able to use the sample implementation without any problems for the SAP_PAYSLIP_DE template provided in 2008 (creation date: 01/04/08) of the payslip because the implementation is based on an older template (SAP_PAYSLIP_DE3, creation date: 04/26/06) whose processing of the periods differ from the procedure in the new template.

The current Smart Forms template processes the two loops, RESULTS and PERIODS. The older versions only contained the PERIODS loop. The structure of the table that is processed in this loop has also changed, which is indicated in the source code of the BAdI. Consequently, if you want to use the BAdI, you should create an implementation based on the sample implementation, and test it before you use the BAdI to estimate the scope of the Customizing work. The old template involved little effort, and consequently the BAdI represented an appropriate solution. In return, the INIT program line and the code initialization were not provided as solutions in the past.

### 4.2.5    Considering the ESS Settings in Infotype 0655

If you want to provide your employees with the payslip in Employee Self-Service (ESS), you can define this in Infotype 0655 (ESS Settings Remuneration Statement) (see Figure 4.42). You can then use the infotype for various checks. For example, you can exclude employees from mass printing if they use ESS and print their payslips themselves. You can integrate this check in the HRFORM_HRF02 BAdI (Enhancements for HR Forms) in the CHECK_PERNR or CHECK_PERSON method if you use multiple payroll. There is a sample implementation for the CHECK_PERNR method that illustrates these aspects in detail (see Section 6.3, Enhancements for HR Forms [HRFORM_HRF02], and Section 6.3.1, CHECK_PERNR Method and CHECK_PERSON Method).

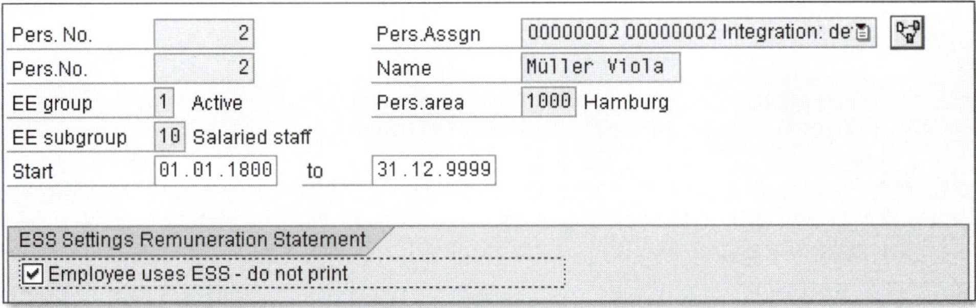


**Figure 4.42**   Infotype 0655

If you collect the employees that are relevant for the payslip using an upstream report, you can also implement a check here.

You can use the procedure just described independently of the layout editor type.

## 4.3    Conclusion

This chapter first described how you create your own payslip before it detailed the related Customizing. We explained the parameters of the selection screen and their meanings and Customizing options. You should now be able to select one of the available report categories or use one of them as a template and customize it accordingly. Next, you learned about the options of grouping wage types and positioning them in the form in the corresponding order. We used an example to illustrate how you can create your own MetaDimension to use your own evaluation class instead of Evaluation Class 02. In addition, we provided a step-by-step guide on the use of cumulation wage types, which enabled you to create your own subapplication and the corresponding cumulation wage types. A detailed description of controlling the printout of retroactive accounting also covered the various procedures, from the XSKIF function, to the HRFORM_HRF02 BAdI, to the program nodes in the forms. Finally, Infotype 0655 (ESS Settings Remuneration Statement) was introduced and the corresponding section described how you can use it in combination with the HRFORM_HRF02 BAdI to exclude employees from mass printing if they use an ESS application for their payslips.

As an alternative to using Smart Forms for the design, you learned that you can design the new payslip with Adobe LiveCycle Designer and you saw how it's integrated with Customizing. We also noted that the procedure of providing data is the same for both Smart Forms and Adobe LiveCycle Designer.

> **Tip**
>
> Because the payslip changes due to legal modifications on a regular basis, you should try to design it as simply as possible to keep the maintenance effort low and transparent.

In the next chapter we will look at the time statement and discuss the templates in the Forms Workplace as well as the time statement-relevant and time statement-specific Customizing — similar to the introduction of the payslip.

# 5 Time Statement — Creation and Customizing

In this chapter, you'll learn how to create a time statement in the design environment — with Smart Forms and Adobe LiveCycle Designer. This chapter frequently overlaps with Chapter 3, Designing the Form Layout with the Form Builder, and Chapter 4, Payslip — Creation and Customizing, so when the details are left out here, we'll ask you to refer back to those chapters.

## 5.1 Creating the Form

The new sample form, SAP_TIM_99, delivered with SAP ERP HCM uses the Form Builder for Smart Forms for the layout design at the time this book went to press. If you want to create the time statement already with Adobe LiveCycle Designer, you should copy the Smart Form and continue the layout design with the Form Builder for SAP Interactive Forms. Section 5.1.2, SAP_TIM_99_0001_P, provides you with information about when the time statement is delivered with the Adobe technology by default and how to proceed.

> **Tip**
>
> You can call the forms using Transaction SFP. However, for HCM forms, you should use Customizing or Transaction HRFORMS to ensure that the form is always correctly integrated with the application.

### 5.1.1 SAP_TIM_99_0002

To create a time statement with Form Builder for Smart Forms, follow these steps:

1. Use Transaction HRFORMS, and select the time statement form (see Figure 5.1).

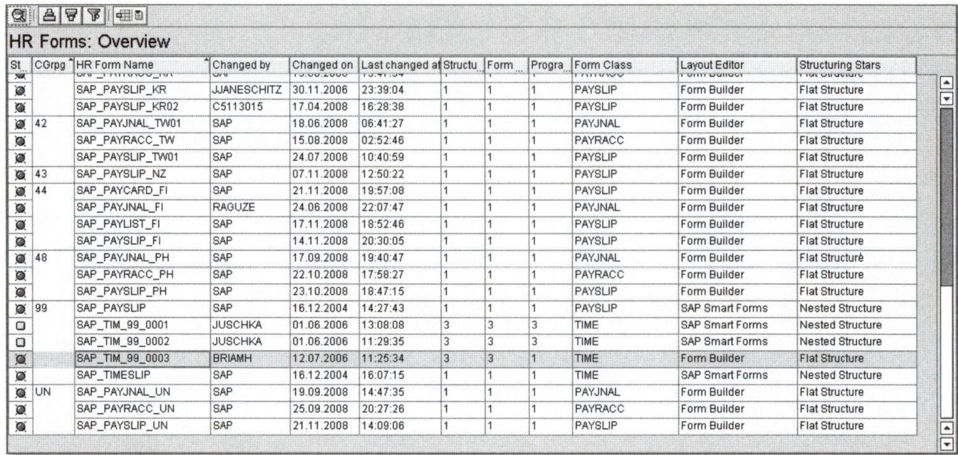

**Figure 5.1**  Time Statement in the HR Forms Workplace

2. Select SAP_TIM_99_0002 in Table HRFORMS. Double-click it to navigate to the data retrieval with the MetaNet, InfoNet, and the properties of the form (see Figure 5.2). The rest of the process is the same as for the payslip in Section 4.1, Creating the Form.

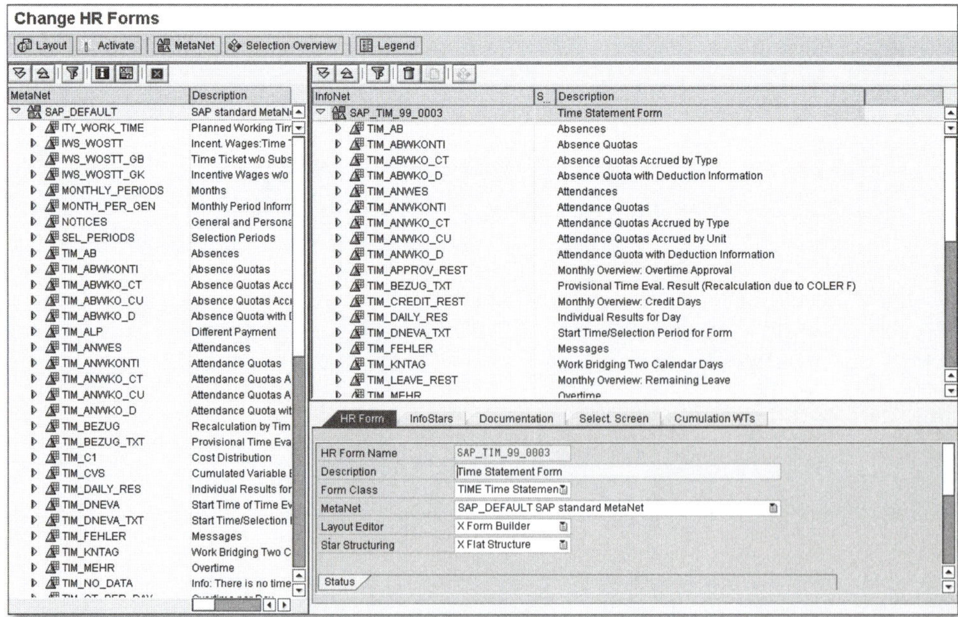

**Figure 5.2**  Data Retrieval in the HR Forms Workplace

3. Click the Layout button to call the Smart Forms editor (see Figure 5.3).

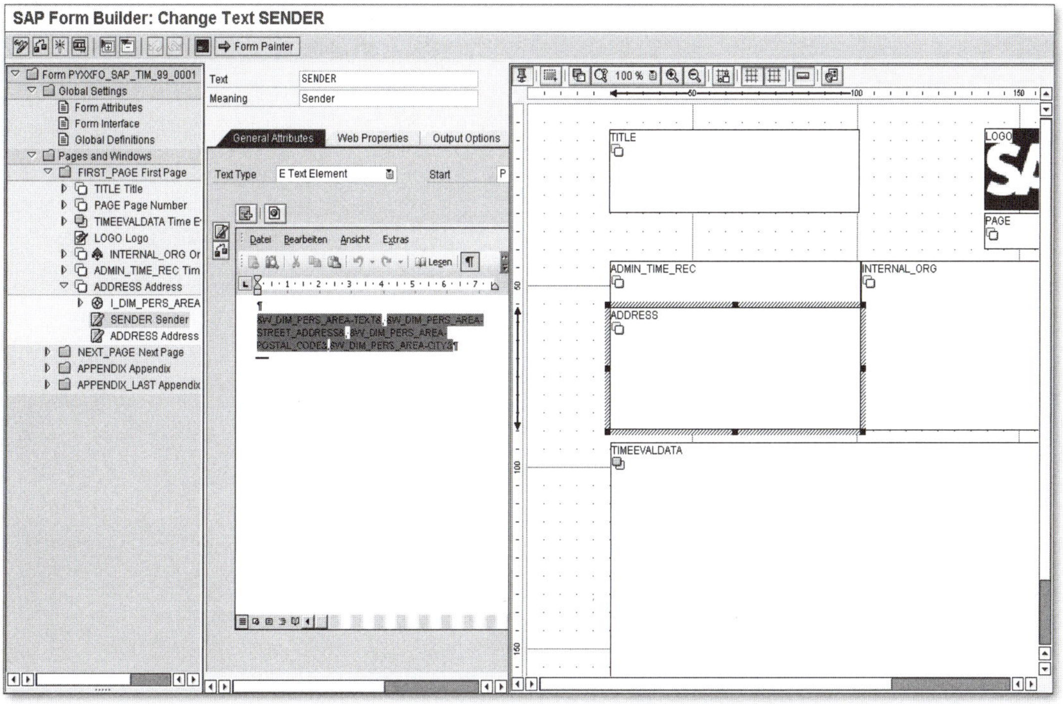

**Figure 5.3** Time Statement in the Form Builder for Smart Forms — Form Painter

4. After you've adjusted the form as required, you can save it and test it just like the payslip via the generated print program. After saving, use the BACK button or press F3.

5. This takes you to the HR Forms Workplace again. Here, you can test the form by selecting the Forms menu and Print Program (Test) or directly call the test parameters by pressing Shift + F5 (see Figure 5.4). At this point, you can transfer the required runtime parameters with the print program and generate the form result.

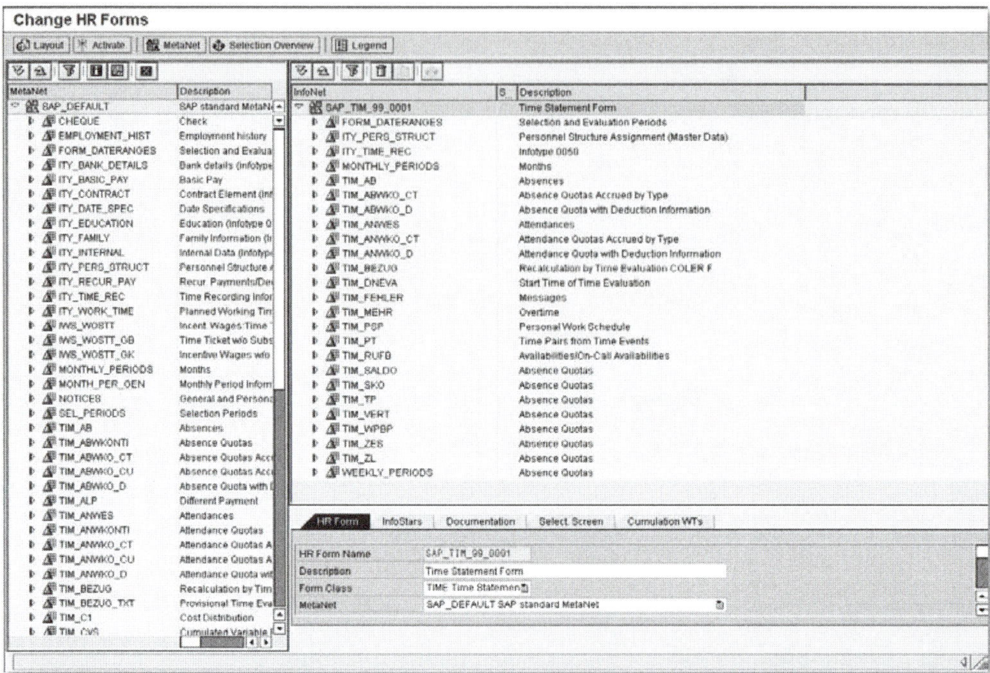

**Figure 5.4** Selection Screen with the Parameters of the Print Program for the Time Statement

### 5.1.2 SAP_TIM_99_0001_P

Currently, the time statement is only delivered for Smart Forms. The PDF-based time statement is provided with EA-HR 06 for SAP ERP 6.0. But you do have the option to generate the time statement as a PDF in the Form Builder (Adobe Live-Cycle Designer); however, this is associated with a corresponding development effort because the preconfigured template isn't delivered yet.

For this process, call the HR Forms Workplace as described in the previous section. To copy the Smart Form, select the row with the Smart Form, SAP_TIM_99_002, and click on the COPY button or press $\boxed{\text{Ctrl}}$ + $\boxed{\text{F5}}$. The row is copied, and you can call this new entry by double-clicking it.

In the form properties, change the LAYOUT EDITOR from SAP SMART FORMS to FORM BUILDER. The result of this change is shown in Figure 5.5.

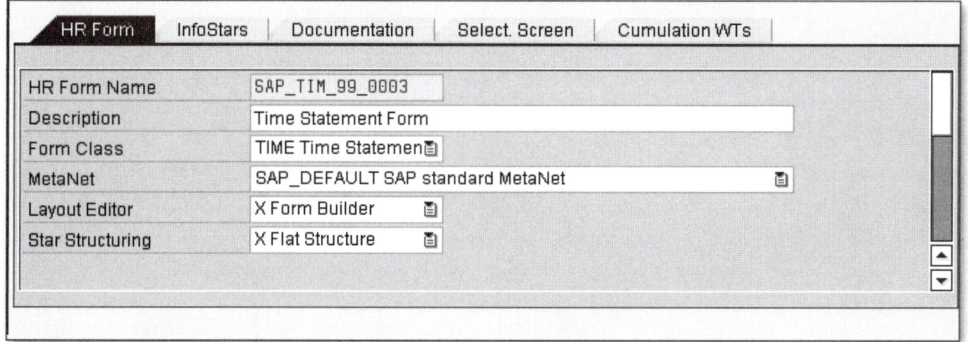

**Figure 5.5**  Changing the Layout Editor in the Form Properties

After you've made these settings, you can use the LAYOUT button or press $\boxed{\text{Shift}}$ + $\boxed{\text{F8}}$ to call the layout environment. Initially, the system takes you to the Form Builder with the fields from the interface (see Figure 5.6).

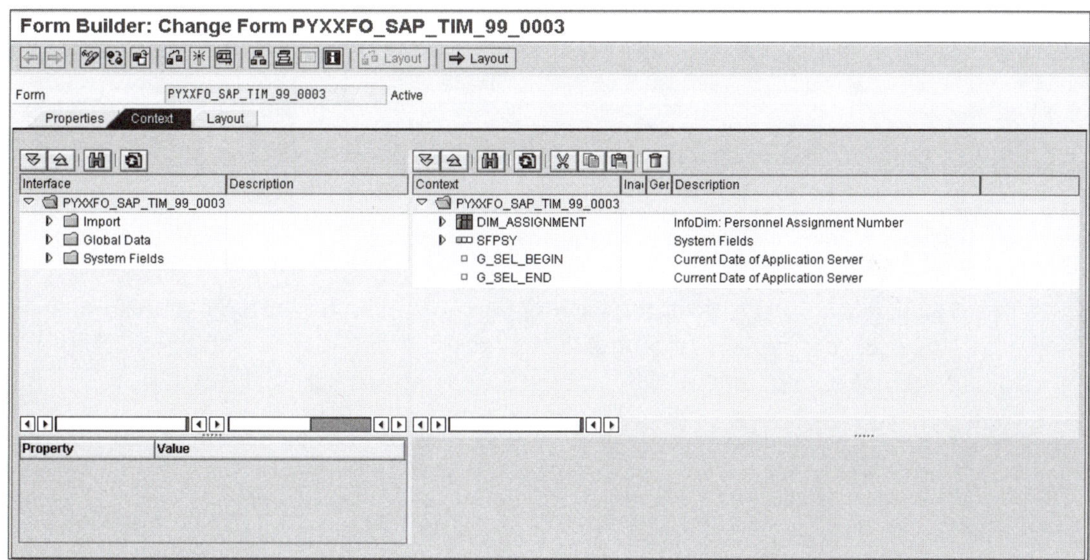

**Figure 5.6**  Form Builder

At this point, you must select the LAYOUT button or press $\boxed{\text{Ctrl}}$ + $\boxed{\text{F12}}$ again to navigate to the corresponding design tool, that is, Adobe LiveCycle Designer (see Figure 5.7). (This must be installed as already described in Chapter 3, Designing the Form Layout with the Form Builder.)

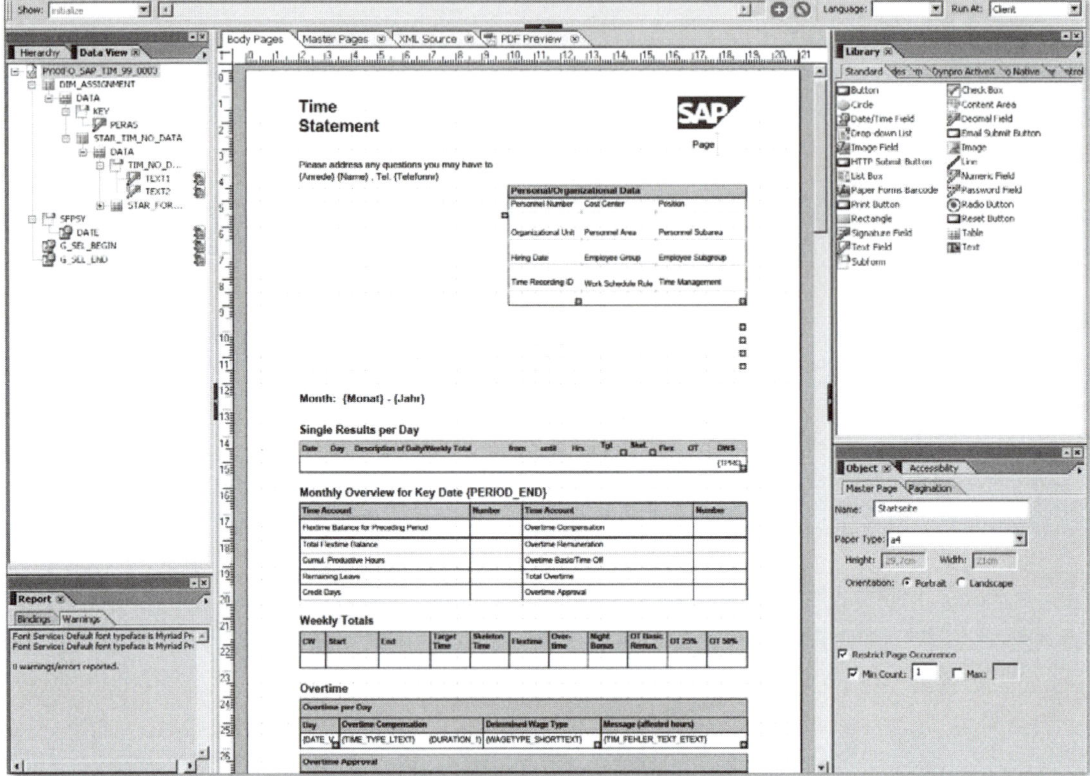

**Figure 5.7** Time Statement in Adobe LiveCycle Designer

The system displays the same view as for the payslip in Section 4.2, Customizing. However, no predefined template is available here; that is, you must create the design of the time statement with the fields on the form.

After you've adjusted the design according to your personal requirements, it's time for Customizing.

## 5.2 Customizing

In addition to creating the form in the Forms Workplace and designing the layout in the Form Builder, you have more Customizing options to modify the form and the output. This section describes how you can modify the selection screen of the print program using default settings and the aspects you should consider for possible recalculation results. You will also learn when it might be necessary to read time data and how you can change the output of industrial times. Similar to the payslip, it may be necessary to exclude the output of the time statement in certain cases, for example, if employees print it themselves via ESS.

Because the activation and deactivation of areas in the form layout is independent of form type, this chapter doesn't outline its use and functionality again. At this point, we just want to draw your attention to this helpful and simple way to edit and test a form, which you can use as part of Customizing. For more details, refer back to Chapter 3, section 3.1.6, Activating and Deactivating Areas in the Layout.

The Customizing steps described in this chapter that require the adaptation of the MetaNet are independent of the tool for the layout design. If you enhance the MetaNet with MetaStars that you want to use in your InfoNet, it doesn't matter whether you create the form with the Form Builder for Smart Forms or with the Form Builder for SAP Interactive Forms. The present descriptions and recommendations are based on the template, SAP_TIM_99_0002, in which the layout design has been implemented using the Form Builder for Smart Forms. Currently, no template is available for a PDF-based form. For this reason, the sections that describe possible adaptations to the layout are limited to the implementation with Smart Forms.

## 5.2.1    The Selection Screen

The selection screen of your print program enables you to choose the data and personnel numbers for the people you want to create the time statements for. You decide whose time evaluation results will be evaluated. You can influence the selection screen of your form via the maintenance of the InfoNet properties in the Forms Workplace in the SELECTION SCREEN tab. The HRF_TIME report category (Time statements) is available to define the number and visibility of the fields in the selection screen. Just like the report categories for the payslip, this report category is also valid for the logical database PNPCE.

> **Tip**
>
> You should use the delivered report categories as templates for your own report categories.

1. Navigate to the maintenance of a report category by double-clicking on it. There you have the possibility to change the available selection fields of the report screen. Select the change mode, and copy the report category to customize it accordingly. Besides the report category, there are optional fields for your selection screen for which you can predefine default values (see Figure 5.8).

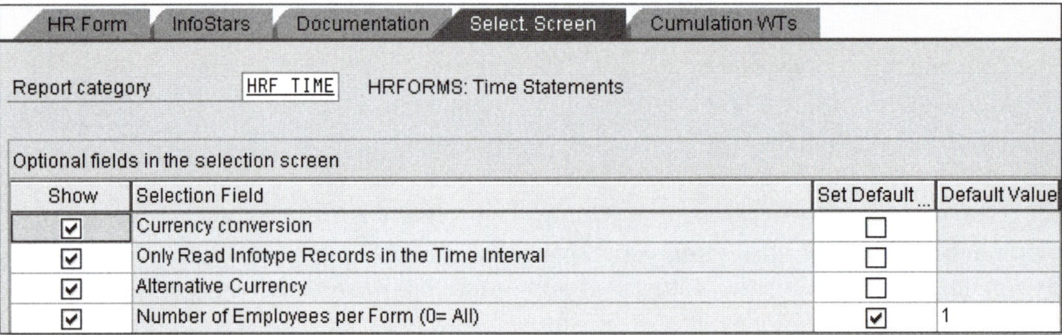



| Show | Selection Field | Set Default ... | Default Value |
|---|---|---|---|
| ☑ | Currency conversion | ☐ | |
| ☑ | Only Read Infotype Records in the Time Interval | ☐ | |
| ☑ | Alternative Currency | ☐ | |
| ☑ | Number of Employees per Form (0= All) | ☑ | 1 |

**Figure 5.8**  Select. Screen Tab

2. By selecting the Show column, you specify whether the field in the selection field of the print program is visible when the print program is executed. Set default values remain valid even if a field isn't displayed in the selection screen.

   Display the parameters for which you set the default values to avoid ambiguities (see Figure 5.9).

3. The parameters for the form-specific settings and the output currency are the same as for the payslip; you can find a detailed description of the parameters in Chapter 4, section 4.2.1, The Selection Screen.

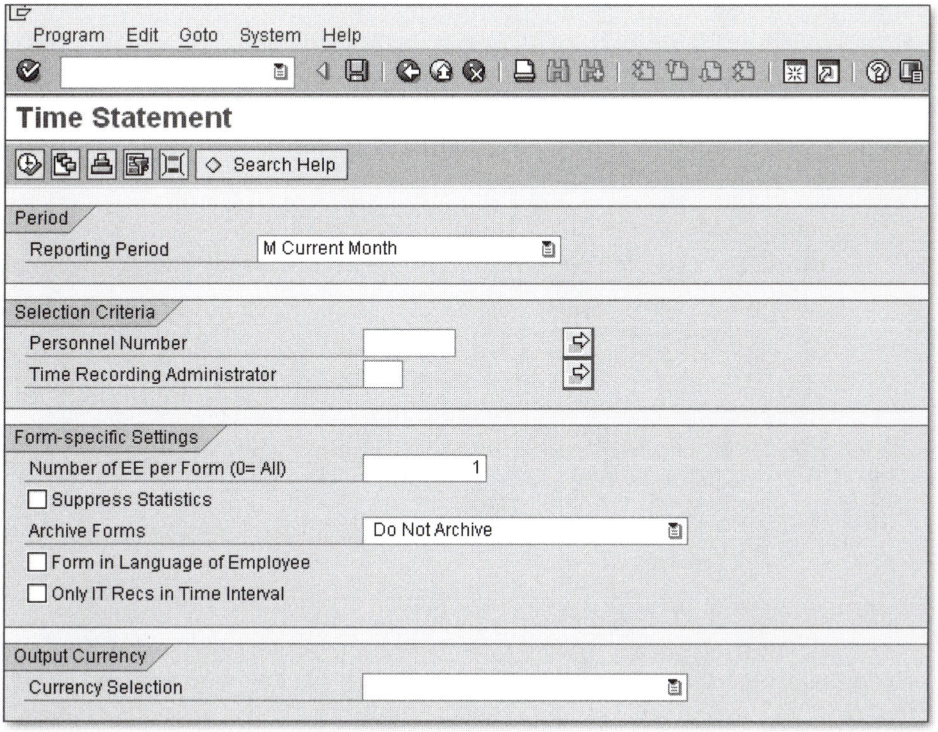

**Figure 5.9**  Selection Screen of the Time Statement Form

## 5.2.2  Notes in the Standard Form

The standard form contains various notes, such as YOUR TIME STATEMENT CANNOT BE DISPLAYED, BECAUSE NO TIME EVALUATION DATA IS AVAILABLE FOR THE SELECTION PERIOD, which are generated by checks, for example, depending on the existence of evaluation results in the selection period. Some of these checks are stored in the form layout within programming code and are difficult to understand due to the complexity of the form.

To help you adjust and control these checks, we'll now show you the areas within the Smart Forms form layout where these kind of checks and conditional outputs of notes occur. Note: Appendix G, Naming Conventions in the Time Statement Form, details the naming conventions for the Smart Forms elements used in the time statement form.

The notes listed in Table 5.1 are all generated in the TIMEEVALDATA main window within the loop element with the name, I_DIM_EMPLOYEE (see Figure 5.10).

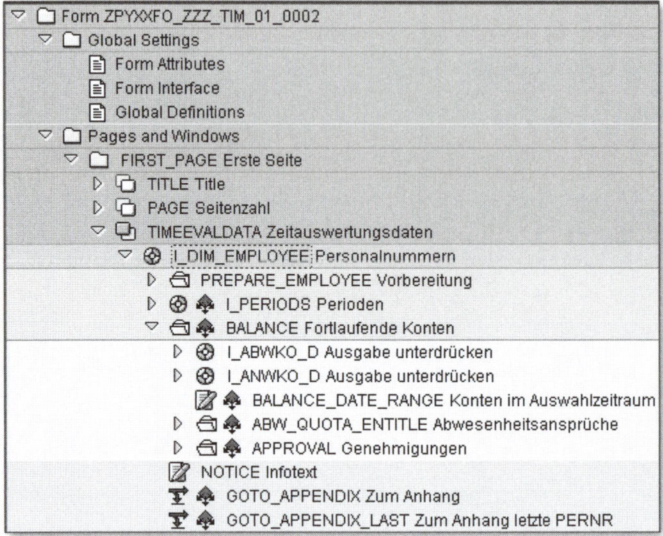

**Figure 5.10** I_DIM_EMPLOYEE Loop

The evaluation period is considered based on the available data that has been evaluated without any errors. If required, it can also be reset. This check is done in the ABAP_SET_DATERANGE program line in the PREPARE_EMPLOYEE folder (see Figure 5.11). The possibly reset evaluation period is also responsible for the output of notes.

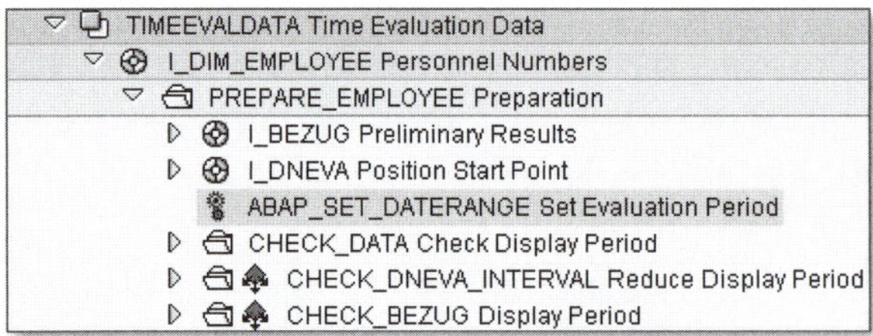

**Figure 5.11** ABAP_SET_DATERANGE Program Line

If you want to change the output of notes, you must consider the evaluation period as well as the conditions set in the elements.

Information is also taken from Cluster B1 (information on time results and status data for time evaluation) as you can see in Table 5.1. You should ensure that the time evaluation function, CHECK NOB1 (No Cluster B1), isn't set. Otherwise, Cluster B1 isn't considered, and no information is imported to and exported from it.

| Problem | Output Note | Area in the Form |
| --- | --- | --- |
| No data exists in Table ZES (Daily Time Balances). This is the case if an employee has not participated in the time evaluation temporarily or at all. | Your time statement cannot be displayed because no time evaluation data is available for the selection period. | Folder CHECK_DATA, loop I_ZES, text ERROR_NO_DATA_IN_INTERVAL |
| The time evaluation finished with an error that is before the evaluation period. There are no evaluation data available within the period. | Your time data could be evaluated without any errors only up to L_DNEVA. | The L_DNEVA variable is populated in the ABAP_SET_DATERANGE program line in the PREPARE_EMPLOYEE folder. The variable contains the previous day of the date up to which an error-free evaluation has been carried out, and it's taken from Table DNEVA (Cluster B1, Table QT, Field DNEVA). |
| The data evaluated without any errors end within the evaluation period. This may occur if the evaluation had to be interrupted due to an error, if the time evaluation has not been carried out up until the end of the selection period, or if the employee is no longer intended for the evaluation due to his status (Time Management status not equal to 1, 2, or 9). | Your time data could be evaluated without any errors only up to and including L_DNEVA. Therefore, your data is displayed up until this date. | The L_DNEVA variable is populated in the ABAP_SET_DATERANGE program line in the PREPARE_EMPLOYEE folder. The variable contains the previous day of the date up to which an error-free evaluation has been carried out, and it's taken from Table DNEVA (Cluster B1, Table QT, Field DNEVA). The message is subordinate to the CHECK_DNEVA_INTERVAL folder and is only processed if the data is contained in Table ZES and if the date that is taken from Table QT is less than the end of the selection period. |
| An error occurred during time evaluation. The reference date (Cluster B2, Table Bezug, Field LAST DAY EVALUATED ) is before the start date of the time evaluation (Cluster B1, Table QT, Field DNEVA). The provisional dates have a gray background. | The results as of W_BEZUG-TIM_BEZUG_ KEY-DATUM are provisional. | The note can be found within the CHECK_BEZUG folder and is output conditionally. |

**Table 5.1**  Notes in the Standard Time Statement

### 5.2.3  Outputting Provisional Time Balances

Time evaluation results, which are based on the evaluation of time data provided by the entry or recording of time data in Infotype 2011 (Time Events) and in time-recording systems, contain the resulting and formatted time pairs in Table PT (Time Pairs) of Cluster B2. If no individual results are available as time results in Table PT (Time Pairs), no individual results are displayed. The weekly totals are output nevertheless. If you still want a display to the day — not of the time pairs, but at least of the time balances — you can take this information from Table ZES (Daily Time Balances). In the InfoNet of the form that contains the InfoStar with the relevant information, however, the TIM_ZES InfoStar doesn't include all time balances that are included in Table ZES of Cluster B2 The cluster tables, ZES (Daily Time Balances), ZL (Time Wage Types), URLAN (Leave Accrual), VS (Variable Balances), QTACC (Absence Quota Generation), and QTBASE (Base Entitlement), are adjusted according to the last day evaluated correctly when reading the time evaluation results. Table entries that follow after this day are deleted. You can find the respective statement in the source code of the HR_TIME_RESULTS_GET function module. If you want these entries in your InfoNet or in the form, you must import this data retroactively into the form via a program line or provide it in a new InfoStar through separate routines.

If you want to provide the data via your MetaNet and consequently as an InfoStar in the InfoNet, you must add a MetaStar to your MetaNet:

1. Call your customer-specific international or national MetaNet. Place the mouse pointer on the TIM_ZES MetaStar. Use the context menu (right mouse button) to copy it to your own namespace. In this example, it's called ZTIM_ZES (see Figure 5.12). All attributes and properties persist in the copy process.

2. Because the standard functionality that populates Time Evaluation Table FT_ZES reads the time balances only up until the last day evaluated correctly, create a separate read function as a function module that imports the entire Table ZES for the selected period. The structure of the imported data corresponds to the line structure, PTR_F_ZES. The corresponding table type is PTT_F_ZES. These types can be found in the HRF_TIM_B2 structure.

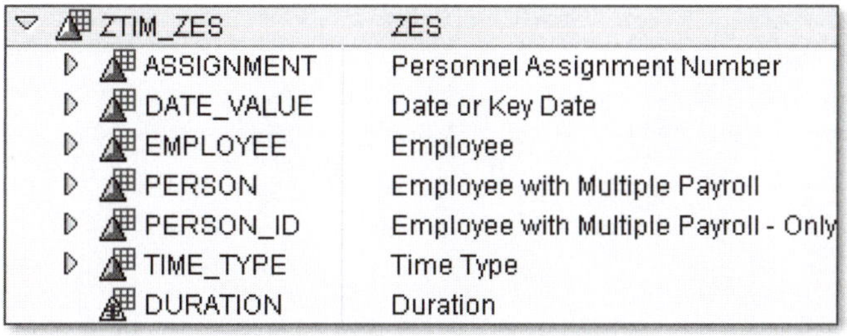

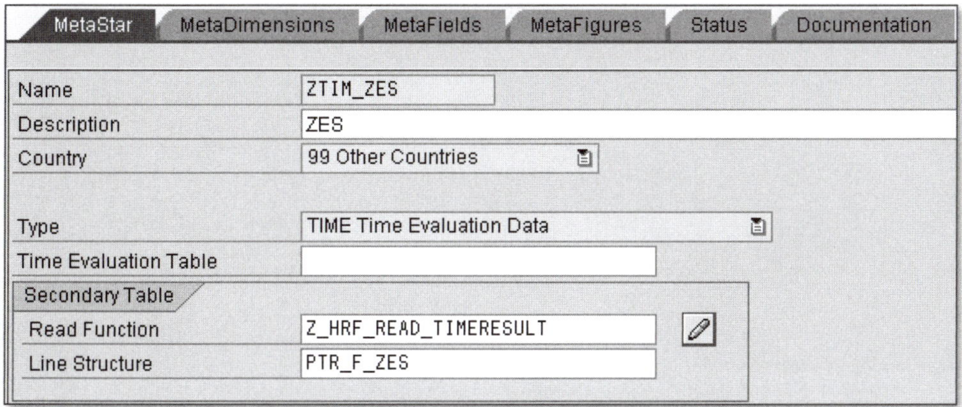

**Figure 5.12**  Customer-Specific ZTIM_ZES MetaStar

3. Enter a name for the read function (here Z_HRF_READ_TIMERESULT), the line structure, PTR_F_ZES, and select the button for creating the function module (see Figure 5.13). The system prompts you to enter a function group to which you assign the function module.

4. If you haven't created any function group for customer-specific objects that you created during the form development, call Transaction SE37 (Function Builder) to generate a function group prior to creating your function module. Then continue to create the function module.

5. Navigate to the interface parameters of your module to change the type of the DATA table parameter. Enter "TYPE" in the TYPING field, and enter the table type, "PTT_F_ZES", in the ASSOCIATED TYPE field. This customizing is necessary because a table is to be populated instead of a structure, and the PTR_F_ZES structure is the initial type. Activate the function module.

**Figure 5.13**  Specifying and Creating the Read Function and Line Structure for the MetaStar

6. Change the entries for the MetaFields as shown in Figure 5.14.

| MetaDimension | Read function | MetaField | Table | Table Field | WPBP Pos | Restriction |
|---|---|---|---|---|---|---|
| TIME_TYPE | ☐ | MOBDE | T001P | MOBDE | ☐ | |
| DATE_VALUE | ☐ | DATE_VALUE | PTR_F_ZES | DATUM | ☑ | |
| TIME_TYPE | ☐ | TIME_TYPE | PTR_F_ZES | ZTART | ☐ | |

**Figure 5.14** MetaFields of MetaStar ZTIM_ZES

7. Call the function module again to fill it with the source code shown in List-ing 5.1. You can enhance or adapt the source code according to your specific requirements. Note that this is a sample implementation that you can copy if you want to use it in your form to resolve the case shown.

```
DATA: i549q TYPE TABLE OF t549q WITH HEADER LINE,
      w_549q TYPE t549q,
      w_dateranges TYPE ptr_f_dateranges,
      w_zes   TYPE pc2b6,
      w_data  TYPE ptr_f_zes,
      w_bezug TYPE ptr_f_bezug.

* Check Table BEZUG whether importing of ZES necessary if required
* Sample coding:
  READ TABLE tim_b2-ft_bezug INTO w_bezug INDEX 1.
* Read selection period to determine periods
  READ TABLE tim_b2-ft_dateranges INTO w_dateranges INDEX 1.

* Check whether last day evaluated correctly
* is before the selection end. Only then re-import ZES
  CHECK w_bezug-datum LT w_dateranges-selendda.

* Determine payroll period
  REFRESH:i549q.
  CALL FUNCTION 'HR_PAYROLL_PERIODS_GET'
    EXPORTING
      get_begda        = w_dateranges-selbegda
```

```
        get_endda        = w_dateranges-selendda
        get_permo        = '01'
     TABLES
        get_periods      = i549q
     EXCEPTIONS
        no_period_found  = 1
        no_valid_permo   = 2
        OTHERS           = 3.

  CLEAR: w_549q.
  LOOP AT i549q INTO w_549q
    CLEAR: b2-key.
    b2-key-pernr = pernr.
    b2-key-cltyp = '1'.
    b2-key-pabrj = w_549q-pabrj.
    b2-key-pabrp = w_549q-pabrp.
    rp-imp-c2-b2. " Macro for reading Cluster B2

    CASE rp-imp-b2-subrc. " Cluster B2 available?
      WHEN 0.
        LOOP AT zes INTO w_zes.
          CLEAR w_data.
          CONCATENATE w_549q-pabrj w_549q-pabrp
          w_zes-reday INTO  w_data-datum.
          w_data-ztart = w_zes-ztart.
          w_data-number = w_zes-number.
          APPEND w_data TO data.
        ENDLOOP.

      WHEN OTHERS.    "No cluster data available

    ENDCASE.
  ENDLOOP.

* Entries that are outside the selection period can
* then be deleted if required
* Sample coding:
  DELETE data WHERE NOT datum BETWEEN
  w_dateranges-selbegda AND w_dateranges-selendda.
```

**Listing 5.1** Source Code of the Customer-Specific Z_HRF_READ_TIMERESULT Function Module

8. If you've created the MetaStar in the international MetaNet (Country Grouping 99), also add it to your national MetaNet. Call the country-specific MetaNet, and drag and drop the MetaStar into your MetaNet. If you've created the MetaStar with a specific country grouping, drag and drop this MetaStar into your MetaNet. You can then use the MetaStar in your form.

9. In the next step, you must create the InfoStar table in your InfoNet (see Figure 5.15).

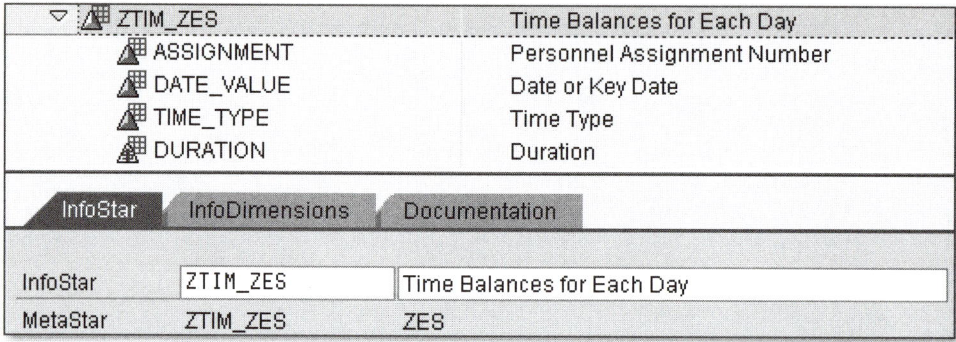

**Figure 5.15**  Creating an InfoStar in the InfoNet

10. Call the print program of your form in the test mode to check whether the cluster data is imported. Set a breakpoint in the source code of the function module also for the test.

> **Note**
>
> The result of setting a breakpoint is that the debugger is called at runtime of the print program, so you can check the data retrieval.

The time balances and thus the TIM_ZES InfoStar below the Individual Results For Day table node (TIM_PSP InfoStar, personal work schedule) are read and processed depending on specific conditions in the form layout. Check them, and, if required, supplement the output of the possible lines (see Figure 5.16).

If you work with the recording of exceptions to the work schedule (negative time management) instead of the recording of all attendances (positive time management), you must check whether the data contained in Cluster B2 is also provided in the InfoStar tables. If the data isn't provided in the InfoStar tables, you can proceed as described in this case. But if this can't be implemented by a similar Customizing, you must create further customer-specific MetaDimensions and MetaStars that retrieve the missing information using the read functions.

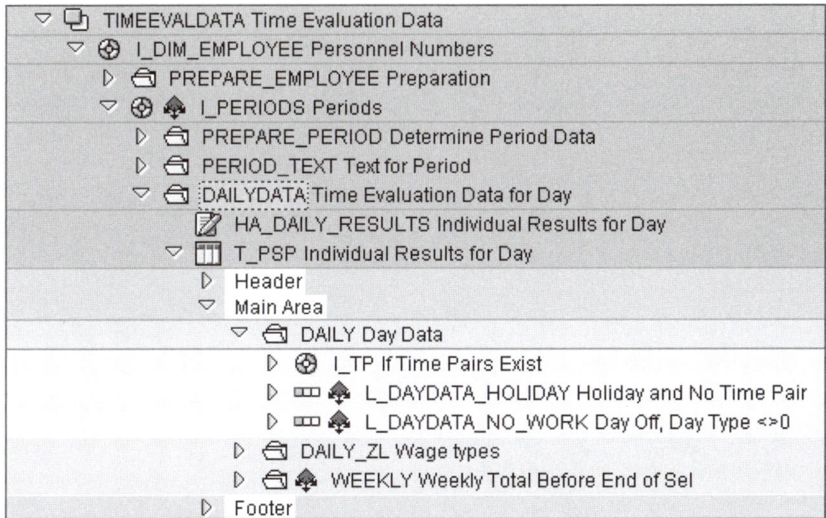

**Figure 5.16**  Individual Results for Day

As an alternative to creating a new MetaStar, you can also call a similar function module within the program line in the form layout of the time statement. For example, you can add the determined entries to the TIM_ZES InfoStar.

You can always import data via program lines into a Smart Form retroactively. The disadvantage, however, is that you can't provide this development to other forms via the common MetaNet as you can for a MetaStar. The development must be integrated in each form individually and maintained in case of a change.

### 5.2.4  Handling Recalculations

Recalculations are caused by changes to an already evaluated period. In Cluster B2 that contains the result tables of the time evaluation, no differentiation is made between In-Periods and For-Periods, as is the case for the payslip. You can use the In-Periods and For-Periods view to track recalculations for the payroll and display them in the time statement. Unfortunately, this isn't the case for the time evaluation results. Here, a note is beneficial to notify employees that a recalculation occurred and when.

No doubt, you can imagine that there are multiple possible solution approaches for each problem, so in this section we'll describe a solution approach that has already been implemented and is currently used.

Table BEZUG (Recalculation data) of Cluster B2 (Time evaluation results) contains the following information that you can use:

- Last day evaluated
- Recalculation period for time statement
- Recalculation period for third-party payroll

For testing purposes, you use the report for displaying the time evaluation results (Transaction PT_CLSTB2).

As determined before, the RECALCULATION PERIOD FOR THIRD-PARTY PAYROLL field is populated with information whether and up to which period recalculation has been implemented (see Figure 5.17).

```
Display Time Evaluation Results (Cluster B2)



Person 00010008 Christina Papadopoulou
Period 09 2008
ClType 1
Table  BEZUG     Recalculation data


Field name                                          Field cont.

Last day evaluated                                  03.09.2008
Recalculation period for time statement
Recalculation period for third-party payroll        08 2008
```

**Figure 5.17**  Table BEZUG — Recalculation Data of Cluster B2

If you had this information at runtime during the design of the layout, you could output a note with the period concerned when necessary. This way, the employee could at least be informed that a change occurred in an already-evaluated period.

Because Table BEZUG isn't available completely in the MetaNet, you need to determine and provide the missing data. Our solution approach is to add a MetaDimension and a MetaStar with all fields of Table BEZUG. If you want to call the time statement for a longer period, you must determine this information period-specifically and person-dependent. This information is available in the standard MetaDimensions and can be transferred to the new MetaStar.

Call the international or a country-dependent MetaNet to create the new MetaDimension and the new MetaStar as well as the read function and line structure. The HR_FORMS_READ_TIME_PERIODS function module, the PTT_F_PERIODS table type, and the PTR_F_PERIODS structure are used as a template for the read function and the line structure. In this example, the international ZZZ_DEFAULT MetaNet, which was also used in the other examples, was customized.

1. Create the MetaDimension and fields as illustrated in Figures 5.18 and 5.19.

| ZTIM_BEZUG | Recalculation data |
|---|---|
| DATUM | Last Day Evaluated Correctly |
| RABRJ | Payroll Year |
| RABRP | Payroll Period |
| RRABJ | Payroll Year |
| RRABP | Payroll Period |

**Figure 5.18**  MetaDimension with Key Fields

Only when you've entered the field type — as shown in Figure 5.19 — can you convert the MetaFields into key fields by selecting the field in the key column of attributes. It isn't necessary to make further entries at this point. You have free choice for the name except for the limitations of the customer namespace.

| Key | MetaField | Field Type | Fixed value of | Description | Restriction for Sel... | Validity of Sele |
|---|---|---|---|---|---|---|
| | DATUM | DATET | | Last Day Evaluated Correctly | | |
| | RABRJ | PABRJ | | Payroll Year | | |
| | RABRP | PABRP | | Payroll Period | | |
| | RRABJ | PABRJ | | Payroll Year | | |
| | RRABP | PABRP | | Payroll Period | | |

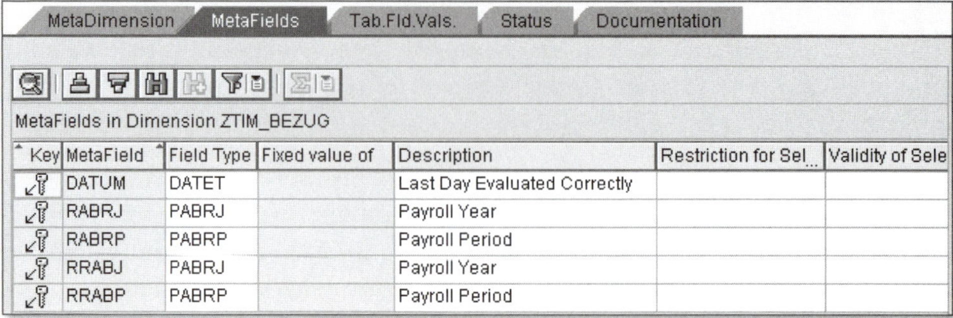

**Figure 5.19** Field Types of the MetaDimension Fields

2. Create a MetaStar that includes the three MetaDimensions, ASSIGNMENT, TIM_PERID, and the new ZTIM_BEZUG (see Figure 5.20).

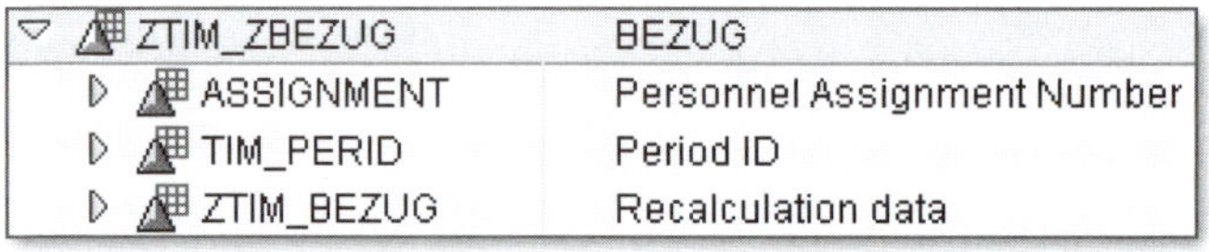

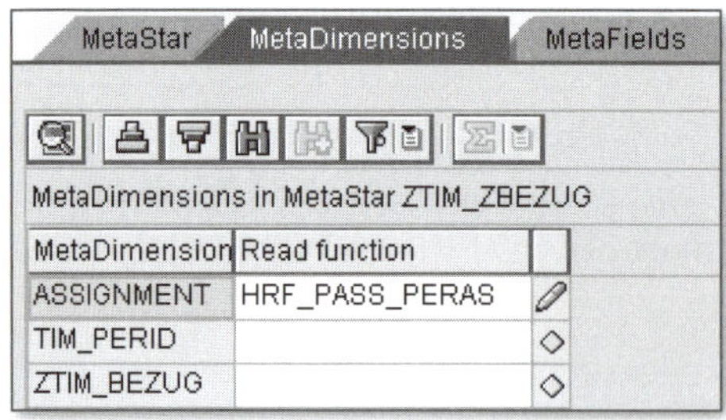

**Figure 5.20** MetaStar with Assigned MetaDimensions

3. Before you assign the MetaDimensions, you must first specify the type of the MetaStar. Select SPECIAL TYPE A (DEPENDENT ON PERSONNEL NUMBER). Then assign the MetaDimensions to the MetaStar via drag and drop. In the METADIMENSIONS tab, enter the default function module, "HRF_PASS_PERAS," as the read function for the ASSIGNMENT MetaDimension (see Figure 5.21).

| MetaDimension | Read function |
|---|---|
| ASSIGNMENT | HRF_PASS_PERAS |
| TIM_PERID | |
| ZTIM_BEZUG | |

**Figure 5.21** Entering the Read Function for the MetaDimension

The two other MetaDimensions or their key fields are populated via the read function to be created and its return structure.

4. Copy the PTR_F_PERIODS structure to your customer namespace. Enhance the new ZPTR_F_PERIODS structure by fields that you've already created in the ZTIM_BEZUG MetaDimension. Copy the PTT_F_PERIODS table type, and replace the line type with the new ZPTR_F_PERIODS structure in the new ZPTT_F_PERIODS table type. You can now use the new table type and the new structure in the function module to be created. Assign the fields of this structure to the key fields of the MetaDimension.

5. Enter the Z_HR_FORMS_READ_TIME_PERIODS function module and the ZPTR_F_PERIODS line structure in the corresponding fields in the METASTAR tab. Add the fixed value "01" (monthly) for the PERMO parameter (period parameter) as shown in Figure 5.22.

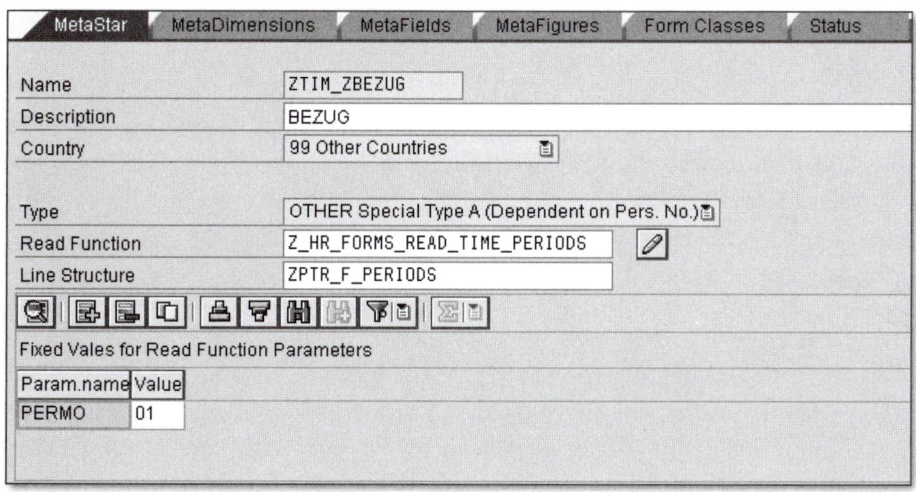


**Figure 5.22** Maintaining the Read Function, Line Structure, and Fixed Value

6. Create the function module as has already been described in Section 2.1.2, Customizing and Enhancing the MetaNet, to automatically obtain the predefined interface. Refer to Appendix E, Source Code of the Z_HR_FORMS_READ_TIME_PERIODS Function Module, where you can find the source code to be used.

7. Assign the fields of the line structure to the key fields of the two MetaDimensions (see Figure 5.23).

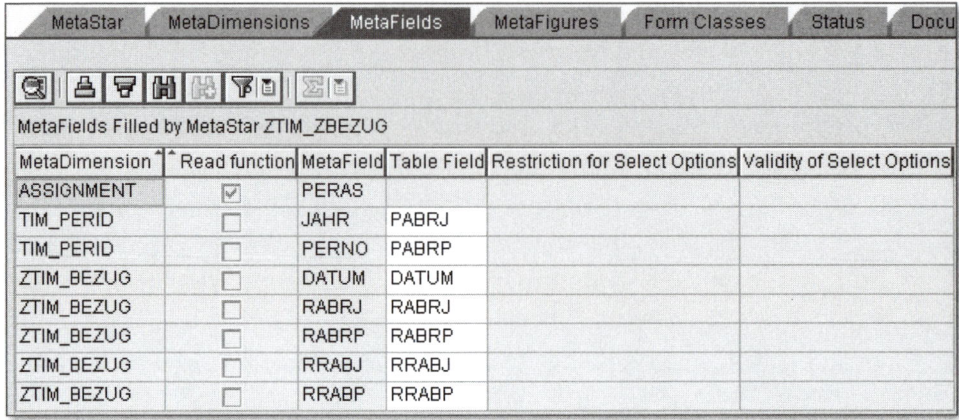

| MetaDimension | Read function | MetaField | Table Field | Restriction for Select Options | Validity of Select Options |
|---|---|---|---|---|---|
| ASSIGNMENT | ☑ | PERAS | | | |
| TIM_PERID | ☐ | JAHR | PABRJ | | |
| TIM_PERID | ☐ | PERNO | PABRP | | |
| ZTIM_BEZUG | ☐ | DATUM | DATUM | | |
| ZTIM_BEZUG | ☐ | RABRJ | RABRJ | | |
| ZTIM_BEZUG | ☐ | RABRP | RABRP | | |
| ZTIM_BEZUG | ☐ | RRABJ | RRABJ | | |
| ZTIM_BEZUG | ☐ | RRABP | RRABP | | |

**Figure 5.23**  Filling MetaFields

The MetaStar is now complete and can be added to your MetaNet. If you add the MetaStar to your InfoNet, you must ensure that all MetaDimensions are added to the InfoStar.

Note that this solution approach is based on the enhancement of the MetaNet. It's also possible to integrate the routine used in the function module as a program line with your Smart Forms.

### 5.2.5  Converting Industrial Time to Standard Hours and Minutes

The presentation of a duration takes place in the MetaStars, TIM_ZES, TIM_ZL, and TIM_SALDO, through the DURATION MetaFigure. The duration is mapped as an industrial time whose presentation of minutes is different from the "normal" time. The hours are displayed identically in both types, with 100 minutes being equal to 1 industrial hour.

If you want to convert the output of a duration, you can do so directly in your form. The following example details how you can create a routine within the Form Builder for Smart Forms that converts the duration format from industrial time to hours and minutes.

1. Call the layout of the form, and select GLOBAL DEFINITIONS (see Figure 5.24).

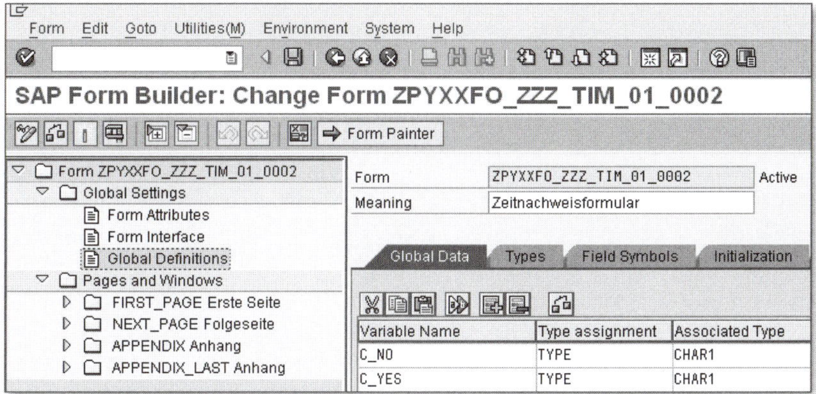

**Figure 5.24**  Global Definitions

Here, you can define a routine in which you can convert the format of the duration. You can then execute this routine in a program line for a specific table and time type or time wage type.

Listing 5.2 shows what the source code and the corresponding call could look like within a program line.

```
PERFORM convert_time_format
                     using number_i " Industrial
                     changing number_n. " Normal


* Routine for the conversion of industrial times into
* hours and minutes
FORM convert_time_format
using number_i type TIM_F_STDNZ
changing number_n type TIM_F_STDNZ.
  DATA: hours    TYPE c LENGTH 10,
        i_minutes  TYPE c LENGTH 10, " Industrial minutes
        n_minutes  TYPE i,        " normal minutes
        number     TYPE c LENGTH 10.

  number = number_i.

  SPLIT number AT '.' INTO: hours i_minutes.
  CONDENSE hours NO-GAPS.
  n_minutes = i_minutes.

  CLEAR: number.
  IF n_minutes < 0.
```

```
      n_minutes = n_minutes * -1.
  ENDIF.

  IF n_minutes <> 0.
    n_minutes = ( n_minutes * 60 ) / 100.
    IF n_minutes < 10.
      i_minutes = n_minutes.
      CONCATENATE '0' i_minutes INTO i_minutes.
    ELSE.
      i_minutes = n_minutes.
    ENDIF.
    CONDENSE i_minutes NO-GAPS.
    CONCATENATE hours i_minutes INTO number
    SEPARATED BY '.'.
  ELSE.
    i_minutes = n_minutes.
    CONCATENATE hours i_minutes INTO number
    SEPARATED BY '.'.
  ENDIF.

  number_n = number.
  IF ms_data-number < 0.
    number_n = number_n * -1.
  ENDIF.

ENDFORM. * End of routine
```

**Listing 5.2** Routine For Converting Industrial Minutes into Hours and Minutes

Alternatively, you can copy the DURATION MetaFigure. For example, add it to the ZTIM_ZES MetaStar (see Figure 5.25). This MetaStar has been created in Section 5.2.3, Outputting Provisional Time Balances. You don't need to customize the MetaFigure because the TIM_F_STDNZ field type is suitable for the input of hours and minutes.

| ZTIM_ZES | ZES |
|---|---|
| ASSIGNMENT | Personnel Assignment Number |
| DATE_VALUE | Date or Key Date |
| EMPLOYEE | Employee |
| PERSON | Employee with Multiple Payroll |
| PERSON_ID | Employee with Multiple Payroll - Only ID |
| TIME_TYPE | Time Type |
| DURATION | Duration |
| ZDURATION | Duration |

**Figure 5.25** New MetaFigure for the Representation of the Duration in Hours and Minutes

2. In the MetaFigures tab, you add a function module to the Read Function field. Click on the Create button to create the function module (see Figure 5.26). If applicable, you must add an import parameter to the function module (see Figure 5.27). The print program terminates if this parameter isn't available.

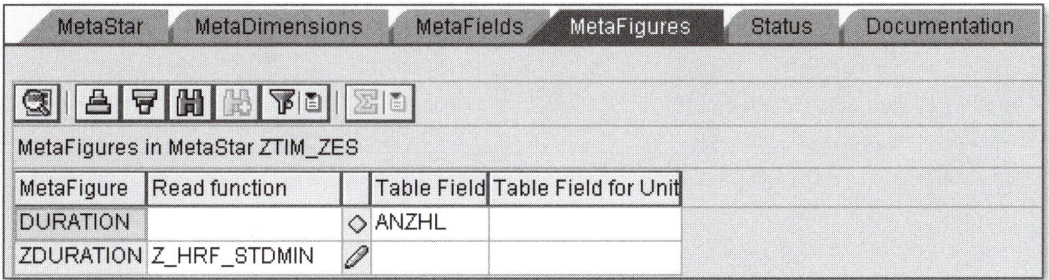

| MetaFigure | Read function | | Table Field | Table Field for Unit |
|---|---|---|---|---|
| DURATION | | ◇ | ANZHL | |
| ZDURATION | Z_HRF_STDMIN | ✎ | | |

**Figure 5.26**  Figure 5.26 Creating the Read Function of the New MetaFigure

| Parameter Name | Type | Associated Type | Default | Opti | Pas | Short text | Lon |
|---|---|---|---|---|---|---|---|
| MS_DATA | TYPE | PTR_F_ZES | | ☐ | ☐ | MetaStar: Line | |
| TIM_B2 | TYPE | HRF_TIM_B2 | | ☐ | ☐ | MetaStar: Line | |
| SELECTIONS | TYPE | HRF_T_SELTOFUN | | ☐ | ☐ | hrforms: Selection in FM | |

**Figure 5.27**  Additional SELECTIONS Parameter

3. Insert the source code provided earlier into your function module. Remove the statements, `FORM` and `ENDFORM`. Instead of the `number_i` and `number_n` transfer parameters, you use the `ms_data-number` and `figure` parameters here.

   The source code of the module is called for each entry of the ZTIM_ZES table. The new ZDURATION MetaFigure is filled with the "normal" time. Figure 5.28 shows that the duration is available in both time formats in the InfoStar.

If you want to use the new MetaFigure, you must add it to your InfoStar. This isn't done automatically. You can't add the new MetaFigure to a standard MetaStar. Copy the standard MetaStar and extend it as described for the customer-specific ZTIM_ZES MetaStar.

| ASSIGN... | DATE_VAL... | T... | TIM... | DURATION | ZDURATI... |
|---|---|---|---|---|---|
| 10008 | 03.09.2008 | 1 | 0500 | 1,00 | 1,00 |
| 10008 | 03.09.2008 | 1 | 0002 | 7,50 | 7,30 |
| 10008 | 03.09.2008 | 1 | 0005 | 1,00- | 1,00- |
| 10008 | 03.09.2008 | 1 | 0050 | 6,50 | 6,30 |
| 10008 | 03.09.2008 | 1 | 0051 | 6,50 | 6,30 |
| 10008 | 04.09.2008 | 1 | 0002 | 7,50 | 7,30 |
| 10008 | 04.09.2008 | 1 | 0005 | 7,50- | 7,30- |
| 10008 | 05.09.2008 | 1 | 0002 | 7,50 | 7,30 |
| 10008 | 05.09.2008 | 1 | 0005 | 7,50- | 7,30- |
| 10008 | 08.09.2008 | 1 | 0002 | 7,50 | 7,30 |
| 10008 | 08.09.2008 | 1 | 0005 | 7,50- | 7,30- |
| 10008 | 09.09.2008 | 1 | 0002 | 7,50 | 7,30 |

**Figure 5.28**  Filled ZTIM_ZES InfoStar

## 5.2.6  Considering the ESS Settings in Infotype 0655

In Chapter 4, Section 4.2.5, Considering ESS Settings in Infotype 0655, we detailed how you can exclude the output of the payslip for employees who use ESS from mass print. This also holds true for printing the time statement. Here again, you can use Infotype 0655 (ESS Settings Remuneration Statement), even if it's intended for the payslip. You're also provided with the CHECK_PERNR or CHECK_PERSON methods in the HRFORM_HRF02 BAdI (Enhancements for HR Forms) if you use multiple payroll (see Section 6.3.1, CHECK_PERNR Method and CHECK_PERSON Method). A sample implementation in which Infotype 0655 is checked exists for the CHECK_PERNR method. At this point, you can also insert another check to distinguish between the payslip and the time statement. If you use a program for the person selection, you can also implement the limitation at this point.

If you want to use Infotype 0655 only for the control of the payslip, you must check whether the CHECKBOX additional field is active in Infotype 0007 (Planned Working Time) (see Figure 5.29). This field can be used to support the control of the time statement's output. Bear in mind, however, that you must create a new infotype record if you set or change the indicator.

**Figure 5.29**  Additional Field in Infotype 0007 (Planned Working Time)

You can query this field and use it correspondingly in the HRFORM_HRF02 BAdI just like the field of Infotype 0655.

> **Tip**
>
> If you need more control indicators at the person level, consider whether you want to create a customer-specific infotype. For example, you could use subtypes to manage the control of the time statement and payslip.

## 5.3    Conclusion

This chapter described the layout design of the time statement using the Form Builder for Smart Forms and the Form Builder for SAP Interactive Forms. Currently, the time statement isn't yet included as a PDF template in the standard delivery, but you learned how to create the time statement as a PDF.

Within the framework of the time statement Customizing, you learned about the most essential points that have recurred in real-world projects during the creation of a time statement using the Forms Workplace. At this point, you should now be able to customize the selection screen, import data that have not been provided in the metadata retroactively, recognize recalculations that have occurred and specify them accordingly in the evaluated period, and convert industrial minutes into hours and minutes through the described extension in the MetaNet. We also taught you how to proceed if you want to produce the time statement in mass print and exclude specific employees who receive their time statement via ESS applications.

During the implementation of your own time statement you'll certainly come across requirements that haven't been mentioned here; however, we hope that we've shown you how you can approach the solution of a requirement by considering the solutions in the customizing of your MetaNet, in the form layout via program lines, or via the provided BAdIs.

In the next chapter we will focus on the enhancements.

# 6    Enhancements with BAdIs

Within the HR Forms Workplace, you have four *Business Add-Ins* (BAdIs) that enable you to influence the processing of your forms at different points. BAdIs are predefined enhancement options that are based on ABAP Objects and can be called in the application programs. Through the implementation of a BAdI method, you intervene in the application program at a specific point. BAdIs contain filters that are used to execute the desired implementation and the associated program section depending on a specific value. The signature of the method contains the parameters that are transferred to this method and are then available for processing. The type of parameter determines whether it can be changed or only used as information. This applies to import parameters whose content you can't change. The content of export, changing, and return parameters, however, can be changed.

The BAdIs described here are classic BAdIs and not "new" BAdIs, which are used within the new *Enhancement Framework*.

You can find all BAdIs in the *BAdI Builder*, which is available via the SAP Easy Access menu (path: SAP MENU • TOOLS • ABAP WORKBENCH • UTILITIES • BUSINESS ADD-INS) or directly using Transaction SE18 (Business Add-Ins: Definitions) or Transaction SE19 (Business Add-Ins: Implementations).

## 6.1    Activating Forms Automatically After Transport (HRFORM_AFTER_TRANSP)

Forms aren't automatically activated after a transport to another system, as the heading suggests, so you must manually make this setting active. The HRFORM_ AFTER_TRANSP BAdI contains the ACTIVATE_FORMS method required for this action. The HRFORM_AFTER_TRANSP implementation exists for the BAdI definition. The BAdI implementation is inactive in the standard delivery, and you must first copy and then activate it for usage. You can then adjust the copy without any risks.

To copy and then activate the BAdI implementation, follow these steps:

1. Call the BAdI Builder using Transaction SE19 (Business Add-Ins: Implementations). Select the option, CLASSIC BAdI • IMPLEMENTATION. Enter "HRFORM_ AFTER_TRANSP" in the IMPLEMENTATION field, and then click the COPY button (see Figure 6.1). You can view the HRFORM_AFTER_TRANSP BAdI definition via Transaction SE18 (Business Add-Ins: Definitions). You can also use this transaction to create an implementation. However, you should use Transaction SE19 to copy an existing BAdI implementation.

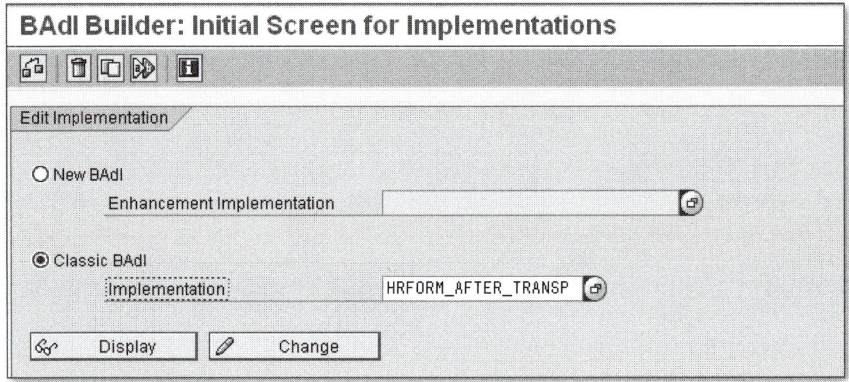


**Figure 6.1** BAdI Builder — Initial Screen for Implementations

2. Assign the implementation to a package, and save it in a corresponding transport request.

3. Call the implementation, and activate it using the ACTIVATE button (see Figure 6.2).

There is no documentation for the standard implementation, so to create documentation for your own implementation, select the DOCUMENTATION button. You should definitely create documentation if you make changes to the standard implementation. But if documentation exists for the BAdI definition, you can view it using the DEFINITION DOCUMENTATION button.

**Business Add-In Builder: Display Implementation ZHRFORM_AFTER_TRANSP**

| | Definition Documenta | Documentation |

| Implementation Name | ZHRFORM_AFTER_TRANSP | Active |
| Implementation Short Text | Activate HR Forms Automatically After Transports | |
| Definition Name | HRFORM_AFTER_TRANSP | |

Attributes / Interface

| Interface name | IF_EX_HRFORM_AFTER_TRANSP |
| Name of implementing class: | ZCL_IM_HRFORM_AFTER_TRANSP |

| Method | Implement | Description |
|---|---|---|
| ACTIVATE_FORMS | ABAP ABAP | Activate Forms |
| | | |
| | | |
| | | |

**Figure 6.2** Activating the Implementation

## 6.2 Formatting a Business Address (HRFORM_BUSINESS_ADRS)

The HRFORM_BUSINESS_ADRS BAdI (Formatting of a Business Address) contains the MAKE_ADDRESS method (format a business address). The BAdI isn't filter-dependent and can't be used multiple times, so you must check carefully how you can use the method. The method is called only if your InfoNet contains the BUSINESS_ADDR MetaDimension. You can integrate it via the PAY_CORP_STRUCT MetaStar. You use the data that is available via the signature to populate the ADRESS export parameter.

You can also import data that you can identify by the import parameter (plant, personnel subarea, company code, address type, personnel number, cost center, etc.). Some of these parameters represent the key of the BUSINESS_ADDR MetaDimension. Even if you don't populate the export parameter, the system creates an entry for the BUSINESS_ADDR InfoDimension that is used in the InfoStar.

Because no implementation exists for the BAdI, you can create it via Transaction SE18 or Transaction SE19. If you use Transaction SE18, select the menu path,

Enhancement Implementation • Create. To create an implementation using Transaction SE19, follow these steps:

1. Select the option, Classic BAdI • BAdI Name. Enter the name of the BAdI definition in the BAdI Name field. Click on Create Impl. as illustrated in Figure 6.3.

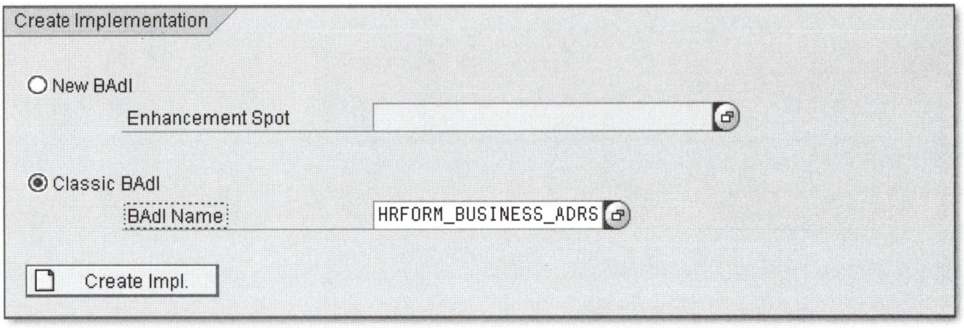

**Figure 6.3**  Creating a BAdI Implementation

2. Assign the implementation to a package, and save it in a corresponding transport request.

3. In the Interface tab, find the MAKE_ADDRESS method. Double-click the method name to navigate to the Class Builder (Transaction SE24). There, you have the option to enter a code. In the signature of the method, you can find the available parameters. Use the button of the same name to hide or show the signature.

4. The buttons, ⬛ and Definition Documentation, enable you to activate the implementation and to add documentation.

## 6.3    Enhancements for HR Forms (HRFORM_HRF02)

The HRFORM_HRF02 BAdI (Enhancements for HR Forms) is available in the Forms Workplace directly via the menu path, Utilities • BAdI Implementation. The following methods are available in this BAdI:

- **CHECK_PERNR**
  Check if the personnel number is rejected or skipped in the form.

- **CHECK_PERNR_LATE**
  Check if the personnel number is rejected or skipped in the form and possible changes to the data.

- **SET_ARCHIVE_INDEX**
  Determine key for optical archiving of the forms.

- **CHECK_PERSON**
  Check whether central person is rejected or skipped in the form.

- **CHECK_PERSON_LATE**
  Check whether central person is rejected or skipped in the form and possible changes to the data.

- **BEFORE_PDF_PRINT**
  Operations immediately before PDF print.

- **AFTER_PDF_PRINT**
  Operations immediately after PDF print.

Using these methods, you can ensure that specific personnel numbers are rejected or skipped, that the key is determined for archiving, and that the print formatting is influenced. You can view the parameters available in the signature of the methods.

Some of these methods have sample implementations that you can copy to your implementation. Copy the HRFORM_HRF02 implementation as previously described in Section 6.1, Activating Forms Automatically After Transport (HRFORM_AFTER_TRANSP), and Section 6.2, Formatting a Business Address (HRFORM_BUSINESS_ADRS). Copy the code of the sample implementation by calling the corresponding function via the menu path GOTO • SAMPLE CODE • COPY (see Figure 6.4). The methods of your implementation are overwritten. Carefully check which methods you can use now or whether you must adjust them.

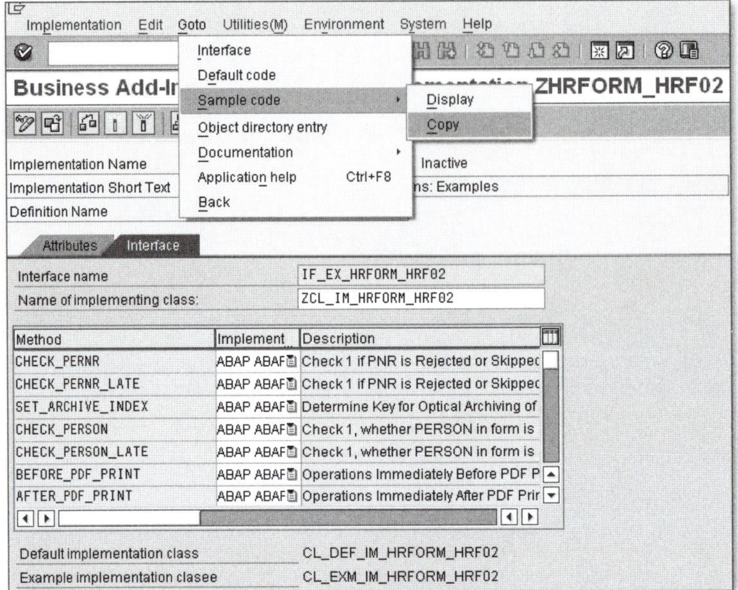

**Figure 6.4** Copying the Sample Code for a BAdI Implementation

### 6.3.1 CHECK_PERNR Method and CHECK_PERSON Method

The CHECK_PERNR method contains a sample implementation which ensures that the system skips employees who have access to Employee Self-Service (ESS). It's assumed that they print their payslip themselves. Infotype 0655 (ESS Settings Remuneration Statement) is checked here. In this infotype, you can set an indicator that informs you whether an employee uses ESS. In this method, you can only exclude one employee from further processing due to the signature. If you use multiple payroll, use the CHECK_PERSON method instead of the CHECK_PERNR method to implement the check. In this case, the method is only implemented for the central person if a person has multiple contracts and consequently multiple personnel numbers. The personnel numbers assigned to a central person are available in the IM_PERSON interface parameter. The CHECK_PERNR method, however, is called per personnel number.

### 6.3.2 CHECK_PERNR_LATE Method and CHECK_PERSON_LATE Method

In the CHECK_PERNR_LATE method — just like in the CHECK_PERNR method — you can exclude an employee from processing. Additionally, the CH_DATA parameter provides you with form data that you can change here or use for further checks. The sample implementation checks to see whether changes exist in the payroll of an employee in comparison to the previous period. Using the source code, you can suppress the output of retroactive accountings. You can find details on the prerequisites for the associated Customizing back in Chapter 4, section 4.2.4, Controlling the Printing of Retroactive Accountings. If you decide to skip irrelevant retroactive accountings, you can also refer to the sample implementation where you find instructions for adjustments that you must implement in the Info-Net. In the meantime, the system also provides a check for this subject in the form layout itself, namely in the MAIN main window of the INIT program node (see Chapter 4, section 4.2.4). You can then decide at which point you want to insert the check. If you use multiple payroll, use the CHECK_PERSON_LATE method instead of the CHECK_PERNR_LATE method, provided that you want to execute the method per person and not per personnel number.

### 6.3.3 SET_ARCHIVE_INDEX Method

You must implement the SET_ARCHIVE_INDEX method if you want to use the optical archiving for forms. In this method, you need to adapt the key for archiving to your specific requirements. You have two changing parameters, ARCHIVE_INDEX (SAP ArchiveLink structure of a DARA line in which you store the index of the document to be archived) and ARCTEXT (SAP ArchiveLink: text information field).

### 6.3.4 BEFORE_PDF_PRINT Method

You can use the BEFORE_PDF_PRINT method to change the program behavior before the print. Here as well, a sample implementation exists which ensures that you can't print the form but can download it. The output parameters and form parameters for the form processing are available as changing parameters in the signature.

### 6.3.5 AFTER_PDF_PRINT Method

Using the AFTER_PDF_PRINT method, you can change the number of forms that are output in the same spool request so that the default value of "50" is overridden. This is also available as a sample implementation. Additionally, the sample source code includes instructions that are required to download the form instead of printing it.

## 6.4 Country-Specific Exit for MetaData (HRFORM_METADATA)

The HRFORM_METADATA BAdI (HR Forms: Country-Specific Exit for MetaData) is implemented depending on filters, in this case, depending on MOLGA (country grouping). The BAdI can't be used multiple times and contains the CHANGE_PAY-ROLL_SPLITS method (process relations between payroll tables).

The implementation of this BAdI is processed as soon as the Metadata Workplace or the Forms Workplace is called. The call isn't done during the execution of a form.

You obtain a table that includes the foreign key dependencies between the payroll tables via the interface of the BAdI. Because the table is a changing parameter, you have the option to process or supplement the dependencies. Also note that the entries of the table are country-dependent, so you should consider this during processing.

## 6.5 Conclusion

You should keep in mind that the existing BAdI definitions you can use for form creation with the Forms Workplace cover a large part of checks and adaptations. Also remember that existing sample implementations support you in the implementation of your requirements. If it's unclear whether your requirement can be covered with a BAdI, you must check which existing BAdI methods could meet your requirement best. Here, you must consider the time of the method call and the interface signature. If there are still ambiguities, create an implementation and test it using the debugging functionality. This is an easy option to determine when the method is called, which information is available, and which data can be changed or enhanced.

In the next chapter we will focus on the integration of forms created using the Forms Workplace in the two SAP HCM components: Time Management and Payroll.

# 7 Integration with the Payroll and Time Management Components of SAP ERP HCM

In this chapter, you'll learn how you can integrate forms you've created using the Forms Workplace with the SAP ERP HCM components, *Payroll* and *Time Management*, particularly the payslip and the time statement. We'll also review how you control the call of forms by using features, and explore how you can decide whether you want to use a SAPscript form, a Smart Form, or an SAP Interactive Form created via the Forms Workplace. In addition, we'll review the standard transactions also available to call the payslip or time statement.

It is important to note that the Forms you create in the Forms Workplace and call in applications pass through an authorization check, as we will discuss in Chapter 8, Authorizations (Authorization Objects). So, they must be considered when calling forms and they must be maintained.

## 7.1 Payroll

The payslip — just like the time statement — is integrated with applications, such as Payroll or Employee Self-Services (ESS), and can be called from there. Because the old payslip was created as an SAPscript form and is still being used, you can call the form via SAPscript and with the new Smart Form or SAP Interactive Form created with the Forms Workplace. You also can create your own transactions with which you integrate the print program, or you can use Transaction PC00_M99_HRF_CALL to select your form and then call it (see Figure 7.1).

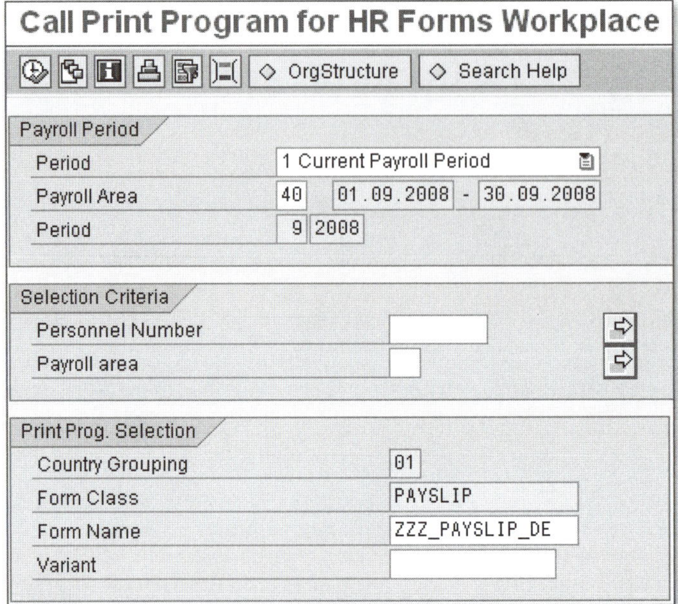

**Figure 7.1** HR Forms Print Program for the Payslip

Some already existing parameter transactions are available in the standard for calling the payslip. The Transaction PC00_M99_HRF, contains the respective country grouping. You can use your own country grouping by replacing 99 in the transaction, for example, PC00_M01_HRF for the German payslip. You can find the country-specific transaction calls for the payslip in the SAP Easy Access menu under SAP MENU • PERSONNEL • PAYROLL • EUROPE (or another continent) • GERMANY (or another country) • PAYROLL.

The country-specific parameter transactions for the payslip are listed in Table 7.1.

| Country | Transaction |
| --- | --- |
| Germany | PC00_M01_HRF |
| Switzerland | PC00_M02_HRF |
| Austria | PC00_M03_HRF |
| Spain | PC00_M04_HRF |
| Great Britain | PC00_M08_HRF |
| USA | PC00_M10_HRF |

**Table 7.1** Country-Specific Transactions for the Payslip

The country-specific transactions differ in their definition through the preassignment of the parameter for the country grouping (P_MOLGA) and the form class (P_FCLASS) that is preassigned with the PAYSLIP value.

You can also create your own transactions in addition to the listed standard transactions. The name of the print program appears in the attributes of your form. In the Forms Workplace, you call your form and select the HR FORM tab. There, you can find the name of the print program in the FORM PARTS area (see Figure 7.2).

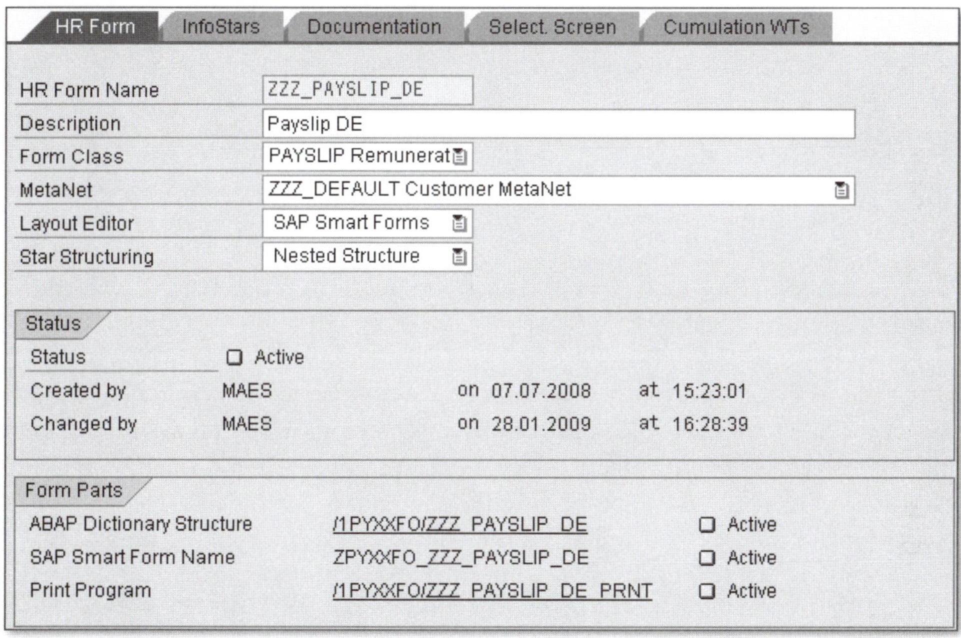


**Figure 7.2**  Form Attributes

Using the HRFOR feature (HR Forms Decision Feature), you can control the call of the payslip from ESS for mass print or the Off-Cycle Workbench. You're given the decision criteria, COUNTRY GROUPING, REPORT CATEGORY, COMPANY CODE, and additional organizational criteria, such as PAYROLL AREA or PERSONNEL AREA. You should use the report category, that is, the criterion that informs you about the application component from which the form is called, in the beginning so that it becomes clear whether it's a call of the payslip or the time statement. The other criteria are primarily used to control the call of a specific payslip, in case, for example, different payslips are used per company code (see Figure 7.3). The documentation of this feature can be found in Appendix F, Documentation of the Relevant Features.

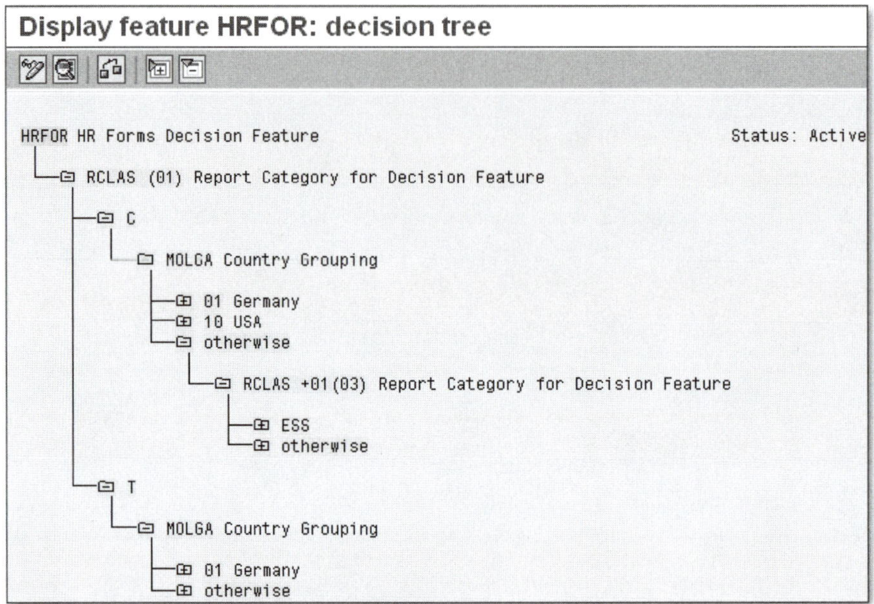



**Figure 7.3** Decision Tree of the HRFOR Feature

Using the PBCHO feature (Pay Bill Choice), you can decide which parameters for the payslip are to be available in the selection screen of the payroll driver. Depending on how you define this feature (see Table 7.2), the system displays *no* parameters, *one* of the two parameters, or *both* parameters for the selection between SAPscript and the form created using the Forms Workplace (see Figure 7.4).

| Value | Description |
| --- | --- |
| 00 | No additional parameters for the selection and display variant of the payslip. |
| 01 | Additional parameter for the selection of the payslip, which was created with the Forms Workplace. |
| 10 | Additional parameter for the selection of the payslip, which was created with SAPscript. |
| 11 | One of the two forms can be selected, whether created with the Forms Workplace or with SAPscript. Both options are provided in the selection screen. |

**Table 7.2** Return Values for the PBCHO Feature

The detailed documentation of this feature can also be found in Appendix F.

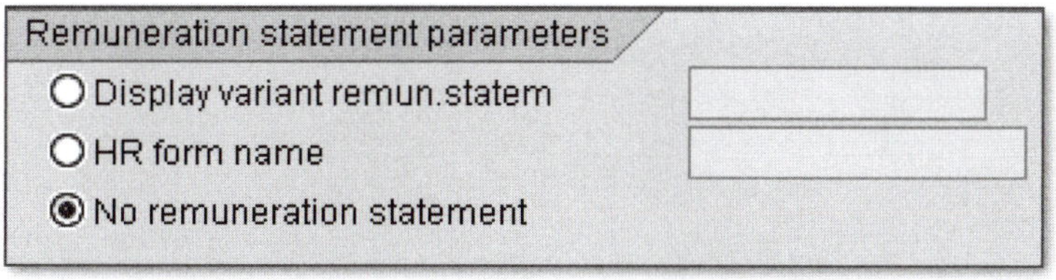

**Figure 7.4** Parameters in the Selection Screen of the Payroll Driver

Remember that the authorization check regarding the selection and execution of the form applies here as well.

## 7.2 Time Management

At some point, the time statement is integrated with the Time Management application, as we'll describe in this section. It's used for the onscreen display for controlling time data or to inform employees as a mass print, or for the targeted call via ESS or the Time Manager's Workplace (TMW).

> **Note**
>
> The Time Manager's Workplace (TMW) was developed by SAP specifically for decentralized time administrators in departments, branches, and so on.

By creating the time statement in the Forms Workplace, you create a print program that can be called within a transaction. You can directly name and integrate the form at other points, for instance, in features, and you can then find the name of the print program in the attributes of the form in the HR FORM tab when you call it in the Forms Workplace (see Figure 7.5 in the FORM PARTS area).

The standard version includes Parameter Transaction PT00_M99_HRF, which you can give to your time administrator. The parameter transaction calls Transaction PC00_M99_HRF_CALL and populates it with default values (see Figure 7.6). Alternatively, you can create your own transaction and assign the print program of your form to it.

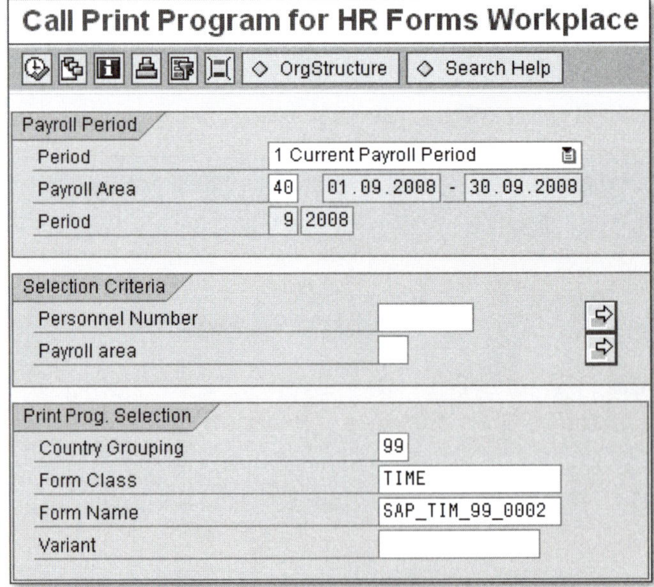


**Figure 7.5** Attributes of the Form



**Figure 7.6** HR Forms Print Program for the Time Statement

If you start the print program with a variant, the system skips the selection screen of the form's print program and outputs the form directly. If you don't specify a variant, the system displays the selection screen of the form's print program. You must create the variant for the print program of the form, and then you can select it via the F4 help.



From the Time Manager's Workplace, you can call the time statement via the menu path, UTILITIES(M) • DISPLAY TIME STATEMENT FORM (see Figure 7.7).

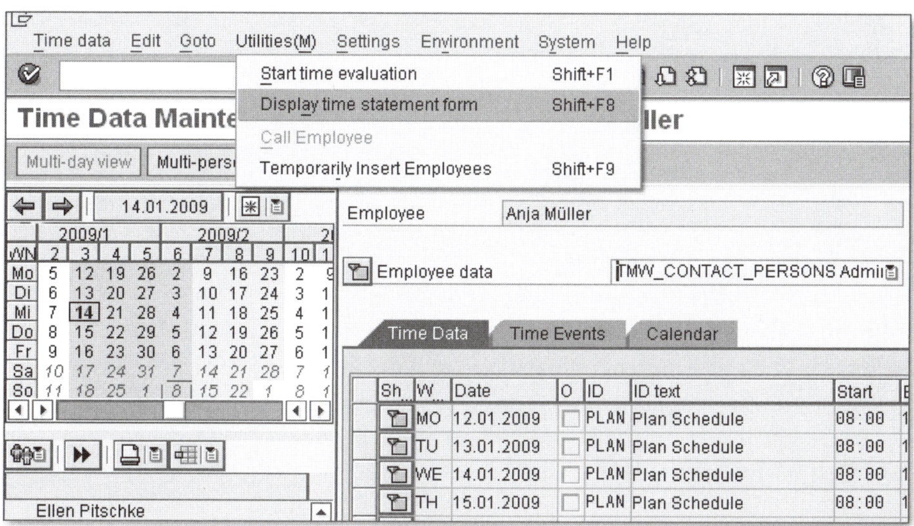

**Figure 7.7** Time Manager's Workplace (TMW)

The type of time statement — SAPscript or a form created with the Forms Workplace — depends on the HRFOR feature (HR Forms Decision Feature). The feature specifies whether and which form is used. You're given the decision criteria, COUNTRY GROUPING, REPORT CATEGORY, COMPANY CODE, and additional organizational criteria, such as PAYROLL AREA or PERSONNEL AREA, to decide which form is to be output. The report category informs you about the application component from which the form is called. It should be used in the beginning of the decision tree to clearly identify the type of call, in this case, the time statement (see Figure 7.8).

The documentation of the feature can be found in Appendix F, Documentation of the Relevant Features. If no entry exists for a report category, the SAPscript form is output. Just as with the TMW, you can use the HRFOR feature to determine the form that will be called in ESS.

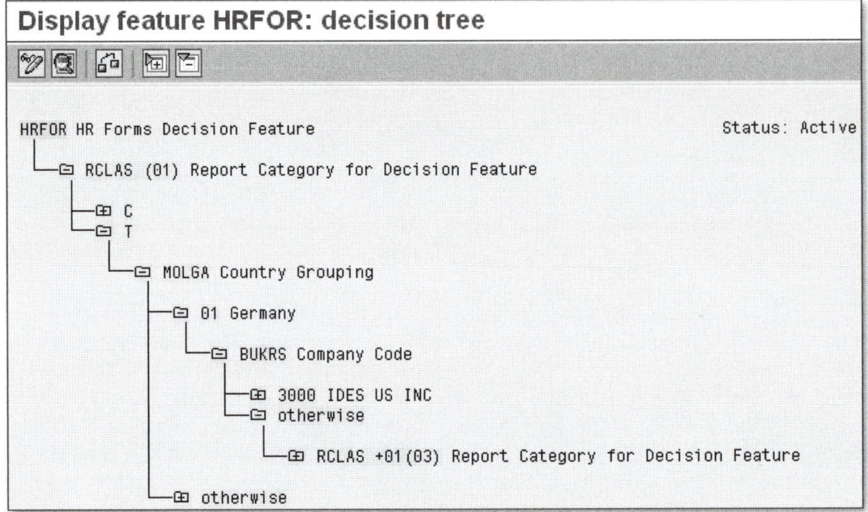


**Figure 7.8** Decision Tree of the HRFOR Feature for Calling the Time Statement

Keep in mind that the call of the time statement form from Shift Planning, Time Management Pool, and Time Evaluation is still done in the SAPscript format.

## 7.3 Conclusion

You should now be able to integrate the call of your own forms, which you create for Payroll and Time Management, with the applications using the available features. Besides the call from the applications, you can also directly call the print program of each form via your own transactions.

The integration of the payslip and time statement with applications of HCM is an ever-changing process. The call from some applications mentioned in this chapter is already supported. But, the integration of the form created with the Forms Workplace is still required at one point or the other, for instance, in Time Evaluation.

# 8 Authorizations (Authorization Objects)

Authorizations play an important role in creating forms because not every user is supposed to have authorization to process or even generate forms. Through authorizations, you can protect the access to forms, which means that you can prohibit the call of a form from any application.

This chapter presents the two authorization objects that control the work with and the call of forms. It is important to remember that a read authorization must exist for the data described in the metadata in addition to the authorizations for the maintenance and call of forms. For example, if an infotype is read, the user must have the authorization to read the data of this infotype. So, you must maintain the authorization objects of Human Resources Management for the user.

Let's look at the two authorization objects for the Forms Workplace and the Metadata Workplace:

1. P_HRF_INFO authorization object — HR: Authorization Check InfoData Maintenance for HR Forms
2. P_HRF_META authorization object — HR: Authorization Check Metadata Maintenance for HR Forms

By using Transaction SU21 (Maintain Authorization Objects), you can view the two authorization objects that you can find within the HR folder (HUMAN RESOURCES).

## 8.1 P_HRF_INFO Authorization Object

The P_HRF_INFO authorization object restricts the access to the forms created in the Forms Workplace. The objects are checked during the call or the processing of a form in the Forms Workplace as well as at any other location where the form can be called, for instance, in the log of the payroll driver.

For this authorization object you're given the COUNTRY GROUPING, INFONET NAME, and ACTIVITY fields (see Figure 8.1). There is no separate check for the objects of the InfoNet, the InfoStars, the InfoDimensions, and the InfoFigures. The values, "02" (Change), "03" (Display), and "07" (Activate and Generate), are provided for the activity.

| Object | P_HRF_INFO | |
|---|---|---|
| Text | HR: Authorization Check Infodata Maintenance for HR Forms | |
| Class | HR | Human Resources |
| Author | SAP | |
| **Authorization fields** | | |
| Field name | Heading | |
| MOLGA | Country Grouping | |
| P_HRF_INET | HR Forms: InfoNet Name | |
| ACTVT | Activity | |
| | | |
| | | |
| | | |

**Figure 8.1**　Authorization Fields of the P_HRF_INFO Authorization Object

## 8.2　P_HRF_META Authorization Object

The P_HRF_META authorization object restricts the access to the MetaNets created in the MetaData Workplace. You need this authorization if you want to process metadata. For example, you can allow the processing of metadata only for a specific country grouping. The check is done when the metadata is processed in the Metadata Workplace, when the metadata is displayed in the Forms Workplace, and for the test call of a form.

You're given the Object Type, Country Grouping, Object Name For Metadata, and Activity fields (see Figure 8.2). The values, "02" (Change) and "03" (Display), are provided for the activity. The object type can contain the following values:

- NET = MetaNet
- STAR = MetaStar
- DIMENSION = MetaDimension
- FIGURE = MetaFigure

▶ SCRFIELD = assignment to the fields of the logic database in payroll

▶ FORMCLASS = form class

| Object | P_HRF_META | |
|---|---|---|
| Text | HR: Authorization Check Metadata Maintenance for HR Forms | |
| Class | HR | Human Resources |
| Author | SAP | |
| **Authorization fields** | | |
| Field name | Heading | |
| P_HRF_TYP | HR Forms: Object Type | |
| MOLGA | Country Grouping | |
| P_HRF_MOBJ | HR Forms: Object Name for Metadata | |
| ACTVT | Activity | |
| | | |
| | | |
| | | |

**Figure 8.2** Authorization Fields of the P_HRF_META Authorization Object

The Object Name For Metadata contains the name of the MetaNet. There is no separate check for the objects of the MetaNet. All data used in the MetaNet or InfoNet that are processed during the form call pass through the standard authorization checks.

## 8.3 Maintaining the Two Authorization Objects

Figure 8.3 illustrates the maintenance of the two authorization objects. The check for the P_HRF_INFO object (Infodata Maintenance for HR forms) allows all activities for all countries of the selected forms. The name of the InfoNet corresponds to the name of the form. If all specifications are allowed, for example, in activities or forms, this is identified with an "*". The check for the P_HRF_META object (Metadata Maintenance for HR forms) allows only the display of selected object types; in the example displayed, all object types were selected. The metadata are also specified, and the form name is selected here. The metadata available in the respective form, which you can limit via the selection of the object types, are then allowed.

```
Manually   Human Resources
  Manually    HR: Authorization Check Infodata Maintenance for HR Forms
    Manually    HR: Berechtigungsprüfung Infodatenpflege für HR-Forms
      * Activity                      All activities
      * Country Grouping              *
      * HR Forms:  InfoNet Name       SAP_PAYSLIP, SAP_PAYSLIP_DE, SAP_TIMESLIP, SAP_TIM_99_0001, SAP_TIM_99<...>
  Manually    HR: Authorization Check Metadata Maintenance for HR Forms
    Manually    HR: Berechtigungsprüfung Metadatenpflege für HR-Forms
      * Activity                      Display
      * Country Grouping              *
      * HR Forms: Object Name for Meta ZZZ_FORMULAR, ZZZ_PAYSLIP_DE, ZZZ_TIM_01_0002
      * HR Forms: Object Type         Figure, Form Class, Net, Assignment of LDB Fields, Star
```

**Figure 8.3** Maintenance of the Authorization Fields in the Authorization Objects, P_HRF_INFO and P_HRF_META

## 8.4 Conclusion

The aim of this chapter was to illustrate that you can also use the SAP authorization concept, which protects against unauthorized access to programs and data, in the area of form design. This means you can use the authorization objects described in this chapter if you don't want to allow all of your users to create and execute forms. Nevertheless, users need additional authorizations that specify the data to be read. So before you wonder why a user isn't allowed to call a form, you should check the authorizations of this user in his authorization profile.

> **Note**
>
> Further information about the topic can be found in the SAP PRESS book, *Authorizations in SAP ERP HCM*. Refer to Appendix H to find a complete list of bibliographical references.

In the final chapter we will give you an outlook of the potential of SAP Interactive Forms by Adobe in the area of form design.

# 9    Outlook for SAP Interactive Forms by Adobe

In this final chapter we'll give you insight to the outlook for the potential of SAP Interactive Forms by Adobe in the area of form design. SAP Interactive Forms support the print forms described in the previous chapters and replace the existing technologies there. Aside from a pure technological change and simplified design and print options, SAP Interactive Forms also offer a decisive added value: the use of truly interactive forms that enable you to support processes that — until now — could only have been implemented manually or via an unstructured communication. They also allow you to eliminate integration gaps and reduce the use of expensive scan solutions with *Optical Character Recognition* (OCR). If you use SAP Interactive Forms, you can create a digital request form directly that supports and accompanies the process and is stored in the electronic personnel file in SAP Records Management for documentation.

All standard SAP print forms have already been switched to the new Adobe technology. These are interactive forms that are ready for input to an increasing degree — particularly in the HCM environment. For example, the portal of SAP ERP HCM provides interactive sample forms for the following processes:

- Birth of a child
- Maternity leave
- Rehiring
- Change in pay

The form offerings continue to be extended and will provide options for changing the classic personnel processes, increasing efficiency, and promoting the transparency of the entire process.

The new functions are provided via the *HCM Processes and Forms* framework, which you can use to define processes and forms in portal roles for online scenarios. In Customizing, these functions appear in the PERSONNEL MANAGEMENT area under ADMINISTRATIVE SERVICES. The functions are available for the *Employee* (ESS), *Man-*

*ager* (MSS), and *HR Administrator* (HRADMIN) roles. For example, the employee can fill out a form directly online within his role.

Figures 9.1 and 9.2 illustrate how an employee can use an interactive form to request maternity leave directly in the ESS Portal.

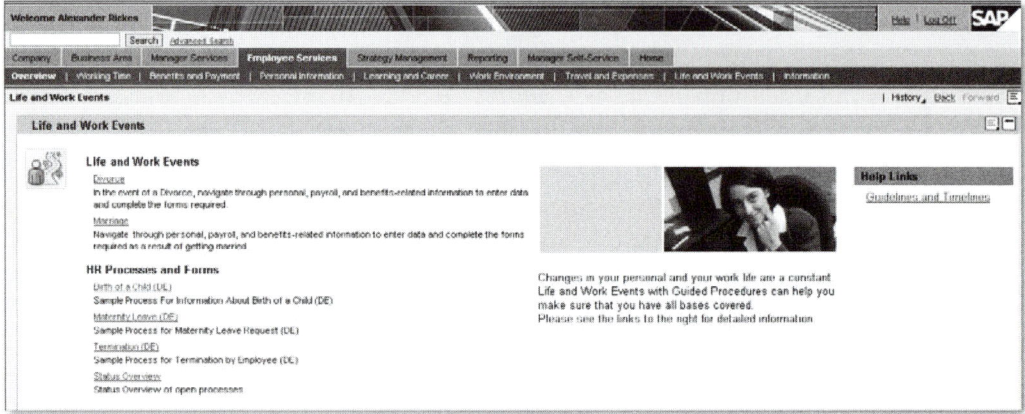

**Figure 9.1**  ESS Role in the Portal — Request Maternity Leave Interactively I

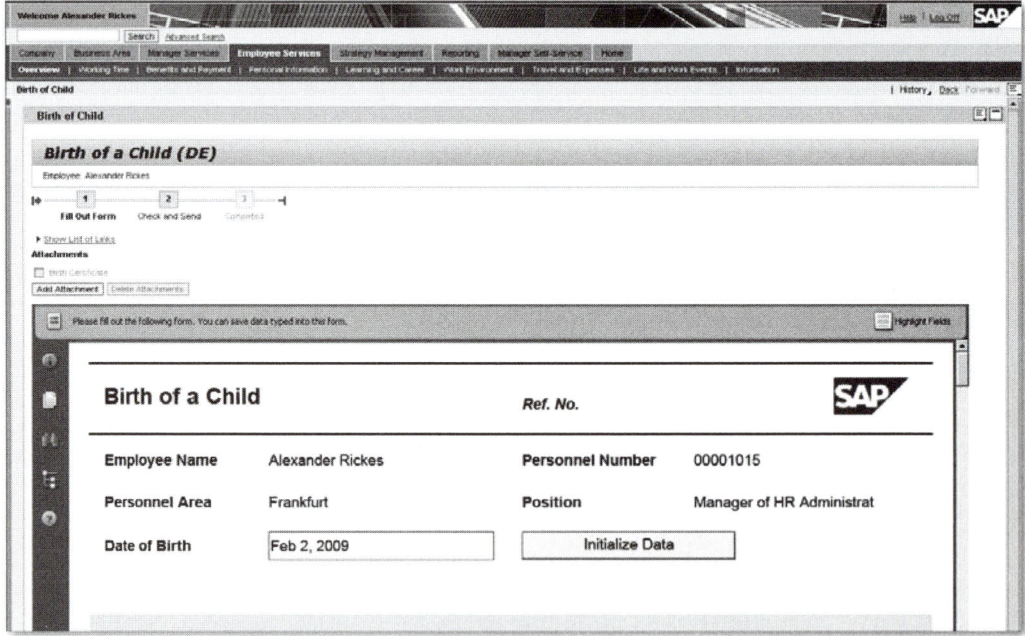

**Figure 9.2**  ESS Role in the Portal — Request Maternity Leave Interactively II

Another example of the added value of interactive forms is the change of the classic process for standard statements, such as employer statements and statements of earnings. For example, employees can use SAP Interactive Forms to directly request statements via their personalized portal role (see Figure 9.3).

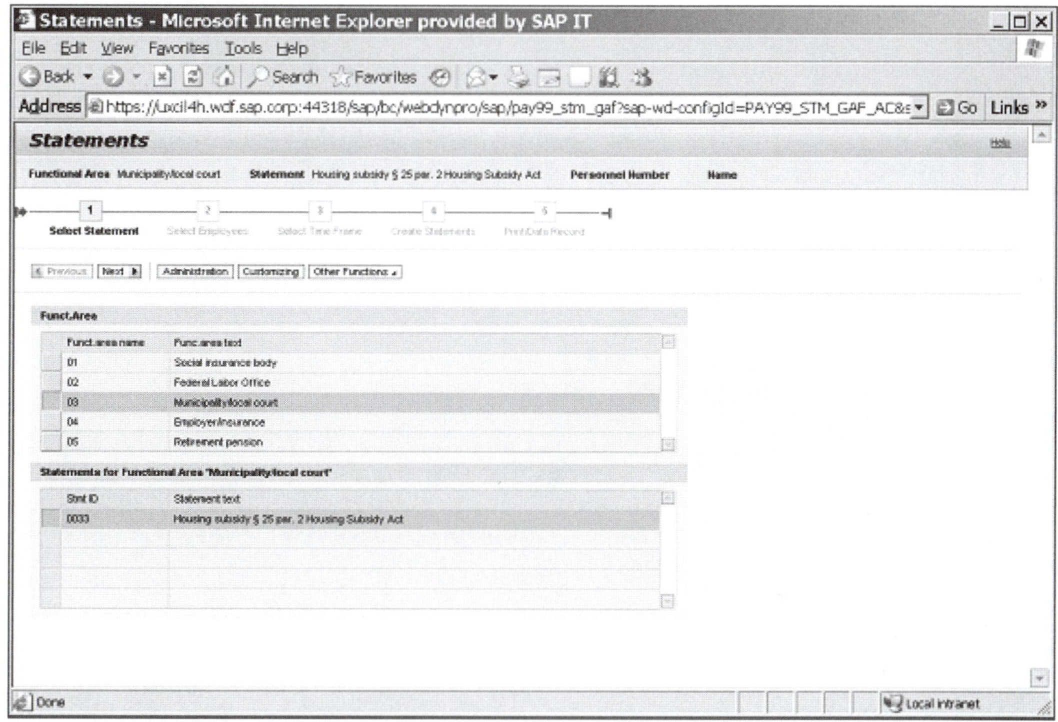

**Figure 9.3**  Requesting Standard Statements I

The statement is created as described in the previous chapters, and the form is made available to the employee via the system.

The created documents can be stored in the personnel file automatically, and the employee can view them via his ESS role in the portal (see Figure 9.4 and 9.5).

> **Note**
>
> The procedure for storing the print documents was described in Chapter 4, section 4.2.1, The Selection Screen. Interactive forms are stored via Customizing of Administrative Services.

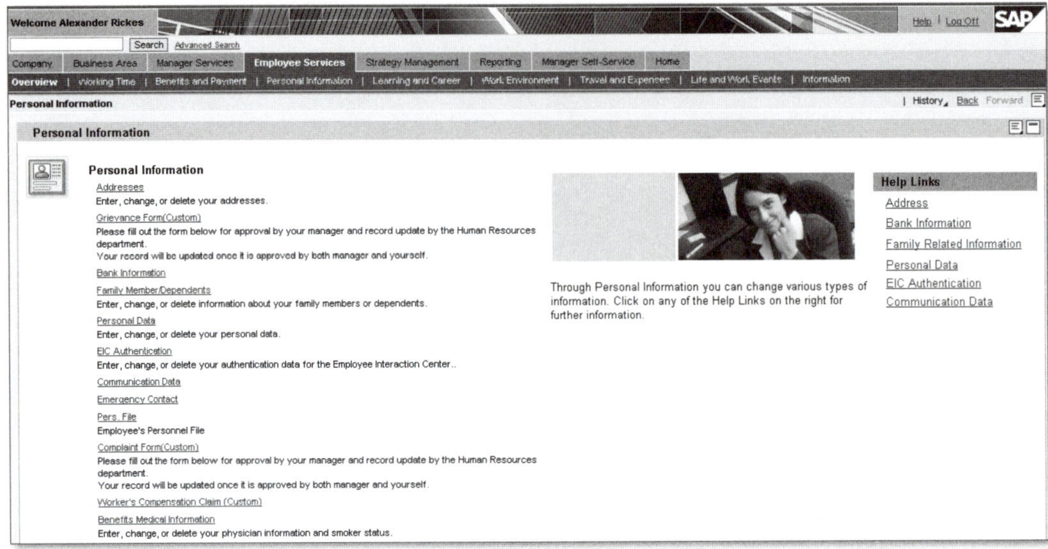

**Figure 9.4** ESS Role in the Portal — Electronic Personnel File

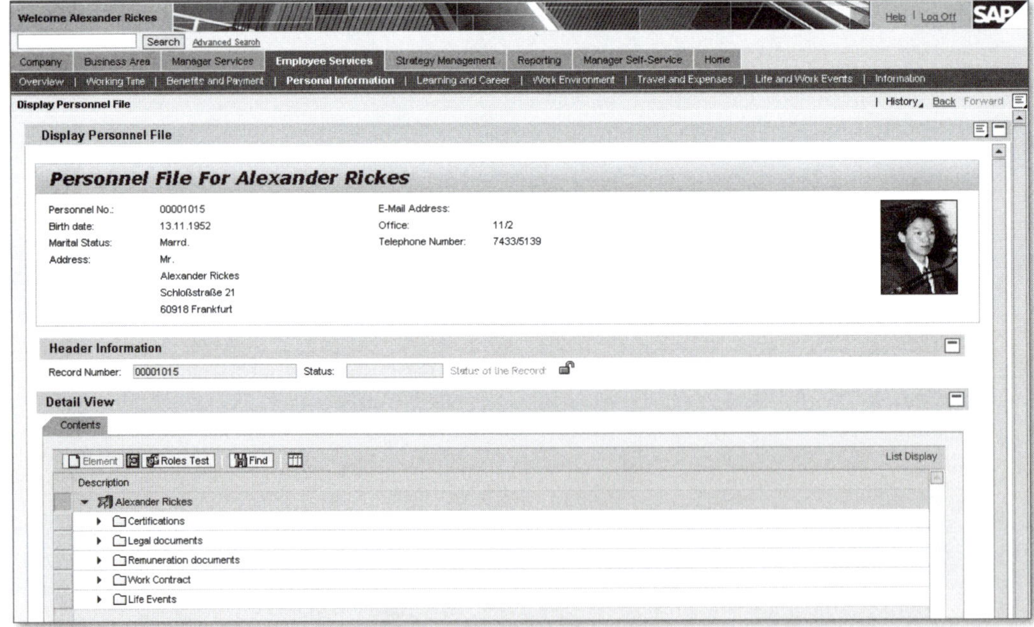

**Figure 9.5** ESS Role in the Portal — Display of Forms in the Electronic Personnel File

This technology ensures that the personnel department is relieved of the routine tasks of daily operations and enables it to provide "contemporary" personnel service to the employees. Of course, this solution path also supports distributed locations and cross-location personnel work, whereas many customer projects revealed that this form technology is used for offline processes in HR, for example, for outsourcing time recording and reporting overtime. The technical prerequisites presented back in Chapter 3, section 3.2.2, Prerequisites for Using SAP Interactive Forms, are identical for the print forms and the interactive forms.

## 9.1    Conclusion

This chapter showed how the use of SAP Interactive Forms by Adobe can lead to more efficient personnel processes.

The appendices that follow include further useful notes for creating forms in SAP ERP HCM.

# Appendices

# A    List of Abbreviations

| | |
|---|---|
| ABAP | Advanced Business Application Programming |
| ADS | Adobe Document Services |
| BAdI | Business Add-In |
| CRT | Cumulated Result Table |
| DDIC | Data Dictionary |
| EA-HR | Enterprise Extension Human Resources |
| ERP | Enterprise Resource Planning |
| ESS | Employee Self-Services |
| HCM | Human Capital Management |
| HR | Human Resources |
| IMG | Implementation Guide |
| ISR | Internet Service Request |
| MSS | Manager Self-Services |
| OCR | Optical Character Recognition |
| PS | Public Sector |
| PDF | Portable Document Format |
| RT | Result Table |
| SAP | Systems, Applications, and Products in Data Processing |
| SCRT | Cumulated Tax Results |
| TC | Transaction Code |
| TMW | Time Manager's Workplace |
| WYSIWYG | What You See Is What You Get |
| XML | Extensible Markup Language |
| ZES | Daily Time Balances |

# B    SAP Notes for the Forms Workplace

Table B.1 provides you with a selection of useful SAP Notes that you can find in the SAP Service Marketplace for the Forms Workplace. Some of these notes were also referred to in the text.

| Note | Subject |
| --- | --- |
| 645158 | New Bar Code Technology for Smart Forms |
| 750784 | SAP Interactive Forms Licenses |
| 782655 | HRFORMS Printing of Monthly Values Without Annual Values |
| 834573 | SAP Interactive Forms by Adobe: Acrobat Reader Version |
| 962763 | Installation of Adobe LiveCycle Designer 7.1 |
| 1009567 | Functional Differences of SAP Interactive Forms and Smart Forms |
| 1034904 | SAP_PAYSLIP_DE — Layout of Retroactive Accountings |
| 1068659 | SAP_PAYSLIP_DE — Old Data in Retroactive Accountings |
| 1121176 | Installation of Adobe LiveCycle Designer 8.0 |
| 1143020 | Information about the Regulation on the Statements of Earnings |
| 1152791 | Statements of Earnings New Conversions |

**Table B.1**   SAP Notes for the Forms Workplace

# C    Form Templates

The form templates provided in Table C.1 are available in the Forms Workplace. The Layout Editor column indicates whether the specific form is based on Smart Forms (= Smart Forms) or SAP Interactive Forms (= Form Builder).

| Country Grouping | Name | Form Class | Layout Editor | Star Structuring |
| --- | --- | --- | --- | --- |
| 01 | SAP_PAYSLIP_DE | PAYSLIP | Smart Forms | Nested structure |
| 01 | SAP_PAYSLIP_DE_P | PAYSLIP | Form Builder | Flat Structure |
| 01 | SAP_PAYSLIP_DE3 | PAYSLIP | Form Builder | Nested Structure |
| 01 | SAP_PAYSLIP_DE4 | PAYSLIP | Form Builder | Flat Structure |
| 02 | SAP_PAYSLIP_CH | PAYSLIP | Form Builder | Nested Structure |
| 03 | SAP_PAYSLIP_AT | PAYSLIP | Form Builder | Nested Structure |
| 04 | SAP_PAYSLIP_ES_1 | PAYSLIP | Form Builder | Flat Structure |
| 05 | SAP_PAYSLIP_NL | PAYSLIP | Smart Forms | Nested Structure |
| 06 | SAP_PAYSLIP_FR | PAYSLIP | Form Builder | Nested Structure |
| 07 | SAP_PAYJNAL_CA | PAYJNAL | Smart Forms | Flat Structure |
| 07 | SAP_PAYSLIP_CA | PAYSLIP | Form Builder | Nested Structure |
| 08 | SAP_PAYSLIP_GB | PAYSLIP | Form Builder | Flat Structure |
| 10 | SAP_PAYJNAL_US | PAYJNAL | Smart Forms | Flat Structure |
| 10 | SAP_PAYJNAL_USCE | PAYJNAL | Smart Forms | Flat Structure |
| 10 | SAP_PAYSLIP_US | PAYSLIP | Smart Forms | Nested Structure |
| 10 | SAP_PAYSLIP_US2 | PAYSLIP | Form Builder | Flat Structure |
| 10 | SAP_PJ_US_CE_PER | PAYSLIP | Form Builder | Flat Structure |
| 10 | SAP_PJUSCE_PERAS | PAYSLIP | Form Builder | Flat Structure |
| 13 | SAP_PAYSLIP_AU | PAYSLIP | Form Builder | Nested Structure |
| 22 | SAP_PAYSLIP_JP | PAYSLIP | Form Builder | Flat Structure |
| 22 | SAP_PAYSLIP_M_JP | PAYSLIP | Form Builder | Flat Structure |
| 22 | SAP_SKPLEDGER_JP | NONE | Form Builder | Nested Structure |

**Table C.1**    Form Templates in the Forms Workplace

| Country Grouping | Name | Form Class | Layout Editor | Star Structuring |
|---|---|---|---|---|
| 23 | SAP_PAYSLIP_SE | PAYSLIP | Form Builder | Nested Structure |
| 25 | SAP_PAYSLIP_SG | PAYSLIP | Form Builder | Nested Structure |
| 28 | SAP_PAYSLIP_CN | PAYSLIP | Form Builder | Nested Structure |
| 37 | SAP_PAYSLIP_BR | PAYSLIP | Form Builder | Nested Structure |
| 99 | SAP_PAYSLIP | PAYSLIP | Smart Forms | Nested Structure |
| 99 | SAP_TIM_99_0001 | TIME | Smart Forms | Nested Structure |
| 99 | SAP_TIM_99_0002 | TIME | Smart Forms | Nested Structure |
| 99 | SAP_TIMESLIP | TIME | Smart Forms | Nested Structure |

**Table C.1** Form Templates in the Forms Workplace (Cont.)

# D  Source Code for the XSKIF Function Program

Listing D.1 provides the extension of the standard program of the XSKIF function as described in Section 4.2.4, Controlling the Printing of Retroactive Accounting. The copied payroll function was saved under the name Z_XSK.

```
*----------------------------------------------------------*
*    Function FUZ_XSK
*----------------------------------------------------------*
* This form adds 'flag-wage-types' to RT. If present,
* they will indicate that the respective sets of wage-
* types have not changed from the previous period. This
* is controlled by table THRFORMS_FLAGWTS.
*----------------------------------------------------------*
  FORM fuz_xsk.
    DATA: wa_rt LIKE LINE OF rt,
          wa_ort LIKE LINE OF ort,
          it_flagwts LIKE TABLE OF thrforms_flagwts,
          wa_flagwts LIKE thrforms_flagwts,
          it_r4flwts LIKE TABLE OF thrforms_r4flwts,
          wa_r4flwts LIKE thrforms_r4flwts,
          prev_flag_wt TYPE lgart,
          prev_endda TYPE endda,
          x_continue TYPE c,
          x_all_wts TYPE c,
          x_new_flag_wt TYPE c.

    PERFORM import_ort.
    SELECT * FROM thrforms_flagwts INTO TABLE it_flagwts
    WHERE molga = calcmolga.
    SELECT * FROM thrforms_r4flwts INTO TABLE it_r4flwts
    WHERE molga = calcmolga.
    SORT it_flagwts BY flag_wt endda DESCENDING.
*==========================================================*
*loop at the main table, where dates match
    LOOP AT it_flagwts INTO wa_flagwts
    WHERE begda LE aper-endda AND endda GE aper-begda.
      x_new_flag_wt = false.
```

```
* I am looping through a sorted table.
* If a new FLAG_WT comes up, I will generate it in RT.
* It will eventually be deleted, if the wage-types
* pass the 'unchanged' test.

        IF prev_flag_wt NE wa_flagwts-flag_wt. "------
          x_new_flag_wt = true.
          x_continue = false.
          CLEAR wa_rt.
          wa_rt-lgart = wa_flagwts-flag_wt.
          wa_rt-number = 1.
          COLLECT wa_rt INTO rt.
          READ TABLE it_r4flwts INTO wa_r4flwts
          WITH KEY flag_wt = wa_flagwts-flag_wt.
* X_ALL_WTS tells if all wage-types must be compared,
* or only a subset.
          IF sy-subrc = 0.
            x_all_wts = wa_r4flwts-x_all_wts.
          ELSE.
            x_all_wts = true. "it should never happen.
          ENDIF.
        ENDIF.
        prev_flag_wt = wa_flagwts-flag_wt. "------
*avoid time splits: only look at the latest record.
      IF prev_endda NE wa_flagwts-endda
      AND x_new_flag_wt = false. "------
        x_continue = true.
      ENDIF.
      prev_endda = wa_flagwts-endda. "------


      IF x_continue = false. "=========================
        IF x_all_wts = false. "----------------------
*only compare certain wage-types.
*check RT against ORT.
          LOOP AT rt INTO wa_rt
          WHERE lgart = wa_flagwts-lgart.
            IF x_continue = true. EXIT. ENDIF.
            CASE as-parml.
              WHEN 'ALL'.
                READ TABLE ort INTO wa_ort
                WITH KEY wa_rt.
                IF sy-subrc NE 0 OR wa_ort NE wa_rt.
                  PERFORM del_entry_from_rt
```

```
            USING wa_flagwts-flag_wt
            CHANGING x_continue.
        ENDIF.
      WHEN 'REL'.
        READ TABLE ort INTO wa_ort
        WITH KEY abart = wa_rt-abart
        lgart = wa_rt-lgart
        betpe = wa_rt-betpe
        number = wa_rt-number
        betrg = wa_rt-betrg.
        IF sy-subrc NE 0.
          PERFORM del_entry_from_rt
              USING wa_flagwts-flag_wt
              CHANGING x_continue.
        ENDIF.
    ENDCASE.
  ENDLOOP. "loop at rt
*check ORT against RT.
    LOOP AT ort INTO wa_ort
    WHERE lgart = wa_flagwts-lgart.
      IF x_continue = true. EXIT. ENDIF.
      CASE as-parm1.
        WHEN 'ALL'.
          READ TABLE rt INTO wa_rt
          WITH KEY wa_ort.
          IF sy-subrc NE 0 OR wa_ort NE wa_rt.
            PERFORM del_entry_from_rt
                USING wa_flagwts-flag_wt
                CHANGING x_continue.
          ENDIF.
        WHEN 'REL'.
          READ TABLE rt INTO wa_rt
          WITH KEY abart = wa_ort-abart
          lgart = wa_ort-lgart
          betpe = wa_ort-betpe
          number = wa_ort-number
          betrg = wa_ort-betrg.
          IF sy-subrc NE 0.
            PERFORM del_entry_from_rt
                USING wa_flagwts-flag_wt
                CHANGING x_continue.
          ENDIF.
      ENDCASE.
```

```
            ENDLOOP. "loop at ort
          ELSE. "if x_all_wts = true. "----------------
*check every wage-type
*check RT against ORT.
          LOOP AT rt INTO wa_rt.
            IF x_continue = true. EXIT. ENDIF.
            CASE as-parm1.
              WHEN 'ALL'.
                READ TABLE ort INTO wa_ort
                WITH KEY wa_rt.
                IF sy-subrc NE 0 OR wa_ort NE wa_rt.
                  PERFORM del_entry_from_rt
                     USING wa_flagwts-flag_wt
                     CHANGING x_continue.
                ENDIF.
              WHEN 'REL'.
                READ TABLE ort INTO wa_ort
                WITH KEY abart = wa_rt-abart
                lgart = wa_rt-lgart
                betpe = wa_rt-betpe
                number = wa_rt-number
                betrg = wa_rt-betrg.
                IF sy-subrc NE 0.
                  PERFORM del_entry_from_rt
                     USING wa_flagwts-flag_wt
                     CHANGING x_continue.
                ENDIF.
            ENDCASE.
          ENDLOOP. "loop at rt
*check ORT against RT.
          LOOP AT ort INTO wa_ort.
            IF x_continue = true. EXIT. ENDIF.
            CASE as-parm1.
              WHEN 'ALL'.
                READ TABLE rt INTO wa_rt
                WITH KEY wa_ort.
                IF sy-subrc NE 0 OR wa_ort NE wa_rt.
                  PERFORM del_entry_from_rt
                     USING wa_flagwts-flag_wt
                     CHANGING x_continue.
                ENDIF.
              WHEN 'REL'.
                READ TABLE rt INTO wa_rt
```

```
            WITH KEY abart = wa_ort-abart
            lgart = wa_ort-lgart
            betpe = wa_ort-betpe
            number = wa_ort-number
            betrg = wa_ort-betrg.
            IF sy-subrc NE 0.
              PERFORM del_entry_from_rt
                USING wa_flagwts-flag_wt
                CHANGING x_continue.
            ENDIF.
          ENDCASE.
        ENDLOOP. "loop at ort
        x_continue = true. "skip to the next flag WT
      ENDIF. "x_all_wts = true or false ? "---------
    ENDIF. "if x_continue = false "==================
  ENDLOOP. "LOOP AT it_flagwts
*=======================================================
  ENDFORM.                        "FUZ_XSK
```

**Listing D.1** Source Code of the Customer-Specific Z_XSK Function

# E    Source Code of the Z_HR_FORMS_READ_ TIME_PERIODS Function Module

Listing E.2 provides the source code of the Z_HR_FORMS_READ_TIME_PERIODS function module. Before you activate the function module, copy the tables and Includes given in Listing E.1 to the global data definitions of the main program for the function module. The Includes contain data definitions that are used in the function module. Also change the type of the MS_DATA interface parameter of the function module. Select the TYPE typing and the ZPTT_F_PERIODS associated type.

```abap
TABLES: pcl1, pcl2. "Tables
INCLUDE rpppxd10. "Includes
INCLUDE rpc2b201.
INCLUDE rpc2b202.
INCLUDE rpc2rx02.
INCLUDE rpcxb200.
INCLUDE rpppxd00.
INCLUDE rpppxm00.
```

**Listing E.1** Global Data Definitions

```abap
 DATA: i549q TYPE TABLE OF t549q WITH HEADER LINE.
 DATA: data TYPE zptr_f_periods.

 REFRESH:i549q.
 CALL FUNCTION 'HR_PAYROLL_PERIODS_GET'
   EXPORTING
     get_begda       = begda
     get_endda       = endda
     get_permo       = permo
   TABLES
     get_periods     = i549q
   EXCEPTIONS
     no_period_found = 1
     no_valid_permo  = 2
     OTHERS          = 3.

 LOOP AT i549q.
```

```
      MOVE-CORRESPONDING i549q TO ms_data.
      APPEND ms_data.
    ENDLOOP.

    LOOP AT ms_data INTO data.
*   Form key for targeted reading
      CLEAR: b2-key.
      b2-key-pernr = pernr.
      b2-key-cltyp = '1'.
      b2-key-pabrj = data-pabrj.
      b2-key-pabrp = data-pabrp.

      rp-imp-c2-b2. " Macro for reading Cluster B2

      CASE rp-imp-b2-subrc. " Cluster B2 available?
        WHEN 0.
  " Write data in return structure
          data-datum = bezug-datum.
          data-rabrj = bezug-rabrj.
          data-rabrp = bezug-rabrp.
          data-rrabj = bezug-rrabj.
          data-rrabp = bezug-rrabp.

          MODIFY ms_data FROM data. " Modify table
        WHEN OTHERS.   "No cluster data available
      ENDCASE.
    ENDLOOP.
```

**Listing E.2** Source Code of the Customer-Specific Z_HR_FORMS_READ_TIME_PERIODS Function Module

# F    Documentation of the Relevant Features

This appendix provides a detailed description of the HRFOR (HR Forms Decision Feature) and PBCHO (Pay Bill Choice) features. These features were mentioned in Chapter 7, Integration with the Payroll and Time Management Components of SAP ERP HCM.

## F.1    Name

HRFOR (HR Forms Decision Feature)

### F.1.1    Task

You use the TASK feature to control which HR form is used in the applications of Human Resources Management. Forms can be provided to employees in ESS or created in mass print just like in the payslip and time statement.

### F.1.2    Usage

You can use decision criteria available for the feature to call the required form from an application. The report category controls which application a form is called from (see Table F.1). In addition, you're given the country grouping as a decision criterion because the forms that you create in the Forms Workplace are country-dependent. You should create country-independent forms with the Country Grouping 99.

| Report Category | Description |
| --- | --- |
| C STD | Salary statement for mass print |
| C ESS | Salary statement in ESS (with or without the $CEDT$ constant) |
| C ESR | Salary statement in ESS for semiretirement (simulation) |
| C EOC | Call of the salary statement from the Off-Cycle Workbench |
| T ESP | Time statement in ESS with input of a period |

**Table F.1**  Report Categories Included in the SAP Standard

| Report Category | Description |
|---|---|
| T ESD | Time statement in ESS with input of a date |
| T TMW | Call of the time statement from the TMW |

**Table F.1**  Report Categories Included in the SAP Standard (Cont.)

## F.2  Name

PBCHO PayBill CHOice

### F.2.1  Task

You use the PBCHO feature (PayBill CHOice) to show or hide the parameters that are possible in the selection screen of the payroll driver for the selection of the payslip.

### F.2.2  Usage

The values shown in Table F.2 can be input in the feature as return values.

| Value | Description |
|---|---|
| 00 | No additional parameters for the selection and display variant of the payslip. |
| 01 | Additional parameter for the selection of the payslip that was created with the Forms Workplace. |
| 10 | Additional parameter for the selection of the payslip that was created with SAPscript. |
| 11 | One of the two forms can be selected, whether created with the Forms Workplace or with SAPscript. Both options appear in the selection screen. |

**Table F.2**  Possible Values of the PBCHO Feature

# G  Naming Conventions in the Time Statement Form

Tables G.1, G.2, G.3, G.4, and G.5 illustrate the naming conventions for the standard form of the time statement with the Form Builder for Smart Forms.

The information is taken from the SAP online library for the time evaluation (source: *http://help.sap.com/erp2005_ehp_03/helpdata/EN/94/8bd39654eeaf439738 64d157f5defb/frameset.htm*).

| Object | Naming Convention | Comment |
| --- | --- | --- |
| MetaStars | TIM_* | |
| MetaDimensions | DIM_* | |
| Folder node | any | |
| Loop node | I_<table name>_<description> | Loop node for the data retrieval |
| Workspace for loops | W_<table name> | Tables from which data is read in SAP Smart Forms |
| Declaration of the workspaces for loops in global data | W_<table name>_LINE OF /1PYXXFO/<form name>-STAR_TIM_[table name] | |

**Table G.1**  General Naming Conventions

| Object | Naming Convention | Comment |
| --- | --- | --- |
| Table node | T_<table name> | Table |
| Table header | H_<table name> | Header |
| Line node | L_<table name> | Line |
| Line type | LT_<table name> | LineType |
| Column node | C_<name>_<description> | Column |
| | C_<name>_H | Header |

**Table G.2**  Output Table is Subset of a Data Table

| Object | Naming Convention |
|---|---|
| Line type | LT_<business-dependent name> |
| Line node | L_<business-dependent name> |
| Column node | C_<table name of data table>_<description> |

**Table G.3**  Names for Output Tables that Summarize Information from Multiple Tables

| Object | Naming Convention | Comment |
|---|---|---|
| Condition query | L_[name] | |
| Condition query | L_DOIT | Query whether nodes and tables in nodes are supposed to be shown. Prior to the output of a table, it's checked whether data is available for the selection period. If so, then L_DOIT > 0. |
| Condition query | L_DOIT_TOO | Like L_DOIT, if additional conditions are to be queried. |
| Condition query | C_ACTIVE | Query whether node is to be output in the form. The query enables the deactivation of individual nodes. C_ACTIVE = BLANK or C_ACTIVE = C_YES indicates that the node is activated. C_ACTIVE = C_NO indicates that the node is deactivated. |

**Table G.4**  Global Variables

| Object | Comment |
|---|---|
| N_MONTH | Number of months that coincide with the selection period. The global constant is set during initialization. |
| N_EMPLOYEES | Number of employees for whom the time statement is printed. The constant is set during initialization. The constant is required to avoid duplicate output of the secondary windows for the last personnel number. |

**Table G.5**  Global Constants

# H    Additional Information

This appendix provides further information on additional literature, relevant SAP trainings, and useful web sites.

## H.1    Additional Literature

Becker, Joachim; Schroeder, Norbert; Spinola, Ulrich: *SAP Records Management.* Boston: SAP PRESS 2009 (forthcoming).

Esch, Martin; Junold, Anja: *Authorizations in SAP ERP HCM.* Boston: SAP PRESS 2008.

Figaj, Hans-Jürgen; Haßmann, Richard; Junold, Anja: *HR Reporting with SAP.* Boston: SAP PRESS 2007.

Hauser, Jürgen; Deutesfeld, Andreas; Rehmann, Stephan; Szücs, Thomas; Thun, Philipp: *SAP Interactive Forms by Adobe.* Boston: SAP PRESS 2009.

Hertleif, Werner; Wachter, Christoph: *SAP Smart Forms.* 2nd, updated and revised edition. Boston: SAP PRESS 2003.

Stefani, Helmut: *Archiving Your SAP Data.* Boston: SAP PRESS 2007.

## H.2    SAP Trainings

- HR 280 — SAP Interactive Forms by Adobe and SAP Smart Forms for HCM
- BC 480 — PDF-Based Print Forms

## H.3    Web Sites

- SAP Service Marketplace: *www.service.sap.com*
- SAP Developer Network (SDN) about SAP Interactive Forms: *www.sdn.sap.com/ irj/sdn/adobe*
  - SAP Developer Network (SDN) about Smart Forms: *www.sdn.sap.com/irj/sdn/ smartforms*
- SAP Help Portal: *http://help.sap.com*

# I    The Authors

**Stefan Kauf** is an administrative chief inspector and computer scientist. Since 2001, he has been working as an SAP NetWeaver Solution Expert ECM (Enterprise Content Management) at SAP Deutschland AG & Co. KG. In this function, he is responsible for the sales of archiving solutions, process-oriented operations and records management, as well as SAP Interactive Forms by Adobe. He also assumed responsibility for the entire HCM implementation at a leading automotive group as the technical project lead. He has supervised various HCM and other technical projects — from the architecture design to the project management to the implementation.

**Viktoria Papadopoulou** is a graduate in Business Information Systems (University Essen, Germany) and initially worked as an SAP ERP HCM developer at myGnosis Consulting Ltd. in Athens, Greece, from 2002 on. In early 2004, she started working for Projektkultur GmbH (*www.projektkultur.com*) in Cologne, Germany, a consulting company within the AdManus consulting network that specializes in Human Resources and SAP ERP HCM, where she now holds the position of SAP ERP HCM consultant and developer. Within the framework of her work, she has implemented numerous national and international HCM projects. For several years now, she has supported customers in the use of the HR Forms Workplace as well as in the creation of Smart Forms and Adobe forms.

Provides an updated guide to integrating CATS with SAP ERP 6.0 components - HCM, Financials, PM, MM, and more

Includes new coverage for using the feature CATEX to determine which data requires approval

Explores the new ERP 6.0 Workflow tasks and covers reporting time and approvals and ESS and MSS

Martin Gillet

# Integrating CATS

## SAP PRESS Essentials #58

Integrating CATS, second edition is a practical Essentials guide that provides detailed, up-to-date instruction on how to use CATS effectively through integration with a variety of SAP ERP 6.0 components, including HCM, Financials, Materials Management, Plant Maintenance, and more.
The new edition is up-to-date for SAP ERP 6.0 components, and provides information on new functionality, including coverage of using feature CATEX to determine which data requires approval, and the new ERP 6.0 Workflow tasks. It also covers creating data entry profiles for Employee Self Services using WebDynpro instead of ITS, and new screens showing approval through the portal feature CATEX, and much more.

232 pp., 2. edition 2009, 68,– Euro / US$ 85
ISBN 978-1-59229-260-8

**>> www.sap-press.de/2000**